SUNNI CHAUVINISM AND THE ROOTS OF MUSLIM MODERNISM

Sunni Chauvinism and the Roots of Muslim Modernism

TEENA U. PUROHIT

PRINCETON UNIVERSITY PRESS

PRINCETON & OXFORD

Published by Princeton University Press
41 William Street, Princeton, New Jersey 08540
99 Banbury Road, Oxford OX2 6JX

press.princeton.edu

Library of Congress Cataloging-in-Publication Data

Names: Purohit, Teena, author.
Title: Sunni chauvinism and the roots of Muslim modernism /
    Teena U. Purohit.
Description: 1st. | Princeton : Princeton University Press, 2023. |
    Includes bibliographical references and index.
Identifiers: LCCN 2022042291 (print) | LCCN 2022042292 (ebook) |
    ISBN 9780691241647 (hardback) | ISBN 9780691241654 (ebook)
Subjects: LCSH: Islamic modernism—History. | Sunna. |
    BISAC: RELIGION / Islam / History |
    SOCIAL SCIENCE / Islamic Studies
Classification: LCC BP166.14.M63 P87 2023 (print) |
    LCC BP166.14.M63 (ebook) | DDC 297.09—dc23/eng/20220912
LC record available at https://lccn.loc.gov/2022042291
LC ebook record available at https://lccn.loc.gov/2022042292

British Library Cataloging-in-Publication Data is available

Editorial: Fred Appel and James Collier
Production Editorial: Nathan Carr
Jacket/Cover Design: Katie Osborne
Production: Erin Suydam
Publicity: William Pagdatoon
Copyeditor: Bhisham Bherwani

Jacket/Cover Credit: توحید (*Tawhid*) by Mohammed Abduh. Translated into Tatar by Gabdulla Bubi (1911).

This book has been composed in Arno

Printed on acid-free paper. ∞

Printed in the United States of America

10 9 8 7 6 5 4 3 2 1

CONTENTS

Acknowledgments   vii

Note on Spelling and Transliteration   xi

Introduction   1

1 Jamal al-Din al-Afghani, Sayyid Ahmad Khan, and
   "Neicheri" Transgression   27

2 Muhammad ʿAbduh, Rashid Rida, and Bahai
   "Esotericists"   61

3 Muhammad Iqbal on the Question of Ahmadi
   Exclusion and Ismaili Inclusion   91

4 Abul Ala Mawdudi's Islamic State and Minority
   Ahmadis   135

5 Postcolonial Legacies of Modernist *Tawhid*:
   A Quest for Justice and the Nation-State   168

Notes   191

Bibliography   213

Index   219

ACKNOWLEDGMENTS

THE BULK of this book's research and writing took place during 2018 and 2021, starting with a Jeffery Henderson Senior Fellowship granted by Boston University's Center for the Humanities for the Spring of 2018. I would like to thank Susan Mizruchi and my fellow participants for their generous criticisms as I began to develop the arc and conceptual framework of the manuscript. Prior to this period, I presented work in progress at NYU (2015), UNC-Chapel Hill (2016), and Oxford (2017) to colleagues whose feedback helped shape the foundational ideas of the book. In 2018–2019, the series of talks I gave at Georgetown, Stanford, Berkeley, FIU, Hebrew University, and Williams College were crucial to sharpening the arguments of the respective chapters. I want to acknowledge those particular institutions and thank my colleagues who invited me and facilitated such productive discussions: Paula Chakravartty, Carl Ernst, Faisal Devji, Jonathan Brown, Thomas Blom Hansen, Abhishek Kaicker, Iqbal Akhtar, Yigal Bronner, and Zaid Adhami.

I am grateful for the critical and insightful feedback of the manuscript's two reviewers as well as the exemplary professional guidance from my editor, Fred Appel, who helped me discover this book's unique intellectual contribution. My colleagues in the Department of Religion at Boston University have been incredibly supportive over the years by reading drafts of chapters, listening to my ideas in seminars, conversing in the hallway, and through informal conversations during time spent at our faculty writing retreats. I want to thank Kecia Ali—a model scholar, department leader, and colleague who patiently tolerated and talked through my complaints and frustrations with the writing process and pushed me to think about new angles at several key junctures of writing. I am lucky to have started my first academic job at Boston University as a new mother with support from my first Chair, Deeana Klepper, who later became my friend and fellow sojourner in the travails of second book writing. Laura Harrington too became a dear friend who skillfully and humorously talked me down from the proverbial ledge of work/relationships/mothering/you name it—on more than one occasion. I'd like also to thank Andrea Berlin, David Frankfurter, Margarita Guillory, April Hughes, Jonathan Klawans, Diana Lobel, Anthony Petro, Steve Prothero, and Michael Zank for their collegial warmth and support in the last five years. I am grateful for the feedback from graduate students who took my Modern Islam class over the years, especially those who helped with research and editing of the manuscript: Elisheva Ash, Ateeb Gul, and Adnan Rehman.

Several friends and colleagues generously listened to and questioned my ideas and/or helped me navigate life's hurdles during the writing process: Manan Ahmed, Iqbal Akhtar, Cemil Aydin, Aparna Balachandran, Ruchi Chaturvedi, Houchang Chehabi, Tanya Cherkerzian, Kavita Datla, Arunabh Ghosh, Chris Gratien, Juliane Hammer, Abhishek Kaicker, Aparna Kapadia, Rajeev Kinra, Rama Mantena, Barbara Metcalf, Farina Mir, Roshni Mohan, Pooja Raval, Riti Samanta, Sharmila Sen, Sadia Saeed, Sunil Sharma, George Stone, Nina Sylvanus, Anand Taneja, SherAli Tareen, Matt Voorhees, Paul Weinfield, Yoon Sun Yang, and Darshana Zaveri.

While writing this book, I have been lucky to recover a part of me that had been dormant for a long time: my love for physical movement. I trained as a *bharatanatyam* dancer for twenty years, but that life of dance came to a screeching halt when I began professional academic life and started a family. Over the last five years, however, I rediscovered movement in a new avatar of weight lifting. As I completed this manuscript, I also competed in my first Strongman competition. Many friends and coaches were instrumental in this journey to my newfound identity as an athlete in middle age—something I could never have imagined. I want to thank Paula Fonseca, Nick Hadge, and Bill Bachand in particular for helping me find my kinetic self and fall in love with movement again.

I am incredibly fortunate to have a close-knit family. My mother Bharti Purohit, my sisters Lopa Kolluri and Deepa Purohit, and my late father Umakant T. Purohit have been the brick and mortar of my emotional constitution—made even stronger with the love and support of my extended tribe: Krishna Kolluri, Sanjit De Silva, Mira, Rania, and Ishan. Our little home trio is my ongoing energy source. Writing was made a little less painful by the wonder that is Sara. Watching her thrive in the transition from childhood to tweenhood—becoming wiser and more confident everyday while continuing to dole out mischief and bear hugs—has been my greatest gift, matched only by the sustenance from my life partner. Sanjay never ceases to surprise me with his perfectly calibrated awareness of when it's time to hear me out on my theories, push back on my assumptions, let me cry, make me a cocktail, or tap into his bottomless magic kit of humor. He makes family life and life of the mind synchronize into a seamless rhythm.

NOTE ON SPELLING AND
TRANSLITERATION

IN THIS BOOK, I have instituted a minimal number of diacritics. Instead of using either the *IJMES* transliteration table or that of the Library of Congress, I have used the everyday spelling for names and terms that most readers would already be familiar with. The one feature that I have retained from the various Arabic-to-Roman transliteration systems is the *'ayn*, but only when it appears at the beginning of a word. Thus: Abu'l A'la Mawdudi would be written as Abul Ala Mawdudi; Abduh would be spelled 'Abduh; *'ulama'* would take the form of *'ulama*; Isma'ili would be without the *'ayn* as Ismaili; and Baha'i would be written as Bahai (without the hamza, except in the case of Baha'u'llah, which is the more standardized orthography of the name in the Roman script).

SUNNI CHAUVINISM AND THE ROOTS OF MUSLIM MODERNISM

INTRODUCTION

WHEN A GROUP OF ISLAMISTS attacked the offices of the French satirical newspaper *Charlie Hebdo* in January 2015 and killed several people, the controversial subject of whether or not Islam needs a reformation began to be debated in media circles shortly thereafter.[1] The discussion amplified over the year, it seems, with the publication of *Heretic: Why Islam Needs a Reformation* by Sudanese-born Dutch activist Ayaan Hirsi Ali. Muslim and non-Muslim journalists writing in major western newspapers weighed in on this topic of Islam's reformation—why it should or should not happen and whether or not it happened already. At stake in this conversation was also the question of leadership—framed in terms of whether there was a need for a "Muslim Martin Luther" to reform Islam and guide the community, since the tradition, according to those who supported the call for a reformation, had been usurped by Islamists. Not surprisingly, there was a flurry of responses, both productive and critical. For example, in January, *Financial Times* journalist Roula Khalaf noted that Egypt's Abdel Fattah al-Sisi had been considered for this role. Later that year, in *The Guardian*, political journalist Mehdi Hasan cautioned against any kind of "Muslim Martin Luther" to unify or purify Islam. Such an endorsement, he argued, provides justification for the rise and mission of figures such as Abu Bakr Al Baghdadi, the recently deceased leader of ISIS.[2]

This particular debate about Islam's reformation was specifically tied to the events of 2015, but similar topics have been recurrent subjects of discussion and disagreement since the early period

1

of Islam. "Reform" is a widely accepted translation of two Arabic terms that share a common meaning: "tajdid" and "islah." *Tajdid* is generally understood as "renewal," or restoration of an original pure Islam, and *islah* frequently translates as "reform" or "repair" of the tradition's current state. Despite these technical variances, both terms communicate a similar conceptual implication: an imperative to unify the Islamic tradition. Furthermore, both ideas have historically aligned with another term, *mujaddid,* or "renewer." The *mujaddid* is the agent of reform, the leader designated to shepherd the community out of its broken or divided state. A well-known hadith, or saying of Prophet Muhammad, states that God will send to the Muslim community, at the beginning of each century, certain individuals who undertake the task to renew Islam. For example, the eighth century Ummayad Caliph ʿUmar ibn ʿAbd al-ʿAziz, the well-known ninth century theologian al-Ashʿari, and the renowned twelfth century philosopher Abu Hamid al-Ghazali are all acknowledged by a majority of Muslims as famous *mujaddid*s.

The discourse invoked in the 2015 debate—reformation, Martin Luther, heretic—represents a constellation of two distinct yet intersecting trajectories in the intellectual history of modern Muslim reform: one Muslim and one European Christian. When Europeans colonialized the Muslim world over the eighteenth to twentieth centuries, Orientalists and Christian missionaries brought with them Protestant conceptions of religion to which Muslims responded—and, in the process, redefined their traditional categories of knowledge. Muslim intellectuals generated new definitions of reform and Islam as a consequence of this entanglement, shaped by the epistemic logics of both the history and debates about *tajdid/ mujaddid* on the one hand and European Christian notions of reform and religion on the other. The fundamental coordinates of this colonial Muslim redefinition project were Protestant in character: there was only *one* legitimate Islam. The implications of this revaluation were twofold: first, the idea of "one Islam" was circumscribed by boundaries largely defined by the beliefs and practices of a Sunni majority. And second, the proponents of this new definition exhibited a

"Sunni chauvinist" tendency that either implicitly criticized or explicitly excluded individuals and/or groups who did not meet the requisite conditions.

Sunni Chauvinism and the Roots of Muslim Modernism examines one specific episode in this European and Muslim interconnected archive of debate about reform: the modernist movement that arose in colonial and postcolonial periods of 1850–1950 in Asia, North Africa, and the Middle East. The late nineteenth and early twentieth centuries were unlike previous eras in Muslim history. Muslim intellectuals were impelled to respond to the new and culturally alien context of colonial modernity—the prosperity of the three Muslim empires had fallen into serious decline and the rise of modern Europe as a serious military, economic, and political presence set in motion the European colonialist enterprise. The Safavid Empire fell in 1736, the Mughal Empire was taken over by the British officially in 1857, and the Ottoman Empire was divided up by the British and the French in the post-World War I mandate. The dissolution of the three great Muslim empires, and the consolidation of British and French rule in India, the Middle East, and North Africa triggered a crisis, as Muslims were no longer in power and had to confront their subservience to European leadership.

This crisis gave rise to a wave of leaders who spearheaded new political and religious movements in response to this cultural transformation. These leaders are largely classified into two categories: traditionalist reformers and modernist reformers. Traditionalists were religious scholars, known as *ʿulama*, whose ideas about reform were shaped in *madrasas* (religious schools). They believed it was necessary to redefine and reinterpret Islam through tradition: by cultivating individual morality, education, ethics, and a renewed commitment to following Islamic law. Modernist reformers, the subject of this study, approached reform from a markedly different perspective than their traditionalist counterparts. The modernists attempted to reconcile Islam in the modern period with western enlightenment values—such as secularism, western education, civilizational progress, democracy, and women's rights.

This volume explores the political and intellectual thought of a select group of modernists: Jamal al-Din al-Afghani (1838–1897), Muhammad 'Abduh (1849–1905), Muhammad Rashid Rida (1865–1935), Muhammad Iqbal (1877–1938), and Mawlana Abul Ala Mawdudi (1903–1979). Although these modernists wrote in different colonial contexts, their responses were uniformly tied together by one main concern: the loss of Muslim political power and the imperialist expansion of Christian Europe. Their reform projects were motivated by the overarching question of how Muslims should orient themselves in a world no longer governed by Muslim rule. It was from this vantage point that modernists sought to redefine Islam in terms compatible with European ideas of education, modern scientific thought, and civilizational progress. It was their aim to transform the cultural fabric of Muslim society on the basis of values and ideas generated through the encounter with enlightenment thought. To clarify, modernists did not want to become secular or European. Rather, they wished to reshape Muslim culture along the lines of their new worldview formulated in response to, yet differentiated from, Europeans. Their distinctive campaign for reform was too delimited and idiosyncratic to take root and effect comprehensive change in society as they imagined it. It is for this reason that I frame modernist reform projects as communicating hopes, visions, and *ideas* of unity.

Sunni Chauvinism and the Roots of Muslim Modernism examines two principal perspectives in modernists' writings: first, their belief that Islam was a unified religion and community; and second, how this claim of unity created mechanisms and boundaries of inclusion and exclusion. Modernists' call for the unity of the Muslim community and concomitant proposals for reform were in theory all-inclusive. However, this desire for unity led many modernists to denounce entire communities, such as the Shia, Bahais, Ahmadis, and Ismailis on the grounds that they undermined or resisted modernist definitions of what it meant to be a Muslim. Consequently, their redefinitions of Islam demarcated insiders and outsiders. Modernists launched criticisms against these aforementioned groups through sustained arguments that relied on implicit or at times explicit "Sunni normative bias": a framework of ideas about the finality of prophecy that provided justification for allegations and accusations of transgression against groups whose ideas contravened their own. To read the movement of Islamic modernism from the perspective of aspiration and exclusion underscores the power structures at work in this implicit Sunni normative bias. Although the modernist project of reform never fully launched in the comprehensive manner they hoped for in the nineteenth century colonial period, the assumptions and epistemic logic of modernist thought about unity and exclusion—made coherent by its implicit Sunni normative bias—persisted well into the second half of the twentieth century.

Sunni Chauvinism and the Roots of Muslim Modernism seeks to understand the logics, biases, and contributions of modernism in this long history of reform and debate about leadership that continues today. It is important to clarify that this book neither stakes a claim in the modern debate about reformation nor intervenes in theological conversations about reform within the tradition. The task here is to outline the history and development of modernist theories of Islam produced in response to European enlightenment concepts over the course of the nineteenth and early twentieth centuries. This project builds on a general consensus about the genesis and development of modernism as articulated in foundational scholarly studies of the topic.[3] This book shares a similar subject of enquiry to two recent monographs that foreground the intellectual contributions of many of the same thinkers discussed herein. Irfan Ahmad's *Religion as Critique: Islamic Critical Thinking from Mecca to the Marketplace* and Khurram Hussain's *Islam as Critique: Sayyid Ahmad Khan and the Challenge of Modernity* both examine key political and religious insights of modernists, challenging the widely held view that "critique" is only possible from the western enlightenment perspective. [4] Hussain, for example, analyzes Sayyid Ahmad Khan's oeuvre and Ahmad examines writings of Mawdudi among others to argue that Islam ought to be understood as tradition of critique, rather than a static entity that simply aspires or responds to the liberal "West."

This monograph does not attempt to reframe modernism as Ahmad and Hussain propose; however, it too calls attention to the limitations and assumptions that are operative in the "Islam" and "West" modernist framework—in particular, the Sunni inflection and bias at work in the "Islam" piece of the dichotomy. It brings into conversation well-known writings of canonically recognized modernists to explore the analogous ways in which modernist theories and definitions of Islam were shaped by a desire to unite the global Muslim community in the name of civilizational progress. Each chapter traces this modernist aim through key figures' writings on *tawhid*—the Quranic theological term signifying unity of God. Modernists reinterpreted this Quranic concept as political unity of the Muslim community, as was the need of the hour. As such, *tawhid* functioned first, as the conceptual medium through which they conveyed their hopes to unify and strengthen the Muslim community, which they believed was fragmented, stagnant, or backward. Second, modernists' statements about *tawhid* opened up discussions about which communities were excluded from the fold of Islam. The Shia, Ismailis, Ahmadis, and Bahais were key groups whose status was up for debate in this frame of inclusion and exclusion. My readings demonstrate how modernists formulated arguments against these communities in terms of "sectarian" deviance, but often their denouncements were specifically targeted at authoritative leaders of these communities. For example, modernist polemics about sectarian transgression were grounded in criticisms of false prophecy and heretical leadership, mounted against figures such as Mirza Ghulam Ahmad, the prophet of the Ahmadis, and ʿAbdul Baha, the leader of the Bahais. I read these accusations as exemplifying a Sunni normative framework of beliefs, ideas, and practices centered on the finality of prophecy, which provided justification for accusations of transgression against groups that believed in more expansive ideas of prophetic continuity and leadership. The modernist writings I analyze put into sharp relief some fundamental biases at the heart of the modernist reform project—the first and foremost being a Sunni majoritarian perspective that deliberates, debates, and frequently denounces altogether the legitimacy of minority groups.

There have been many books written on individual minority Muslim communities such as the Ahmadis or Ismailis. However, these studies tend to be monographs focused on one particular community. Moreover, they all address in some manner the relationship and/or tension with ideas and authoritative claims of the Sunni tradition. No book on modernism thus far has addressed how the debates about the role of minority groups have been central to the modernist project. Nor has any book on modernism identified an underlying Sunni normative bias that explicitly or implicitly operates as an essential component and force of canonical modernist thought. Each chapter describes the contours of arguments and accusations constructed by modernists and tries to understand possible motivations for what at times comes off as sheer antipathy and vitriol against certain communities and their leaders specifically. The modernists I read all convey some form of Sunni chauvinism, albeit in different ways, and against different groups. There has yet to be a study of modernism that has made the claim that the debates and positions of minority communities have been integral to the formation of modernist thought itself.

Before I explicate these unexamined assumptions of modernist arguments, let me turn to a brief discussion of what characteristics modernists share. Modernists were set apart as a group of Muslim reformers in that they were unambiguous about promulgating "modern values"—that is to say, values clearly identified with the modern world, such as rationality, science, civilizational progress, constitutionalism, and human equality. As the scholar of modern Islamic thought Charles Kurzman has noted, the modernist movement, roughly spanning the period 1850–1950, was not simply modern (as in taking root in the modern period, or feature of modernity), but explicitly a proponent of modernity. Modernist reformers were unambiguous supporters of freedom of speech, unapologetic about their endorsement of enlightenment ideas, and wholly committed to disseminating their views on reform. Modernists participated in political parties, lectured at universities, and published their ideas in local newspapers, but it would be misleading to assume that the modernist movement created an autonomous Muslim public sphere. Over the course of the eighteenth and nineteenth centuries, traditional structures of power in the Muslim colonial context were weakened by growing European presence. This specific political transformation limited internal economic growth, which necessarily restricted the development of independent institutions of learning. With notable exceptions like Sayyid Ahmad Khan, who founded Aligarh Muslim University in India, modernists did not establish schools or official educational organizations. Despite this lack of formal institutions in the colonial context, they were determined to debate and broadcast their positions on reform. They relied on informal leadership and mentorship as well as the written word. For example, Afghani was the revered mentor of Muhammad ʿAbduh and Rashid Rida, who gathered and taught students in coffeehouses, at the university, and in Freemason societies in Cairo. Although many modernists took to traditional literary forms of expression such as poetry and debate to convey their ideas, the most common medium through which they conducted their campaigns to redefine Islam in modern terms was the printing press. The periodical press was established in Muslim communities throughout India, North Africa, and the Middle East. It was the primary vehicle through which modernists addressed the issues they felt were the most pressing: Muslim cultural revival, women's rights, political reform, modern science, and western education.

Modernist ideas generated and transmitted through intellectual lineages and print from the mid-nineteenth to the mid-twentieth century were principally motivated by the existential condition of colonial occupation. When modernists stood as political representatives, gave speeches in universities, or composed opinion pieces in the press, they often did so from a defensive and/or nationalist perspective, undoubtedly under pressure to respond to European criticisms of Islamic civilization. That is to say, their ideas were certainly circulated and debated within Muslim public spheres, but the content itself was largely formulated as responses to European ideas and theories of science, philosophy, and history. Modernists wrote in reaction to books written in and about Europe, and specifically on topics generated by Orientalists, such as the periodization of the "Golden Age" of Islamic civilization and the rise of Islamic decadence associated with the Ottomans prior to the arrival of the Europeans. They were motivated by concerns about the weakness of Islam as civilization, which they believed could be saved through their modernist program of reform.

Recently, the global historian Cemil Aydin has demonstrated how a unified Islamic civilization or "Muslim world" never existed. The "Muslim world" represented an idea rather than any kind of reality, and this concept of civilizational unity took substantive shape and form in Muslim intellectual and political thought during the late Ottoman and Indian nationalist period—roughly 1870–1930s. [5] The modernists analyzed in this volume held the view that Islam was a discrete civilization and religion, thereby promulgating the coherent idea of the Muslim world Aydin identifies. They defined Islam as such against and in response to European Orientalists and Christians, who were the first to describe and translate Islam as a religion equivalent to Christianity. Modernists offered their various interpretations of Islam, sometimes in agreement and sometimes in disagreement with western ideas. What is interesting to note is that all those involved in the conversation—Europeans and Muslim elites—acceded to the belief that Islam was bounded and definable just like Christianity.[6]

The overarching argument of this volume about aspirational unity and exclusion is examined through the writings of modernists on the subject of *tawhid*. *Tawhid* was originally a Quranic idea that refers to God's unicity and theologically implies the assertion of monotheism. Herein, I analyze the writings of Afghani, ʿAbduh, Rida, Iqbal, and Mawdudi to demonstrate how they offered a new interpretation of *tawhid* to describe the unity of the Muslim community. Their understanding of *tawhid* as political and social unity conceptually functioned in a bifurcated manner. It represented an ideal of both the past and the future. It signified, on the one hand, a description of a "Golden Age" when the Muslim community was once united politically and socially, and on the other hand, an aim for a similar future. In this sense, it was the idiom through which modernists expressed both lament as well as aspiration.

Tawhid served as the platform through which this group of modernists communicated a host of concerns that were tied to the anxiety of civilizational decline. First, underlying their analysis of *tawhid* as social unity was an assumption that Islam had become fractured because of practices associated with "sects" such as Sufism and Shiism as well as the Bahai and Ahmadi traditions. Modernists viewed what the historian of Islam W. C. Smith called the "cumulative tradition" of Islam—the multiplicity of religious practices, notions of religious authority, interpretations of scripture, art, and music that change and develop throughout history—as "accretions" that compromised *tawhid*.[7] For these particular modernists, historical diversity of the Islamic tradition precluded the possibility of a future Islam that could become unified as it had been in the past. The prescription they offered to the problem of religious "accretions" was an argument that the Quran serve as the exclusive source of authority for all Muslims. Modernists embraced a *sola scriptura* position—one that emphasized the importance of individual rationalist interpretations of the Quran—over and against a heterogenous understanding of Islam as a diverse tradition of beliefs, practices, and interpretations of the Quran mediated through figures such as imams, pirs, and clergy. They made the case that if Muslims relied exclusively on an intellectual and individualist approach to the Quran and denounced devotional practices—such as memorizing the Quran or visiting the tombs of saints—the community as a whole could unite again as it had done so in the past.

Second, their anxiety about *tawhid* was explicitly tied to leadership, often associated with communities they criticized, such as the Bahais, the Ismailis, the Ahmadis, and the Shia. Modernists were highly dismissive of local community leaders such as imams, pirs, and even the 'ulama. They claimed that that there had been only one paradigmatic leader in the history of Islam, Prophet Muhammad. Consequently, they made the case that mediating figures of authority were unnecessary and in fact contradictory to the essential principles of Islam. There was a fundamental tension and contradiction in their views on this topic, however. On the one hand, they felt it imperative to assert that no prophetic leader could follow or replace Prophet Muhammad. On the other hand, they also asserted that the contemporaneous time in which *tawhid* was compromised required new modern leadership to shepherd the divided Muslim community, a position which many modernists saw themselves as filling. To be clear, I am not saying that they believed they were literally prophets of Islam. Rather, they saw themselves as exceptional men and bearers of special wisdom. As I discuss further below, their self-assertions as authoritative guides involved the strategic undermining of groups that had officially recognized leaders already, such as the Bahais, Ahmadis, and Ismailis.

Unlike reformers of earlier periods or traditionalist reformers of the same period, modernists argued that it was possible to reach across the various schools of Islamic law (*maddhabs*) and/or bypass the traditional schools altogether. For them, primacy was given to the Quran—and it was necessary to reconcile this foundational source of Islam with human reason. The modernists were in general quite critical of the 'ulama and traditional institutions of seminary training, and in fact claimed that they, rather than the traditional legal and religious scholars, were equipped to reinvigorate and redefine the Islamic tradition in the modern period. Furthermore, they deployed distinctive modes of expression to transmit their ideas. Modernists published their ideas in media such as newspapers and journals, but they also found ways to convey their intellectual positions in traditional Muslim genres of expression, such as poetry and debate, modifying and reconfiguring the content with their views about the compatibility of western science, education, and progress with Islam in the modern period.

One of the main differences between the traditionalists and the modernists was their respective positions on *ijithad*, or reinterpretation, of Islamic sources and concepts. Unlike the *ʿulama*, modernists thought it was possible and at times necessary to bypass the legal schools in order to provide fresh interpretations of Islamic ideas that could speak to modern changing conditions.[8] In fact, modernist reformers explicitly worked to renew and reinterpret Islam against and in conversation with enlightenment ideas of the colonial West. ʿAbduh, Rida, and Iqbal followed in the footsteps of their predecessors, al-Afghani and Sayyid Ahmed Khan, who believed that the tradition of Islam required renewal in the wake of secularization and the discovery of science in Europe. In response to these developments, Muslim intellectuals in the Middle East and India were concerned that Islam, as a religion and culture, was in a state of weakness, particularly after the decline of the Ottoman, Safavid, and Mughal Empires and the rise of colonialism. The modernists indeed sought to reform Islam like many earlier reformers—but the conditions in which they did so were altogether new, insofar as they operated in a milieu that was dominated by European cultural mores, political rule, and economic power.

The modernists' distinctive perspective is illuminated by comparison with that of traditionalist reformers writing in the same time period. The traditionalists, as mentioned earlier, were primarily members of the clergy, the *ʿulama*, or Sufis who oriented their projects of reform through the structures and institutions of particular legal or Sufi schools of interpretation. In India, for example, the disintegration of the Mughal Empire and the hierarchical structure of the royal court society of Persianate imperium ushered in a new audience for reformist literature. The language of composition changed from Persian to Urdu and the theological content of this reformist tradition was simplified and narrowed, with the primary topics of study focused on the Quran and the hadith. This Protestant approach to scripture served as a theological

"leveler," as the masses could access the Quran and hadith literature on the subject of piety, composed in Urdu for the people, in
a way that was not possible through the hierarchical structure of
the royal court.[9] The ultimate goal for traditionalist reformers was
to disseminate the traditions of Quranic interpretation and hadith
exegesis to a wider Muslim community. *Tawhid*, from a traditionalist perspective, functioned in a theological capacity. This new
traditionalist religiosity emphasized the unicity of God and individual piety for all.

Piety was not front and center of the modernist project. Certainly, many of the modernists were religious men, and some
trained as and were mentored by the *'ulama*, such as Muhammad
'Abduh and Rashid Rida. However, their intellectual campaigns,
unlike the traditionalists' projects, did not revolve around the restoration of piety. What distinguished the modernist worldview
was their preoccupation with how Islam as a civilization could
prosper again as it had in the past. Modernists formulated arguments that reflected on the past, though they weren't historians.
They were ideologues who glorified a golden age of Islam, bemoaned
the present, and directed their visions for reform toward the
future. *Tawhid* served as a conceptual medium through which they
conveyed their reflections on Islam as a religion and a civilization.
Each chapter in this book, therefore, is framed by an analysis of
modernists' reinterpretation of *tawhid*, which provides an opening
into two lines of thinking that have yet to be analyzed by scholars
in the study of Islam: first, the ways in which modernist thought
created a new form of Muslim majoritarian logic that demarcated
specific groups as minority sects; and second, how many of the
modernist reformers saw themselves in a salvific role, of a "Martin
Luther"-type reformer, with a mandate and mission to restore Islam
to its early glory.

As I mentioned in the opening, there are certain figures that are
recognized as *mujaddids* within the Islamic tradition. Many of the
modernists mentioned thus far, such as Muhammad 'Abduh and
Muhammad Iqbal, are commonly identified as crucial members

of this group, either specifically in accordance with the hadith about *tajdid,* or as subjects in academic studies of seminal reformers in the modern period. The contributions of the Bahais, Ismailis, and Ahmadis—communities whose ideas have always been part and parcel of the history of Islam and whose charismatic leaders were so critical to the reform period of the nineteenth century—rarely inform discussions about *tajdid* or *islah* in scholarly accounts of modern Islamic reform movements. Why these groups have been relegated to "sectarian" status and their interventions in Islamic reform denied in standard narratives of *tajdid* are questions that have yet to be interrogated by scholars in the study of Islam. One possible reason is that traditionalist/modernist frameworks, the binary through which modern reform is examined, cannot account for their contributions. It is certainly the case that Ahmadis and Ismailis do not fit into the traditionalist paradigm, as neither were their leaders trained members of the ʿ*ulama* nor were their teachings focused on piety according to Islamic law. However, there are many components of their beliefs that align with modernist reform. Take for example the Ahmadis. The founder of the Ahmadi community, Mirza Ghulam Ahmad, from Qadian, Punjab, claimed to receive God's revelation, and in 1888 called on Muslims to pledge their allegiance to him and to a new movement to reform Islam. He declared that he was the Promised Messiah, the Mahdi of the Muslims, and appeared in the likeness of both Jesus and Prophet Muhammad. Mirza Ghulam Ahmad instigated much controversy as a consequence of his radically new ideas, experiences with the divine, and approach to Muslim reform centered on his prophetic authority. He participated in polemical debates with Arya Samajis and Christian missionaries while simultaneously advocating for British rule.[10] Mirza Ghulam Ahmad endorsed *ijtihad,* wrote about the importance of the state (in this case his support of the British), and engaged Europeans and non-Muslims as well as Muslims about Islam. It is obvious that Mirza Ghulam Ahmad's ideas do not fit into the traditionalist model of reform; but surprisingly, his contributions to Muslim reform are never included in standard accounts of modern reform of the nineteenth and early twentieth centuries, when in fact many of his positions fit into the modernist paradigm. I would argue that this occlusion can be attributed to scholarly accounts of modernism that have given primacy to canonical modernist figures such as Afghani, 'Abduh, Rida, and Iqbal. It is not a coincidence that these canonical modernist thinkers have articulated criticisms of sectarian groups such as Ismailis, Ahmadis, and the Shia. It is likely that the implicit Sunni normative bias adopted by modernists has shaped the study of modernism itself. This has led, I argue, not only to an overall neglect of Shii and Sufi perspectives, and a disavowal of the impact of charismatic leaders such as Mirza Ghulam Ahmad, but also to a delimited understanding of modernism that is fundamentally majoritarian.

The major difference between Mirza Ghulam Ahmad and the canonical modernists was that he believed that he was a messiah, having arrived in the likeness of Muhammad as well as Jesus to renew Islam, as he explains in the following passage from 1900:[11]

> I am both Jesus the Messiah and Muhammad Mahdi. In Islamic terminology, this type of advent is called a *buruz* [re-advent, or spiritual reappearance]. I have been granted two kinds of *buruz*: one is the *buruz* of Jesus, and the other is the *buruz* of Muhammad. . . . In the capacity of Jesus the Messiah, I have been assigned the duty of stopping the Muslims from vicious attacks and bloodshed. . . . In the capacity of Muhammad Mahdi, my mission is to re-establish Tauhid in this world with the help of Divine signs.[12]

For Mirza Ghulam Ahmad, *risalat*, prophetic calling, was the solution to the crisis of Islam and the disintegration of *tawhid*. As the above passage illustrates, Mirza Ghulam Ahmad was impelled to find an appropriate solution to the problem of compromised *tawhid*; but in this case, the answer was his prophetic calling. Herein lies the connection with the canonical modernist response: both see the world temporally bifurcated. There was an ideal *tawhid* of the past and a possibility of an ideal *tawhid* in the future. For the Ahmadis—as well as the Bahais and Ismailis—official charismatic leadership of the respective communities helped navigate this existential condition in ways that were not possible for the canonical modernists.

Afghani, ʿAbduh, Rida, Iqbal, and Mawdudi all implicitly or explicitly espouse a Sunni normative position in their writings. Therefore, it is possible to interpret their arguments against the Ismailis, Bahais, and Ahmadis in a sectarian framework. That is to say, it is possible to interpret modernists' statements about deviation as a kind of assertion of Sunni orthodoxy. However, it is clear from the subject matter of their treatises, as well as their trenchant criticisms that often border on antipathy, that these target groups all, in some form, posed a threat to modernist leadership and authority. In this way, it is important to regard their accusations of theological transgression with suspicion. As I address in the chapters, modernists' polemical arguments are generally directed toward the specific leaders of these communities, and their motivations are oftentimes political or personal rather than theological. Furthermore, many of the modernists, such as Afghani and Mawdudi, often suggest their own credentials for leadership over the Muslim community in their writings. Even more surprising is that these same modernists sometimes adopt ideas and beliefs of these communities that have well-established structures centered on a charismatic figure. As I discuss below further in the first chapter: Afghani, for example, describes his own qualifications as a potential leader by appropriating and reworking ideas of prophecy that originate from the Shia and the Bahais—groups whom he accuses of heresy.

The canonical modernists refer to communities they perceive as violating the terms of unity as "sectarian," but as I have argued previously, the underlying logic of "sect," which presumes a corporal center, the "church," cannot be mapped upon the Islamic tradition in which no centralized institution or authority exists.[13] Moreover, there was never any kind of formal institutional decision or event in the history of Islam equivalent to the Protestant Reformation that demarcated different Muslim communities into sects. It would, therefore, be helpful to think about the Ahmadis, Ismailis, and Bahais in terms that are more capacious than "sectarian."

One concept that might be useful is "esoteric." Historically, esoteric refers to "hidden" knowledge accessible to a private community focused on practices of interior reflection. Esoteric groups, for the most part, never self-identified as such, as "esoteric" was more of an approach or way of comprehending the world rather than a structured system of belief and practice. Ancient and medieval esoteric traditions such as Gnosticism and Hermeticism, for example, were deeply intertwined with Christianity and also scientific practices. Recent scholarship on western esotericism has shown, however, that the Enlightenment ushered in a new framework for understanding esotericism. It created divisions between "secular" and "religious" disciplines and in turn established esoteric traditions as a separate sphere from both religion and science.[14]

This enlightenment categorization functioned in a similar manner as the new taxonomy of religion established by Orientalists starting in the nineteenth century. Orientalists inaugurated a novel classification system of religion, which was informed by comparisons to Christianity and theories of language and race. One crucial figure in this enterprise was the British philologist William Jones, who discovered "Indo-European"—the linguistic relationship between European and Indian languages—in the late eighteenth century. Jones's finding was premised on the categorization of languages into groups, such as "Aryan" and "Semitic." Over the course of the nineteenth century, Orientalists adopted this philological paradigm to outline theories of race. For example, the nineteenth century French philosopher and philologist Ernest Renan offered extensive explanations of Jews as Semites on the basis of Indo-European linguistic categories, most well known of which was the argument that the Semitic race was inferior to the Aryan race. New interpretations of religion also emerged from this paradigm.

Hinduism was considered "Aryan" in origin and Islam was classified as a "Semitic" religion, like Judaism. The logic herein created divisions within Islam as well. Sufism was identified as having roots in the "Aryan" race, as opposed to the "Semitic" race and religion of (presumably) Arab Sunni Islam. In this regard, the Orientalist framework of categorizing religion ultimately divided Muslims into separate identities and effaced religious components that were unrecognizable in this philological/race model.

This Orientalist paradigm that has become foundational to the comparative religion model of organization and classification has never recognized Ismailis, Bahais, or Ahmadis—yet, all three groups have been intertwined with the history of Islam, just as esotericism was historically imbricated within the Christian tradition. No doubt, the Ismailis, Bahais, and Ahmadis are distinct groups whose histories, community structures, fundamental theological premises, and practices preclude any kind of collective categorization. Bahais have roots in Islam but don't identify as Muslim, Ahmadis identify as Muslim but many Muslims don't recognize them as such, and Ismailis are generally understood as a sect of Islam. Despite these historical and theological differences there is a basic set of common features that these three groups share, which illustrate an "esoteric" orientation: first, they adhere to the belief in hidden truths; second, they proclaim that prophecy and/or revelation continued in some form after Muhammad and the Quran; and third, they believe their leaders possess hidden or special knowledge to guide their respective communities. All three groups in the nineteenth and early twentieth centuries were organized around charismatic leadership: that of Mirza Ghulam Ahmad, the Aga Khan, and ʿAbdul Baha. To analyze Ismaili, Ahmadi, and Bahai approaches to reform as "esoteric" helps elucidate two main points integral to this study: (1) the unacknowledged representation of these three communities in traditional models of classification endemic to the study of religion/Islam; and (2) their distinctive approach to reform based on hidden knowledge, continuous prophecy, and living religious leadership.

The Ahmadis, Bahais, and Ismailis are the main target groups analyzed here, but canonical modernists also identify "Sufis" and the "Shia" as communities that at times undermine the social and political unity of the Muslim community as they perceive it. I would argue that the Shia and Sufis would also qualify as "esoteric" insofar as they acknowledge hidden meanings of the Quran and continuous prophecy, as I outline above. However, they function slightly differently in canonical modernist criticisms: Sufi and Shia beliefs and practices are regarded with suspicion, but these groups lack the publicly recognized leadership and routinized bureaucratic structure that developed with the Ahmadis, Bahais, and Ismailis, whose successful organization and mobilization, shepherded by their respective communities' charismatic leadership, set them apart as sources of threat and/or envy to the authority of modernists.

Both the canonical and esoteric modernists were concerned with the problem of a fractured Islam and wrote about Islam in the modern period in terms that were inflected by the values of the enlightenment. However, each group assumed different positions when it came to the leadership of the Muslim community. The esoteric modernists, by virtue of their belief in possibilities of continuous prophecy, ultimately resolved the question of who exactly is the reformer of the time. The canonical modernists officially claimed that prophecy was over, and so the question of who should lead the community remained open. What I wish to underscore in my analyses is how many canonical modernists saw themselves as leaders who could serve in a prophetic capacity for the Muslim community. However, they were unable to make this claim explicit because of their commitment to a Sunni normative paradigm that precluded the possibility of prophetic authority after Muhammad. They, in turn, felt the need to deride and undermine groups that were unambiguous about the existence of continuous prophecy and its fulfillment by their charismatic leaders, such as 'Abdul Baha and Mirza Ghulam Ahmad.

This volume explores the boundaries of modernists' definitions of Islam through close readings of their polemical arguments. The modernists I study, on the one hand, make claims about Islam that are universal in character. They will often simply claim "Islam is x" or "What it means to be a Muslim is y." On the other hand, these same reformers' formulations are defined by parameters of inclusion and exclusion. Each reformer takes explicit positions on what beliefs, ideas, and people are outside the pale of their respective definitions of Islam as unity. This study focuses on how canonical modernists arrived at the conclusion that specific groups were excluded from the fold of Islam. Afghani's polemics were aimed at the followers of Sayyid Ahmad Khan as well as the Ismailis and the Bahais. For ʿAbduh, it was the Shia, and Rida believed that the Bahais as well as the Ahmadis and the Ismailis transgressed the boundaries of Muslim identity. Iqbal and Mawdudi both made pronouncements that the Ahmadis were heretics of Islam. Each chapter takes up a discussion of one particular modernist in light of the theme of Islam as unity, examines the contours of the modernist argument against a particular group or groups, and reflects on the reasons and driving forces behind the argument.

Canonical modernists' arguments fundamentally rely on the logic of western enlightenment ideas, such as reason, scriptural authority over popular practice, and, most importantly for this study, civilizational progress. As I began to outline above, their claims about Islam as cohesive and unified assume a Sunni normative bias that excludes groups such as the Shia, Ahmadis, Ismailis, and Bahais. However, canonical modernists often adopted esoteric concepts from these excluded groups—in particular, prophecy. The canonical modernists denounce Ahmadi, Bahai, and Ismaili ideas of prophetic continuity and authority; but their positions and arguments are often imbricated within many of the same logics and arguments about continuous prophecy that are practiced by these same communities. This is not altogether surprising, as esoteric ideas were in many ways woven into the historical fabric of Islam's cumulative tradition, as I noted above. What is quite remarkable to think about, however, is how Islamic modernists developed many of their reformist ideas based on the simultaneous exclusion *and* appropriation of esoteric thought.

The conceptual distinction between "esoteric" and "canonical" modernism helps draw attention to a central line of investigation in this study: namely that Muslim modernism was given meaning and legitimacy through proclamations about exclusion. It is important to clarify that this argument is based on the writings of five main modernists at the center of this study—Afghani, ʿAbduh, Rida, Iqbal, and Mawdudi, who collectively illustrate a continuous line of thinking that developed over a wide geographic range starting in the nineteenth century and extending into the late twentieth century. Despite the different contexts and time periods in which each of these figures produced their ideas, they all demonstrate a consistent pattern of argumentation about unity and exclusion based on the redefinition of Islam as unity. I illustrate this continuity through their respective statements on *tawhid* but also outline the salient differences by analyzing the writings of the selected modernists in three phases over the period of approximately 1870–1980. Afghani and ʿAbduh represent early modernist thinking, as their positions on *tawhid* and exclusion are conveyed within the context of colonial rule. Rashid Rida too produced his works in the context of the colonial empire, but his views on *tawhid* were motivated by concerns about community that were nationalist in character. These positions mirrored Iqbal's, who wrote at approximately the same time as Rida and with similar nationalist concerns but in colonial India. Mawdudi, a late modernist, constructed his vision of *tawhid* with the question of the state—the postcolonial state specifically—front and center. This focus on the state distinguished his and Sayyid Qutb's modernism (or what is generally referred to as "Islamism") from that of the earlier group of modernists. The concluding final chapter examines the legacy of this modernist line of thinking about *tawhid* as unity through discussion of variegated Muslim political thinkers in the postcolonial period—as diverse as Fazlur Rahman, Ali Shariati, and leaders of Al Qaeda.

This group of modernists all provide sustained arguments about the boundaries of unity that implicate the esoteric modernists through the conceptual framework of *tawhid*. Moreover, they all reveal contradictions in their writings: on the one hand, they make pronouncements about heresy and exclusion; on the other hand, they are open to "heretical" ideas. For example, Iqbal is sympathetic to Sufi ideas of continuous prophecy while at the same time declaring Ahmadis heretical. Mawdudi reflects on the importance of a modern Mahdi to guide the community while also formulating arguments against Ahmadi religious authority. There is no single answer as to why this is the case. However, each chapter reflects on possible reasons for the contradictory and seemingly arbitrary positions on unity and exclusion. It is important to note that the spectrum of intention is quite broad in modernist thinking too: some modernists had deeply humanistic goals and, as I demonstrate in the concluding chapter, modernism also opened up reactionary and destructive ideas. This study aims to unpack how a pattern of thinking about unity and exclusion developed and persisted over a century in Muslim political thought, despite variegated intentions and consequences.

Chapters

The first chapter, "Jamal al-Din al-Afghani, Sayyid Ahmad Khan, and 'Neicheri' Transgression" takes up a discussion of Jamal al-Din al-Afghani (1838–1897), the most renowned and earliest of the modernists. Afghani was a political activist and agitator, orator, teacher, and journalist who traveled and spread his ideas throughout the Middle East, South Asia, and Europe in the late nineteenth century. He spent two years in Hyderabad, India (1879–1881), where he composed a series of essays, the most well-known of which was "The Truth about the Neicheri Sect and an Explanation of the Neicheris," which was later translated as "The Refutation of the Materialists." The subject of this first chapter is an interrogation of Afghani's understanding of "neicheri." The closest English equivalent of "neicheri" is "naturalist." However, this definition is not simply descriptive. It was a derogatory neologism that Afghani invoked in his essay to describe heretical groups—Zoroastrians, Ismailis, and Bahais, as well as the followers of Sayyid Ahmad Khan (1817–1898). The chapter analyzes Afghani's arguments about heresy in tandem with his position on *tawhid* (as political unity), which he believed was compromised at the time, primarily because Muslims were lacking proper leadership. Turning to a discussion of his time as a political and social leader in Egypt, I show how Afghani was recognized as a quasi-prophetic guide by a contingent of students and activists in Cairo. The question that animates this analysis is why Afghani condemns Sayyid Ahmad and his followers as heretical "neicheris" especially when Sayyid Ahmad shared many of the same values about Islam's civilizational progress as Afghani. The chapter concludes with the suggestion that Afghani undermined the ideas and followers of Sayyid Ahmad Khan because he resented his achievements as a successful leader of Muslims—a position Afghani sought for himself.

The second chapter "Muhammad 'Abduh, Rashid Rida, and Bahai 'Esotericists'" discusses Muhammad 'Abduh (1849–1905) and his student Rashid Rida (1865–1935). Together with Afghani, these three are widely regarded as the founders of Islamic modernism. The chapter begins with an examination of one of Muhammad 'Abduh's most famous treatises, "Theology of Unity," in which he accuses the Shia for having undermined Muslim unity, and which is followed by an analysis of a less known exchange between 'Abduh and Rida about Bahai beliefs, practices, and leadership. 'Abduh's mentor Afghani made public proclamations against the Bahais, and 'Abduh's student Rashid Rida vehemently opposed Bahai beliefs and practices. Rida explicitly denounced the authority of this group, describing them as "propagandists" similar to Ismailis and Sufis. But 'Abduh, on the other hand, was quite sympathetic to Bahai ideas. This chapter calls attention to a surprising contradiction at the heart of many modernists' positions: Even though Afghani and 'Abduh claim that specific groups explicitly undermined Muslim political unity, their writings also reveal how they have been shaped and influenced by the esoteric components of Shia, Ismaili, and Bahai thought. I discuss this problem in Afghani's and ʿAbduh's writings in terms of the issue of prophecy—specifically how both ʿAbduh and Afghani rely on ideas of continuous prophecy from Shii and Bahai thought to establish their own views on religion and religious authority despite their strident positions against these groups.

The third chapter, "Muhammad Iqbal on the Question of Ahmadi Exclusion and Ismaili Inclusion," addresses the controversy about Ahmadi ideas of continuous prophecy through a study of Muhammad Iqbal's writings, in particular, his famous book-length essay titled *Islam and Ahmadism*, in which he makes the argument that Ahmadis should be considered a separate community from Muslims because of their heretical beliefs and practices. The chapter begins with Iqbal's views on *tawhid* as social and political unity, followed by his criticisms of the Ahmadis. Iqbal's idea of prophecy was fundamentally at odds with Mirza Ghulam Ahmad's interpretation. Iqbal claimed that prophecy manifested itself in a unique way in Islam, and what distinguished Islam from Christianity, as well as Judaism, was the special status of Muhammad as *nabi* (prophet). Ahmadi endorsement of continuous prophecy not only undermined the idea of *nabuwwat*, but also, through its belief in messianic salvation in the figure of Mirza Ghulam Ahmad, disempowered both the individual as well as society at large. Scholars have argued that Iqbal's denouncement of the Ahmadis must be understood as an ethical and theological violation of the doctrine of Muhammad's final prophecy. This theological reading, I contend, does not provide a complete picture of why Iqbal would denounce the Ahmadis as heretics. This chapter engages the writings of several sociologists—Zimmel, Zito, and Bourdieu—to investigate the theory of the heretic. The intervention I offer to this debate about Iqbal's denouncement of the Ahmadis is that Iqbal perceived Mirza Ghulam Ahmad and his followers as "backward," and ultimately threatening to progressive ideas of community and leadership. The

Ahmadis in short precluded civilizational progress of the Muslim community from modernity. By way of comparison, I turn to Iqbal's statements about the Ismailis and their leader, the Aga Khan, whom Iqbal praises for their integration and accommodation into the Indian Muslim community. Whereas Afghani writes about the Ismailis as *"neicheri,"* Iqbal claims that Ismailis represent the paradigmatic sectarian Muslim community, something to which the Ahmadis ought to aspire.

The fourth chapter, "Abul Ala Mawdudi's Islamic State and its Minority Ahmadis," focuses on the thought of Islamist theoretician Sayyid Abul Ala Mawdudi (1903–1979). Although there are clear distinctions between modernists and Islamists, the chapter examines modernist lines of thinking that continued with the rise of Islamist ideology. One of the key features of Islamism, outlined by Mawdudi, was the goal of an Islamic state. Whereas the earlier modernists wrote within the domain of colonial empire, Islamists like Mawdudi in India and Sayyid Qutb in Egypt wrote during the transition to and after the rise of the nation-state. Despite these distinct historical moments there were still connections and shared viewpoints between modernism and Islamism, found in conceptions of *tawhid* as political unity. Mawdudi, similarly to his modernist predecessors, deployed ideas of *tawhid* that represented political unity and civilizational progress; however, in Mawdudi's writings, *tawhid* stands at the center of his call for an Islamic state in which God is the only sovereign. Furthermore, the chapter calls attention to the ways in which his polemical writings against Ahmadis—in particular his call for their status as non-Muslims— draws from components of Iqbal's arguments, and how Mawdudi, like Afghani, exhibited aspirations to be recognized as a reformer and leader of the modern Muslim community.

The final chapter, "Postcolonial Legacies of Modernist *Tawhid*: A Quest for Justice and the Nation-State," reflects on the repercussions of the nineteenth century idea of Islam as political unity, through an analysis of various statements on unity and *tawhid* in the postcolonial period. The view that Islam was a cohesive tradition continued into the 1950s, and the examples I briefly discuss all reflect on the subject of social and political unity from a perspective that can be broadly defined as "ethical." This chapter begins with a study of unity in the writings of Fazlur Rahman, the Pakistani modernist Quran scholar. Rahman shares many of the perspectives of his modernist predecessors, such as a Sunni normative bias that maligns groups such as the Shia and the Sufis. However, exclusion is not exactly front and center in Rahman's writings. In response and in contrast to Islamist and clerical interpretations of law and the Quran, Rahman claims that the Quran offers systematic moral and ethical guidelines based on the early community of the Prophet that can be applied to the contemporary context. Thereafter, the chapter analyzes how this ethical approach enjoined in discussions of *tawhid*/unity is given new meaning in the postcolonial period by political thinkers such as Ali Shariati in Iran, Farid Esack in South Africa, and the Afghanistan-based Al Qaeda. Ali Shariati, one of the seminal founding ideologues of the Iranian Revolution, casts *tawhid* into a Shii and Marxist framework that offers a corrective to what he identifies as the unjust social and political order of Shah Reza Pahlavi's state rule. South African scholar of Islamic studies, Farid Esack, examines how Muslims fighting against apartheid in the 1980s invoked *tawhid* as part of a larger campaign against racial and political oppression of the South African state. And finally, the chapter concludes with a discussion of Al Qaeda, as a way to explore the reactionary turn and manipulation of modernist and Islamist views of unity and religious authority. Al Qaeda appropriated the Islamist idea of the vanguard and discursively legitimized terrorism against superpower western nation-states as a salvific project aimed to rescue a once unified but now fractured Muslim community.

1

Jamal al-Din al-Afghani, Sayyid Ahmad Khan, and "Neicheri" Transgression

JAMAL AL-DIN AL-AFGHANI (1838–1897) was the earliest, most widely traveled, and globally recognized modernist. He was a political activist, orator, teacher, and journalist who spread his ideas throughout the Middle East, South Asia, and Europe in the late nineteenth century. He was born and educated in Iran, participated in Afghan politics, taught at universities in Istanbul, spearheaded anti-colonial agitation in Egypt, and spent time writing and publishing in India, England, and France. In terms of scholarly interventions, he was the first Muslim intellectual to engage in formal debates with European scholars. Afghani's modernist positions are exemplified in the famous exchange with the nineteenth century French Orientalist Ernest Renan on the topic of Islam and science, wherein Afghani made the case, in response to Renan, that Muslims were just as capable of scientific thinking as Europeans. What is less known about Afghani is his time in India and the set of writings he produced during his two-year stay in Hyderabad (1879–1881). During this period, he composed a series of strident polemics against Sayyid Ahmad Khan (1817–1898) and his followers, the most well-known of which was "The Truth about the *Neicheri* Sect and an Explanation of the *Neicheris*," later translated

27

as "Refutation of the Materialists." The term "neicheri" is most frequently interpreted as "naturalist"; however, it is important to note that "neicheri" was a nineteenth century neologism. At the time it was invoked by critics to describe Sayyid Ahmad Khan's approach to reform which was premised on a fundamental compatibility between religion (Islam) and western science. Afghani specifically used the term "neicheri" to malign the followers of Sayyid Ahmad Khan as well as various groups he believed to have denied the existence of God—such as the Greek Cynics, Zoroastrians, Ismailis, and Bahais. The chapter analyzes "The Refutation of the Materialists"— as well as two other pieces titled "The Materialists in India" and "Commentary on the Commentator," respectively—to understand Afghani's ideas about Islam and *tawhid* as political unity, and his position on Ismailis, Bahais, and the Shia. Afghani branded these esoteric groups as "neicheri," as they threatened *tawhid*, the political unity of the Muslim community.

In this selection of writings, Afghani assumes a line of reasoning that is straightforwardly "orthodox." That is to say, the logic of his argumentation assumes a recognizable Sunni normative intolerance of sectarianism. There are two main scholarly interpretations of Afghani's alleged orthodoxy. The Arab historian Albert Hourani has made the point that Afghani actually thought that Sayyid Ahmad Khan was a naturalist who denied the existence of any divine order, and thus interprets the "Refutation of the Materialists" as a defense of orthodoxy against heterodoxy.[1] From this perspective, the polemic against Sayyid Ahmad Khan is understood as theological. According to the Iranian historian Nikki Keddie, who has provided the most systematic history and biography of Afghani, the denouncement of Sayyid Ahmad Khan was politically motivated, which is to say that Afghani's religious rhetoric was a cover for his criticism of Sayyid Ahmad Khan as a Muslim leader who was pro-British.[2] Both of these readings, however, don't fully account for the vitriolic accusations against Sayyid Ahmad Khan and his explicit statements that Indian Muslims needed a more suitable political leader than him.

I argue that Afghani saw in Sayyid Ahmad Khan a constellation of leadership roles that he once held—teacher, intellectual, political leader, and spiritual guide—especially during his time in Egypt. Afghani gathered a following of students on the basis of his eccentric ideas about religion and politics, which he disseminated in coffeehouses and Freemason societies in Cairo. He also helped mobilize forces during the nationalist Urabi revolt. In terms of credentials, Afghani's claim that he could provide leadership for Indian Muslims was not altogether out of the realm of possibility. Afghani saw himself, and was recognized, as more than just a worldly political or intellectual figure, as many of his students described him in the language analogous to that of a Sufi *pir* or master. Moreover, in many of Afghani's writings, he offers suggestions about a potential leader more qualified than Sayyid Ahmad Khan at the same time that he intimates that he could serve in the role of a Mahdi—a similar religiopolitical position as the contemporaneous Sudanese Mahdi. This was of course ironic, considering that the language he invoked to describe his potential leadership positions—such as Mahdi and guide of the *ikhwan*—was drawn from Ismaili and Shii traditions, both of which he maligns in the "*Neicheri*" piece. Below, I explain how he at once denounced the practices and beliefs of these esoteric groups while simultaneously adopting esoteric concepts of continuous prophesy to legitimatize his claims to leadership.

Before delving into the specific teachings and practices that were crucial to Afghani's intellectual formation, it is important to understand his early background. The traditional biographical sources—those by Muhammad ʿAbduh and Jurji Zaidan—rely on Afghani's words about his biography. But according to Nikki Keddie, there is ample evidence that these sources are not completely accurate as they cast Afghani as unquestionably orthodox and Sunni. This account, Keddie explains, must be understood as attempts by his biographers to counter charges against Afghani as a religious deviant.[3] It is now abundantly clear, for example, that Afghani was not born and raised in Sunni Afghanistan as his traditional biographers recount, but rather in Shiʾi Iran—which is demonstrated by the Government of India documents that describe how Afghani entered Afghanistan for the first time in 1866. Furthermore, Persian sources explain that he was born in Asabad and attended school in Qazvin and later Tehran, where he was trained in traditional Shii education as well as Islamic philosophy and mysticism.[4] There is also quite a bit of evidence in Afghani's writings that shows the influences of religious and political Shiism as well as messianic Babism, which I will explicate further below.

Afghani travelled to India for the first time when he was approximately 18 years old. It is difficult to reconstruct from the sources where exactly he lived and travelled, but it is likely that he spent several formative years there. Afghani was first exposed to the presence of the British at this time, witnessing firsthand the ways in which the British displaced the old Muslim ruling elite. He was also introduced to Western science, civilizational theories, and religion during this period. His exposure in India to Western ideas of science, combined with the Shii religious climate of his early years in Iran, came to shape a peculiar understanding of religion that was evolutionary in nature. That is, he developed a theory that "simpler prophetic religion was useful for less advanced peoples, and a more rational reformed religion was what the masses needed later."[5] As I will discuss further below, this progressive idea of religion was crucial to the logic at work in his accusation of heresy against Sayyid Ahmad Khan.

After his first trip to India, he made a short trip to Mecca and then traveled to Afghanistan. Although his biographers claimed he "returned" to his homeland, Government of India documents point to the fact that Afghani arrived in Afghanistan, for the first time, in 1866. There, he aligned himself politically with the new Amir Azam Khan in Kabul and, according to British documents, urged him to support the Russians and fight the British. After Azam Khan was defeated by his brother Shir Ali, Afghani lost his position as a political ally, as the new Amir exiled Afghani from Qandahar in 1868. From there he travelled to Bombay, Cairo, and, by 1869, Istanbul. In Istanbul, he joined many of the leading figures of the Tanzimat reforms and supported the development of educational reforms in the university. Afghani was selected to give a keynote lecture at the opening of the new university. His speech underscored the virtues of Western science and education and the necessity to emulate the "civilized" nations.[6] Shortly after, he was appointed as an official of the Council of Education. In this post, he allegedly gave a controversial speech that caused his expulsion from Istanbul. Instead of lecturing on the expected topics of science and the workings of modern industries, he discussed "heretical" ideas of Islamic philosophy and prophecy. Afghani's ideas offended the sensibilities of Sunni westernizing reformers as well as the ʿulama.[7]

Afghani returned to Cairo in 1871 until he was expelled in 1879. He arrived at the invitation of Riyad Pasha, a prominent politician, but most of Afghani's activities were conducted in informal sectors of teaching and mentoring. It is clear that people were drawn to Afghani—politicians as well as students and intellectuals—because of his charismatic personality. Students were attracted to Afghani's peculiar background in Islamic philosophy. For example, it was at this time that Muhammad ʿAbduh, the famous Egyptian legal scholar and reformer, was introduced into the circle of Afghani's followers. Afghani was popular because he taught about subjects such as medieval Muslim philosophy, which spoke to many of the Muslim intellectuals' nationalist spirit. Many of his philosophical and radical ideas served, in some ways, as an alternative to and intellectual escape from Egypt's political and social crisis. Nationalist sentiments against Western domination—especially Egypt's dependence on European bankers and capitalists—were on the rise. Afghani stepped in and encouraged his followers to set up newspapers and write about their political grievances. By 1878 and 1879, he began composing incendiary public speeches against the British and developed his reputation as a popular leader and orator. However, in 1879, the new Khedive, Tawfik Pasha, demanded that Afghani be expelled.

From Egypt, Afghani traveled to Hyderabad via Bombay, where he stayed for two years. In 1881, he wrote "The Truth about the *Neicheri* Sect and an Explanation of the *Neicheris*," which was later translated as "Refutation of the Materialists," which was supposedly a response to a query from a local teacher, as indicated in the preface to the piece. At the start of the "Refutation," Afghani presents a note from a mathematics instructor, named Muhammad Vasil, who writes to Afghani from a local madrasa, "Madrasa-i-A'izza," in Hyderabad, to inquire about the identity of the *neicheris*:

> These days the sound, "neicher, neicher," reaches us from all over India—the Western and Northern states, the Punjab, Bengal, Sind, and Hyderabad in the Deccan. Some men called "neicheris" are to be found in every city and town. It seems that this group is constantly growing, especially among the Muslims. I have asked many of this group: What is the truth about neicher, and when did this school appear? Is this neicheriyya group trying to reform civilization by its new policy or do they have a different aim? How might one compare its total effects on civilization and the social order with those of religion? Also, if this is an ancient sect, then why has it not begun to spread in the world until now? If it is recent then what effects will result from its existence? But not one of these people gave a decisive and adequate answer to my questions. Therefore, I pray that Your Honor explain for me in details the truth about neicher and nicheriyya.[8]

Before launching into the formal statement on the matter, Afghani offers a preliminary short response to Vasil, explaining that *neicher* means "nature" and that "the *neicheriyya* school is the same as the materialist school of ancient Greece of the third and fourth centuries." The first doctrine of the "*neicheriyya* sect," he explains, is "the overthrow of religions," and the sect's sole purpose is to "lay the foundations of license and communism among all peoples." They have existed in many nations and in "various guises" and their principal aim has been the "ruin of civilization and corruption of the social order."[9] He then states that he will explain these ideas further in his treatise.

Afghani's initial rejoinder to Vasil sets the groundwork for the ensuing discussion in the piece, which is divided into the following subject headings:

- "The Greek Materialists,"
- "The Modern Materialists, Especially Darwin,"
- "The Social Virtues of Religion and the Social Harm of the Materialists,"
- "Religions' Three Beliefs,"
- "The Three Qualities Produced by Religion,"
- "How the *Neicheris* Undermine the Six Beliefs and Qualities,"
- "How the Materialists Undermined the Great Nations of the Past,"
- "Why the *Neicheris* Undermine the Restraint of Passion," and
- "The Evils of the *Neicheris* and Virtues of Religion."

Afghani uses the terms "*neicheri*" and "materialist" interchangeably throughout the piece. According to him, at the most rudimentary level, the materialists/*neicheris* are those who deny religion and attempt to destroy civilizational progress. It is important to note that his argument is ahistorical, even though it purports to provide a chronological account of the matter. The piece is fundamentally polemical, as it maligns various groups as political and religious deviants.

The opening sections explain that the first materialists were one of two groups of Greek philosophers in the third and fourth centuries (the other being the theists). Whereas the theists believed in a creator, the materialists believed that nothing existed but matter. These two opposing groups set the foundation for the discussion about "the corruption that has come into the sphere of civilization from the materialist or *neicheri* sect." To put it in simple terms, there are those who fall in the theist category (followers of religion) on the one hand, and those who deny God (the *neicheris*) on the other hand. After establishing this division, he then turns to the subject of the "virtues, advantages, and benefits of religions, especially the Islamic religion."

His exposition on the "Religions' Three Beliefs" section begins with an explanation of how first, "there is a terrestrial angel (man) and that he is the noblest of creatures," second, "the certainty that his community is the noblest one, and all that are outside his community are in error and deviation," and third, "the firm belief that man has come into the world in order to acquire accomplishments worthy of transferring him to a world more excellent, higher, vaster, and more perfect than his narrow dark world. . . ." These "three beliefs" make no reference to the Quran or any other Muslim religious beliefs or practices. His ideas of the individual, the community, and the necessity of self-improvement are abstract and universal statements, functioning, it seems, to set the terms for his argument about progress.[10] He writes: "His ascent on the ladder of civilization proceeds in proportion to his progress in the intellectual sphere."[11] These ambiguous ideas about progress serve as the framework through which he conveys his aspiration for the unity of the community. He draws connections between individual progress and the progress of the community, which ultimately leads to his point about community pride or the belief that one's community is the best of all. He writes:

> one of the consequences of the certainty that one's own community is the best one and all others are in error is that the man who believes this will inevitably enter into rivalry and competition with other communities; will compete against them in the arena of virtues. . . . Such a man will never be satisfied with decline, baseness, or ignobility for himself and his community.[12]

Afghani's arguments about religion as community pride and progress have been interpreted as an expression of pan-Islamist politics.[13] Keddie claims that the reason why Afghani writes in support of pan-Islamism is that it was a means by which he could ingratiate himself with Sultan Abdulhamid (1842–1918).[14] Basically, if Afghani wanted to appeal to Sultan Abdulhamid and those around him, it was necessary to frame his political vision in terms of religious orthodoxy.[15] It is for this reason, as well as his desire to win the support of Abdulhamid, Keddie contends, that Afghani presents his calls for Muslim unity in terms of orthodoxy.

It is more than likely that this piece was politically motivated, as Keddie claims. However, there are several aspects of Afghani's rhetoric that are not necessarily or exclusively politically instrumental in ways that Keddie suggests. Let's turn to his idea of religion as explicated through *tawhid*. Afghani begins his closing remarks in the piece with this Quranic theological idea. He writes: "the first pillar of Islamic religion is that by the luster of unity [*tawhid*—the absolute unity of God], it purifies and cleans off the rust of superstition, the turbidity of fantasies, and the contamination of imaginings."[16] It becomes clear as he explicates this idea of *tawhid* thereafter, that he is not concerned with the question of God's unity; rather, he is concerned with the Muslim community. This interpretation of *tawhid* as social unity provides the basis of his argument about Islam and allows him to make comparisons with other religious traditions. In this comparative move he asserts that, Christianity, "Brahman religion," and Zoroastrianism are divided and hierarchical religions. For example, the "Brahman religion," he writes, "divides men into four classes." This missing principle of social unity, he contends, "may be considered one of the main causes for the lack of proper progress among the followers of this religion."[17] Afghani draws a direct connection between social unity inherent to a specific religion and the progress of the people, noting in the case of the "Brahman religion" a lack of both. In Afghani's view, Christianity fares a bit better than the "Brahman religion" as he contends that the Christian religion does not make distinctions in social classes. However, the problem with Christianity is that it too eventually divided when the "followers of that religion . . . gave so much honor to the class of priests that it became a cause for lowering others." As long as the priesthood remained a powerful institution, Afghani explains, "no progress was achieved among that community."[18] Whereas the Hindus lack this doctrine of unity altogether, the Christians were led astray from this original principle by the Catholic Church. There was, however, a specific figure in history that changed this course for the Christians, and that was Luther. He then turns to the French historian Guizot to explain what happened with Luther and his reformation: "One of the greatest causes for European civilization was that a group appeared, saying: 'Although our religion is the Christian religion, we are seeking the proofs of the fundamentals of our beliefs.' ... When the group became strong their ideas spread; minds emerged from their state of stupidity and dullness into movement and progress."[19]

This reference to Guizot provides another dimension into Afghani's understanding of the relationship between religion and progress. Luther was the key figure who reversed the downward spiral of Christians from their "state of stupidity and dullness" into "movement and progress." Luther disrupted the power and the authority of the priesthood and salvaged Christianity from Catholicism; that is, from any form of mediation and popular belief. It is interesting to note that before he describes Luther's intervention, via Guizot, he makes the point that Luther took his ideas about Protestantism from Muslims.[20] Afghani thus draws a direct correlation between religions that are unified (as opposed to divided) and social progress of its people. In this schematic argument, the "Brahman religion" is inherently divided and therefore its followers backward. Christianity was unified, hit a theological and social setback when it became divided through the institution of the church, but then was redeemed from the path of "stupidity" to "progress" through Luther.

This discussion of Islam's unity by comparison to other religions provides important background to the central subject of the essay, the *neicheri*. He begins with the point that this *neicheri* group has focused throughout history on one goal: "to extirpate ... human happiness that is built of those three noble beliefs and three great qualities."[21] All the points that Afghani delineates thus far in his explication of religion rhetorically function to underscore the ways in which the *neicheris* actively seek to thwart the progress of civilization. Afghani remarks that the *neicheris* believe that there is no distinction between man and other animals, there is no life after death, and their most important values are communist ideals of sharing and of banning of privilege. The *neicheri* worldview can be summarized as follows:

> The happy man is he who attains in this world animal appetites and pleasure. Because of this false opinion, they gave currency to the misfortunates of perfidy, treachery, embezzlement . . . and prevented man from discovering truths and traveling toward perfection.[22]

Who exactly were these *neicheris* in history? According to Afghani, some of the first *neicheris* were the Cynics, who over time:

> influenced the souls and minds of the Greeks. They brought intellects to the point of stupidity; the bazaar of knowledge and wisdom became sluggish, and manners became corrupt. . . . In sum, all six pillars of their castle of happiness and all the foundations of their humanity were overturned.

Among the Persians, there was the *neicheri* Mazdak (a sixth-century Zoroastrian reformer who became prominent under Sassanian rule), who Afghani claims replaced the laws, norms, and customs established by men with the sacred law of "*neicher*" that "established the right of sharing all food, drink, and women" and made it "incumbent on every person . . . to obtain his rights in property and women in whatever way he can, in accord with the sacred law of nature."[23] Basically, for Afghani, the Zoroastrian *neicheris* were communists.

It is clear that the *neicheri* is not really a "sect" as the title of the piece claims. Unlike the recognizable divisions or schools of thought within Islam, such as Shii or Sufi, or Mutazilite, *neicheri* is simply a pejorative designation of specific groups who are unrelated historically and theologically. Moreover, the *neicheri* functions like a dormant virus that keeps recurring no matter how much effort is made to destroy it. For example, Afghani explains that even though Anushirwan killed Mazdak and his followers, he was unable to get rid of the teachings. Consequently, they reappeared in the fourth century, this time in the guise of the *batiniyya*. He writes:

> The Muslims were a community . . . in whom the bases of those six pillars were so firm, that in one century, as a result of those beliefs and praiseworthy qualities, they occupied lands from the Alps to the wall of China. . . . The superiority and greatness of this noble community remained until the fourth century [h] . . . the *neicheris* or naturalists appeared in Egypt under the name of the *batiniyya* and the knowers of the hidden. They spread their program to all sides and corners of the Muslim world, and especially to Iran.[24]

These *batiniyya neicheris* were different from earlier *neicheris*, in Afghani's view. Central to their mission was to "first create doubt in the Muslims about their beliefs; and after the establishment of doubt in their hearts take an oath . . . and promise to the eyes of the Perfect Guide."[25] The distinguishing feature of the Ismaili *neicheris* is that they directed their devotion to their leader, a shared feature with the "Babis," whom he describes as "the apprentices of those same *neicheris* of Alamut," thereby making an explicit link between Ismailis and the Bahais.[26] Thereafter, he moves from a discussion of Iranian *neicheris* to *neicheris* in the contemporaneous Ottoman Empire. Here the targets are specific figures "who committed treason in the recent war and were the cause of ruin and destruction [and who] were the same ones who marched in the *neicheri* road, and considered themselves holders of new ideas."[27]

Afghani's explication of the *neicheri* relates specifically to his conclusions about Islam, which he defines as a civilization that was once unified. He contends that Islam is the only religion that is both undivided and intrinsically rational, yet has not achieved progress, as his closing remarks indicate:

> If someone says: If the Islamic religion is as you say, then why are the Muslims in such a condition? I will answer: When they were [truly] Muslims, they were what they were and world bears witness to their excellence. As for the present, I will content myself with this holy text: 'Verily, God does not change the state of the people until they change themselves inwardly.'[28]

Despite possessing the fundamental principle of *tawhid* and inherent rationality—the two elements that he outlines as necessary for progress—it is apparent from his concluding citation from the Quran that he believes Islam was unable to open up a path to progress as did Christianity. Why is this the case? How can this failure of Islam be understood? This lack of progress is altogether more puzzling considering that Afghani argues that Luther appropriated his ideas from Islam.

It seems that Afghani's argument operates on a fundamentally inconsistent logic. Afghani does not draw a distinction between the "religion" and the "people" when he introduces the principle of *tawhid* that is built into the religion of Islam. Nor does he mention the people when he makes his comments about Islam as the only rational religion because it is based on proofs and reason. However, when he discusses the contemporaneous state of Islam, he refers to the past as a time when Muslims were "truly Muslim" as opposed to the present time, when Muslims are in a "sad condition." At this juncture in Afghani's argument, he relies on an idea of Islam that is divided between the ideal past and the broken present.

The *neicheris* contribute in a fundamental way to his narrative of decline. As noted above, he explains that, "The Muslims were a community. . . . The superiority and greatness of this noble community remained until the fourth century,"[29] at which point the "*batiniyya*" began to spread their teachings, which they inherited from their predecessors, the Babis. The *neicheris* are the primary target for this civilizational decline. The comparison with Christianity highlights further the contours of this bifurcation enjoined in his conception of religion. Afghani sees a direct parallel between Islam and Protestant Christianity. Both are similar in one feature: an original set of core beliefs, the power to abrogate divisions and hierarchy based on that foundation principle of unity, and finally the tendency for rational thought. If there is this similar structural parallel, why then does Afghani end his piece lamenting the present condition of Muslims? For Afghani, first, there is Islam, on the one hand, and Muslims on the other. Islam was perfect, complete, and undivided in the past and thus has the potential to be perfect, complete, and undivided in the future. However, it is the present that is the problem since Muslims have fallen into a "sad condition," and the only way that they can pull themselves out of this state is through self-awareness and self-improvement—which is what Afghani outlines as his basic interpretation of religion in his essay. As for the differences and similarities with Christianity, Afghani describes a parallel course and bifurcation between Christianity and Christians. Christianity too was undivided, complete, and perfect until Christians instituted the priesthood and clergy that created divisions and hierarchy. The difference, however, is that Christianity had a Luther to help facilitate the return to the original teachings and tenets.

Christians were able to confront and overcome the problem of divisions and return to unity because of Luther; but Muslims have yet to spur a movement by a group of people equivalent to the Protestants, who were moved by rational thought to return to their fundamentals, as the quote from Guizot—"Although our religion is the Christian religion, we are seeking the proofs of the fundamentals of our beliefs"—indicates. This is why Afghani laments the current "state of the people" who fail to look inwardly and change themselves.

This same temporal bifurcation and distinction between Islam and Muslim people is enjoined in Afghani's response to Renan. The "Answer to Renan" was a response to Ernest Renan's lecture on "Islam and Science" that he delivered at the Sorbonne and published in 1883 in *Journal des Debats*. Afghani's piece was published in the same journal a couple of months later. Renan made the argument that Islam as a religion was opposed to scientific thought and that Arabs, by virtue of their Semitic race, were incapable of scientific thinking. In Renan's view, science and philosophy made their way into the Arab world via the Persians and Greeks (implicitly, those "Aryan" or "Indo-European" races). Afghani again draws a parallel with Christianity, relies on a progressive view of civilization development, and invokes his hopes for the possibility for Islam to follow in the footsteps of Christianity:

> If it is true that the Muslim religion is an obstacle to the development of sciences, can one affirm that this obstacle will not disappear someday? How does the Muslim religion differ on this point from other religions? All religions are intolerant, each one in its way. The Christian religion . . . seems to advance rapidly on the road of progress and science, whereas Muslim society has not yet freed itself from the tutelage of religion. Realizing, however, that the Christian religion preceded the Muslim religion in the world by many centuries, I cannot keep from hoping that Muhammadan society will succeed someday in breaking its bonds and marching resolutely in the path of civilization after the manner of Western society, for which the Christian faith, despite its rigors and intolerance, was not at all an invincible obstacle. No, I cannot admit that this hope be denied to Islam.[30]

Here we find the same structural comparison between Islam and Christianity. The first few sentences set out an equivalence between the "Muslim religion" and "all religions," and especially "the Christian religion." The separation between the religion and the people appears in the fourth sentence: "The Christian religion . . . seems to advance rapidly on the road of progress and science, whereas Muslim society has not yet freed itself from the tutelage of religion." On this subject of progress, we see that he moves from specifically religion to society, indicating that the Muslims are behind the Christians when it comes to progress. In fact, he makes this essential coordinate of his argument—that religion and society are two distinct phenomena—perfectly clear when he remarks that Muslims have not freed themselves from "the tutelage of religion." However, his aspiration is that they will "march in the path of civilization" in the future.

Religion, in this particular account, represents that which prevents the exercise of rational thought, which again he sees as part of the history of Christianity in the "Answer to Renan." He writes, "In truth the Muslim religion has tried to stifle science and stop its progress. It has thus succeeded in halting the philosophical or intellectual movement. . . . A similar attempt, if I am not mistaken, was made by the Christian religion, and the venerated leaders of the Catholic church have not yet disarmed so far as I know."[31] Again, here it is the leaders of the Church whom he blames for having stifled progress for Christianity.

In the "Refutation," Afghani defends religion, and, in "Answer to Renan," Afghani makes the argument that religion keeps the masses in a backward state. Is it possible to reconcile this contradiction? It might not be necessary if we understand that religion is a moving target, and that his real concern is actually civilizational progress. If that is the case, there is a consistency between the two pieces. Afghani speaks about Islam and how Islam/Muslim society will eventually progress as did Christianity, thereby appropriating the same progressive and evolutionary understanding of religion that can be applied to both religions. In this piece, he contends that all religions are equal, as he notes in the conclusion: "Religions, by whatever names they are called all resemble each other." He makes this point to illustrate what he claims is a diametric opposition between religion and philosophy. He believes this to be the case with not just Islam but also Christianity. In this analysis, the target is in both cases the masses: "So long as humanity exists, the struggle will not cease between dogma and free investigation, between religion and philosophy; a desperate struggle in which I fear the triumph will not be for free thought because the masses dislike reason."[32]

To recap, the "Refutation" as well as the "Response to Renan" demonstrate that Afghani's interpretations of religion are based on an understanding of Islam as unified in the past and having the possibility of unity in the future. Education and Enlightenment ideas of rationality are necessary for the Muslim community to progress toward unification. Islam is trailing behind Christianity; but, in his view, it will get there. What is also needed is leadership— an equivalent to Luther to help guide the community. The next section will examine "The Materialists in India" wherein Afghani discusses Sayyid Ahmad Khan: the figure he believes is the wrong leader for Muslim reform, despite the fact that he shares many of his values.

Whereas the "Refutation" purports to defend Islam against the *neicheris*, identified by groups as diverse as Greek Cynics, Ismailis, Bahais, Zoroastrians, and Ottoman political dissidents, "The Materialists in India" focuses specifically on the figure of Sayyid Ahmad Khan as a *neicheri*. Afghani first wrote the piece in Persian and titled it "The Truth of the *Neicheri* Sect"; however, since the reference to the "*neicheris*" was only relevant to Indians, he later dropped the word from the title and renamed it "Refutation of the Materialists." He then published "The Materialists in India" in the Arabic newspaper *al-Urwa al-Wuthqa* three years later in 1884, in which he takes this subject of the *neicheri* sect and directs it specifically to the figure of Sayyid Ahmad Khan.

Afghani begins with an explanation of why and how Sayyid Ahmad Khan became a "*neicheri*." First, Afghani explains, Sayyid Ahmad Khan defended the Torah and the Gospel; second, he declared himself Christian; and finally, he decided to take "another road in order to serve his English masters, by sowing division among the Muslims and scattering their unity."[33] He writes:

He appeared in the guise of the naturalists and proclaimed that nothing exists but blind nature . . . and began to seduce the sons

of the rich, who were frivolous young men. Some of them in-
clined toward him, escaping from the bonds of the Law of
Islam, and pursuing bestial passions. His doctrine pleased the
English rulers and they saw in it the best means to corrupt the
hearts of the Muslims. They began to support him, to honor
him, and to help him to build a college in Aligarh called the
Muhammadan College.[34]

Although Afghani frames criticisms of Sayyid Ahmad Khan and his
followers in theological terms of religious deviance, it is apparent
that the charge is a political rather than religious one—consistent
with the logic of the earlier piece on the *neicheri* sect. Afghani's
account of *neicheris* in "Materialists in India" focuses on Sayyid
Ahmad Khan's support for the British as its launching point.
Sayyid Ahmad Khan and his followers exhibit the same *neicheri*
tendencies that Afghani outlines in his earlier "Refutation." The
neicheris in both cases are described as morally depraved, manipu-
lative, and conniving. In the "Refutation," however, he ascribes these
characteristics to multiple groups of people—such as the Greek
materialists, the Ismailis, and the Bahais. Here, the single source
and object of *neicheri* criticism is one local leader and his followers,
who have, in Afghani's words, indulged in "bestial passions." He
does not explain what exactly these "passions" involve and instead
redirects his attack against the British, whom he sees as having
worked hand in hand with Sayyid Ahmad Khan to "corrupt the
hearts of Muslims."

Afghani claims that Sayyid Ahmad Khan's activities were driven
by his desire to cause division within the Muslim community, as
demonstrated by the account of how he became a *neicheri*: according to Afghani, Sayyid Ahmad Khan asserted the ultimate truth of
the Bible, declared himself a Christian, and then finally decided
he would become a naturalist and denier of God, when the previous two weren't enough. Afghani also claims that Sayyid Ahmad
Khan wrote a commentary on the Quran that distorted what
God revealed, and believed that denouncing all religions was the

only way that Europeans progressed in civilization. According to Afghani, Sayyid Ahmad Khan created rifts within the Muslim community by encouraging godlessness as well as disloyalty. He writes:

> For whoever abandons religion in Western countries retains love for his country, and his zeal to guard his country from the attacks of foreigners is not diminished. . . . But Ahmad Khan and his companions, just as they invited people to reject religion, [also] disparaged to them the interests of their fatherland.[35]

In the "Refutation," Afghani explains how *neicheris* are first and foremost political deviants—communists—who do not simply keep to themselves, but actively seek to attract a following.[36] Afghani claims that Sayyid Ahmad Khan too adopted this *neicheri* practice when he took advantage of "weak Muslims" with promises to "raise their hopes that if they followed him, he would bring them into government service."[37] Ultimately, Afghani remarks, Sayyid Ahmad Khan's followers "became an army for the English government in India."[38] Afghani thus tries to expose Sayyid Ahmad Khan as a traitor as well as a collaborator with the British. In this regard, the *neicheri* accusation is a way to usurp and undermine Sayyid Ahmad Khan's political and religious authority.

Much of what Afghani has to say about Sayyid Ahmad Khan is fabrication, or at the very least, distortion. Sayyid Ahmad Khan never disavowed Islam or religion. In fact, it is well known that he felt the need to respond to critical commentaries written by Christian missionaries as well as British civil servant historians, such as William Muir. Many of Sayyid Ahmad Khan's writings were devoted to defending Islam and Muhammad. In addition to the apologetic literature, such as the *Khutabat-i-Ahmadiyya* (*Essays on the Life of Mohammed*), he wrote on 'ilm al-kalam, in which he argued that a new modern *kalam* was necessary to respond to the changing times and, most importantly, to speak to the issues that arose with modern science and how exactly this new modern science is (or is not) compatible with Islam.

Sayyid Ahmad Khan believed the ʿulama were incapable of responding to modern western scientific developments, and so he took on the practice of *ijtihad* himself. He presented his ideas in a literary journal, *Tahdhib al-Akhlaq,* and in a commentary on the Quran. Sayyid Ahmad Khan's ʿIlm al-Kalam rested on four basic points: (1) that God and his Word are true, which science cannot falsify; (2) that there is no distinction between the Work of God and the Word of God; (3) that the "'law of nature' is God's manifest covenant and His promise of reward or retribution is His verbal covenant"; and (4) that in order to undertake the burden of religion, man possesses reason.[39] In terms of his politics, Sayyid Ahmad Khan explains his own position in the following way: "I am in favour of the consolidation of the British Government, not because of any love or loyalty to the British but only because I see the welfare of the Indian Muslims in that consolidation. And I feel that they can emerge from the present state of decline only with the help of the British government."[40]

Afghani and Sayyid Ahmad Khan certainly had very different formations. Sayyid Ahmad Khan was shaped by and concerned with the specific territory and life of Indian Muslims, and Afghani was completely disconnected from his homeland and spent his time as an itinerant teacher and orator. Sayyid Ahmad Khan studied and educated himself within recognizable fields of theology and mysticism (some of his earliest writings were on the Naqshabandi sect to which his family was tied), whereas Afghani's writings illustrate no formal training or association to any particular school of legal or philosophical thought. Sayyid Ahmad Khan was an institution builder and educator grounded in colonial India, whereas Afghani was a charismatic teacher and speaker and, wherever he travelled, a political agitator. Despite these differences, both individuals were the earliest of modernist Muslims to understand and define "Islam" in relation to the "West"—as W. C. Smith has described as "connoting correlative—and of course antagonistic—historical phenomena."[41]

What is therefore surprising about Afghani's denigration of Sayyid Ahmad Khan is that they in fact shared many of the same values and concerns. The issue that both of them recognized as integral to the development of Islam as a religion and civilization was education, specifically modern western scientific thought. Afghani's response to Renan provides the most detailed argument about his advocacy for science. In the following section, I will examine Afghani's "Lecture on Teaching and Learning" given in Calcutta in 1882 and compare its logic and arguments to Sayyid Ahmad Khan's lecture on Islam, which he gave in 1884 before the *Anjuman-i-Himayat-i-Islam* (Islamic Protection Association) in Lahore, to show how these two figures adhere to a similar logic—one that defines Islam as a glorious civilization of the past that has the possibility of this greatness for the future.

The subject of the "Lecture on Teaching and Learning" is science. In it, Afghani writes: "The benefits of science are immeasurable.... If someone looks deeply into the question, he will see that science rules the world.... If we look at the Chaldean conquerors ... the true conquerors were not the Chaldeans but science and knowledge."[42] He continues to explain that it was science rather than people or person—whether the Egyptians, Phoenicians, or Alexander the Great—that made conquest successful, and now it is the Europeans who are in control of expanding and successfully conquering the world through science: "Thus it is evident that all wealth and riches are the result of science.... In sum, the whole world of humanity is an industrial world, meaning that the world is a world of science."[43]

On the one hand, Afghani contends that science alone is responsible for progress. On the other hand, as the lecture develops, he makes the point that science cannot be isolated from philosophy, or *falsafa*, the second piece of his argument. In early Islam, he maintains, there was an active "philosophic spirit" that made the early Muslims receptive to the sciences, which they translated into Arabic. He proceeds to explain how both the Ottoman government and the Khedivate of Egypt attempted to establish teaching of the sciences in schools, but because the culture and institutions lacked any kind of philosophy in their respective curricula there was no way the sciences could succeed. As a consequence of this oversight and neglect of philosophy, Muslims missed the opportunity to benefit from logic, rhetoric, and philosophy, and instead "ma[de] grammar a goal in itself."[44] Moreover, he asserts that those who study the rich philosophical tradition of the *shari'a* do not apply it in such a way to help understand the ways law can help civilizational progress.[45]

Here, Afghani deploys the now recognizable rhetorical move of blame. This time the recipient is not the *neicheri*, or the masses, but the *'ulama,* whom he describes in the essay as "a very narrow wick on top of which is a very small flame that neither lights its surroundings nor gives light to others."[46] The problem with the *'ulama* is that they claimed to be scholars, but rather than teaching and enlightening the masses they transmitted to the people their narrow ideas, thereby playing a key role in civilizational decline. He remarks in the closing line of the lecture: "If one considers, he will understand this truth, that the ruin and corruption we have experienced first reached our *'ulama* and religious leaders, and then penetrated the rest of the community."[47]

Sayyid Ahmad Khan makes a similar point about the crucial intervention of science in Islam and shares in a similar, albeit milder, critique of the *'ulama* as upholders of tradition who have very little salutary relevance to Islam. Sayyid Ahmad Khan also highlights a golden period of scientific thought in his account of Islamic history. This "zenith" was the Abbasid period (750–1258), when "Greek philosophy and natural science had gained popularity among Muslims."[48] He provides a more specific analysis to his understanding of this period, namely that many who acknowledged these philosophical and scientific tenets began to cast doubts on Islam; and how, as a consequence, the *'ulama* developed an *'ilm al-kalam*, or a science of argumentation to deal with this tension. According to Sayyid Ahmad Khan, the *'ulama* at the time "made great efforts to protect Islam and to make it triumph."[49] Now, Muslims are in a somewhat similar situation because they must find a way to respond to new scientific and philosophical ideas. However, the situation is different because science itself has changed, as it is now grounded in experiments and observation. He writes:

> My friends! Another problem is the big difference between critical research today [and its results] and the tenets of Greek wisdom of old because the tenets of former wisdom were based on rational and analogical arguments, and not upon experience and observation. It was very easy for our forbears, whilst sitting in the rooms of mosques and monasteries, to disprove teachings arrived at by analogous reasoning. . . . But today . . . doctrines are established by natural experiments [that is, experiments in natural science] and they are demonstrated before our eyes. These are not problems of the kind that could be solved by analogical arguments, or which can be contested by assertions and principles which the ulama of former times have established.[50]

As a result of this situation, he finds a pressing need to respond to modern science: "Today we need, as in former days, a modern *'ilm al-kalam* by which we either render futile the tenets of modern sciences or [show them to be] doubtful, or bring them into harmony with the doctrines of Islam."[51] He then proceeds to explain the nature of this new modern *'ilm al-kalam*, which he insists is necessary for those in whom doubt about Islam and religion has arisen as a consequence of modern developments in philosophy and natural science. Sayyid Ahmad Khan sees himself as implicated in the problem: "But since I have striven to spread among Muslims those sciences which, as I have just stated, are to a certain extent in discrepancy with contemporary Islam, it was my duty . . . to protect Islam and to show forth to people the original luminous face of Islam."[52] He continues to explain that his efforts in teaching about science have resulted in people calling him "*kafir*" or "*nechari.*" He then gives an example of what distinguishes his understanding of Islam from that of the 'ulama and the maulavis. According to Sayyid Ahmad Khan:

> the only criterion for the truth of the religions which are present before us is whether the religion [in question] is in correspondence with the natural disposition of humankind, or with nature. If yes, then it is true. . . . But if this religion is against the nature of humans and their natural constitution . . . then there can be no doubt that this religion is not sent by the One that created humankind. . . . So I have determined the following principle for discerning the truth of the religions and for testing the truth of Islam—that is, is the religion in question in correspondence with human nature or not.[53]

He then concludes this proposition and argument with the following statement: "Islam is nature and nature is Islam."

If science is one point on which both Sayyid Ahmad Khan and Afghani agree, so too is the subject of education more broadly. Sayyid Ahmad Khan believed that education was the means through which Muslims would progress and reform in the modern period. Afghani shares this basic supposition on education, as he writes in his essay "Commentary on the Commentator":

> Education, if it is good, produces perfection from imperfection, and nobility from baseness. . . . When this is understood, one must realize that if a people receive a good education, all of its classes and ranks, in accord with the natural law of relationships, will flourish simultaneously and will progress.[54]

Afghani's position on education is consistent with everything he outlines about religion in the neicheri piece. The same ideas— nobility of the soul versus base animal instincts and the endorsement of the former as the means to progress—are applied specifically to the subject of education here. However, in this "Commentary" piece, he moves from a discussion of the importance of education to an attack on Sayyid Ahmad Khan. Afghani writes about Sayyid Ahmad Khan's alleged inability to deliver on education, with particular focus on how his interpretation of the Quran and Muhammad's prophecy was inaccurate and too secular:

> Since he claims to have written this commentary for the improvement of the community, I was certain he had in the introduction of his book described and explained in a new manner, with the light of wisdom, those divine policies and Koranic ethics that were the cause of the superiority and expansion of the Arabs in every human excellence. . . . When I read the commentary I saw that this commentator in no way raised a word about these matters or about divine policy. . . . Even stranger is the fact that this commentator has lowered the divine holy rank of prophecy and placed it on the level of reformer. . . . If the goal of this commentator is, as he says, the improvement of the community, then why does he try to end the belief of the Muslims in the Islamic religion.[55]

Herein Afghani claims that Sayyid Ahmad Khan misled Muslims by distorting the meaning and significance of Islamic beliefs and practices. This accusation is completely unsubstantiated and slanderous. It necessitates the question of why Afghani would write such demeaning statements about Sayyid Ahmad Khan, especially when Afghani endorsed the same values of science, education, and progress. It seems Afghani's position on religious leadership provides some insight into why he would be compelled to undercut Sayyid Ahmad Khan. In this piece, Afghani writes:

> There is no doubt that in the present age, distress, misfortune, and weakness besiege all classes of Muslims from every side. Therefore every Muslim keeps his eyes and ears in expectation—to the East, West, North, and South—to see from what corner of the earth the sage and renewer will appear and will reform the minds and souls of the Muslims, repel the unforeseen corruption and again educate them with a virtuous education. Perhaps

through that good education they may return to their former joyful condition.[56]

Afghani makes clear in the above passage the need for a "sage" to help redeem Muslims. Keddie has argued that Afghani likely "pictured himself in this role" of renewer for the time.[57] Her point is corroborated by his own words in the "Commentary" piece, wherein he explains, after the above statements, that he in fact sees himself as playing a vital role in the reformation of Muslims. He remarks:

I more than others expect that the minds and souls of the Muslims will very soon be enlightened and rectified by the wisdom of a sage. For this reason I always want to keep abreast of the articles and treatises that are now appearing from the pens of Muslims, and be thoroughly acquainted with the view of their authors. I hope that in these readings I may discover the elevated ideas of a sage who could be the cause of good education, virtue, and prosperity for the Muslims. I would then hope to the extent of my ability, to assist him in his elevated ideas and become a helper and associate in the reform of my people. [58]

The above passage underscores Keddie's observation that Afghani saw himself as the reformer of the time. She describes this role as a kind of "Muslim Luther" who could revolutionize Islam along the lines of the Protestant reformation.[59] What is interesting about the above passage is that Afghani does not make an explicit self-proclamation as reformer. He leaves it open, and instead situates himself as the person who *recognizes* the sage, and someone who has the powers to assist with the dissemination of the new ideas to the masses. Afghani's reformer is configured not in Protestant terms but within a messianic Shii frame: There is an "expectation" and anticipation of the Muslim reformer whose appearance can arrive from any region of the world, and whose presence will "repel the unforeseen corruption" and help people "return to their former joyful condition."

Whether implicitly or explicitly, Afghani considered himself fulfilling the role of a Mahdi for the people. He wouldn't be the first to make such a claim. The task of serving as Mahdi for the people was happening during his lifetime, specifically with the Sudanese Mahdi—Muhammad Ahmad in 1881 claimed to be the Mahdi of the Sudan, having led a successful revolt against the Khedive and the British. After Afghani's stay in India, he travelled to Paris and London in the years 1882–1884. His time in Paris coincided with the rise of the Sudanese Mahdi. During this period, Afghani wrote for a newspaper entitled *L'Intransigeant*, edited by Henry Rochefort.[60] Rochefort's newspaper published two pieces by Afghani—one entitled "Lettre sur L'Hindustan," in April 1883, which was an attack on British rule in India, and the second, published in December that same year, entitled "Le Mahdi." Muhammad Ahmad rose to prominence on the public stage after he defeated the British general Hicks in 1883. The British were threatened by Muhammad Ahmad, the "Mahdi," and were concerned about whether Muslims outside of Sudan would give their support to him. According to Keddie, when Afghani wrote these articles for *L'Intransigeant,* he had in mind hopes for an anti-British alliance of France, Russia, the Ottoman Empire, and Afghanistan. This is in fact the subject of his first article on India. In it, he argues that in their aim to control India, the British ruined Indian trade and industry and incited in her people, regardless of caste or religion, a hatred for them. And since the British had severed relations with the Afghans since the second Afghan war, the Afghans too were aligned against the British and with the Russians. He therefore hoped for a Franco-Russo-Ottoman alliance. Building on this observation about the state of political affairs and success of the Sudanese Mahdi, he explains that even though there have been mahdist movements in Islamic history, none of these earlier mahdis was the unique Mahdi. He writes:

In a word, under this name, how many Muslims have accomplished brilliant and considerable acts, and have they not brought about a very serious change in the world of believers? . . . In brief, however diverse these beliefs may be from the point of view of form, it is no less true that every Muslim awaits a Mahdi, ready to follow him and to sacrifice his life to him, along with all he possesses. The Indian Muslims especially, given the infinite sufferings and cruel torments they endure under English domination, are those who await him with the most impatience.[61]

Both Keddie and Kedourie describe Afghani's understanding of messianism in "Le Mahdi" as political. That is to say, they claim that he writes the piece to a European audience with the purpose of suggesting another successful uprising on the part of the Sudanese Mahdi, which, Afghani explains, would lead to Muslims worldover in joining him. Keddie notes that Afghani was not interested in putting forth any kind of religious theory of the Mahdi but rather hoped to get Europeans to respond to Muslims with some sort of compromise, especially having the French exert pressure on the British to negotiate with the Egyptians and Sudanese.[62] It is for this reason he exaggerates the effects of Mahdist victory and its repercussions for Europeans and the Ottoman Sultan. Despite the fact that he had these politically instrumental motives in mind, it is noteworthy, as demonstrated in the above quote, how he writes about the idea of the Mahdi. He explains that even though there have been mahdis in history, "it is no less true that every Muslim awaits a Mahdi, ready to follow him and to sacrifice his life to him, along with all he possesses." Afghani saw for himself the possibility to occupy this role, especially among "Indian Muslims."[63]

    It is evident that Afghani could not claim any kind of Mahdi role in the North Africa/Middle Eastern regions, as that position was very much taken over by the Sudanese Mahdi. However, India, it seems, remained a prospective opportunity. There was one big challenge to this possibility: the person who was actively disseminating new ideas and imparting wisdom as an ideal "sage" was supposed to, was of course Sayyid Ahmad Khan. It is no coincidence that he was subjected to Afghani's most vehement denouncements. He rose to prominence in a way that Afghani likely hoped for himself.

But why would Afghani think that he would be able to acquire such a role as Mahdi, sage, and/or political leader of Muslims worldwide? I contend that this is because Afghani had experience in this role earlier in his life, as a political agitator and charismatic leader during his time in Egypt. While in Egypt, Afghani taught many students and disciples, mostly "rebellious Azharites" in coffeehouses and bars in Cairo. But in terms of formal, institutional spaces, it was in the lodges of the Freemasons where he was known to spend time with a community of like-minded individuals. The Freemasonry brought to Egypt by the French was mostly the space of Europeans, but by the 1860s and 1870s, Egyptians began to enter the lodges, mostly for political reasons.[64] Afghani applied for membership to join a masonic lodge in 1875 and the sources indicate that he was invited to sessions of Italian lodges and the Eastern Star Lodge (affiliated with the Grand Lodge of England) during the period of 1877–1879.[65] The year 1877 in particular was a crucial turning point for Afghani's political activities. Afghani and his followers began to exert influence outside their small circle with the publication of articles critical of the government.[66]

When Afghani first arrived in Egypt in 1871, he was supported by a government pension and taught at al-Azhar, but soon was not welcome there by the 'ulama because of his reformist ideas. This was a period in which Egypt was undergoing dramatic economic, political, and social changes under Khedive Ismail. It was at this time that Afghani turned to the Masons as a place to organize and lead his political agitations against the British. While Freemasonry in Europe was focused on the promotion of philanthropy and brotherhood, in Egypt it was the organization that attracted those who were interested in subverting the authority of Khedive Ismail. Afghani and Prince 'Abd al-Halim were the two leading figures of this mission. According to Afghani's records, his initial reason for joining was political. His first contact was in 1875, when he requested admission into one of the masonic centers in Cairo. The documents indicate that he was invited to sessions in various lodges until the time of his exile from Egypt, and that between 1877 and 1879, he belonged to the National Grande Lodge of Egypt and was a leading member of the Star of the East Lodge in Cairo (which eventually included Tawfiq Pasha, Ismail Pasha's son, as a member). The documents together suggest that he maintained ties with multiple lodges, and the lodges were the means through which he agitated against the state, called for reforms, and reached out to nationalist leaders.[67]

The Freemason societies were also the places where, due to their culture of secrecy, it was possible to cultivate "heterodox" ideas and practices. They were the sites of secret initiations and esoteric discussions about religion and philosophy. Kedourie writes:

> In an application to join a masonic Lodge in Egypt in 1875, [Afghani] describes himself as a 'teacher of philosophical sciences' and addresses the Masons as *ikhwan al-safa . . . wa khullan al-wafa '*—i.e., 'sincere brethren . . . and faithful companions,' clearly in deliberate allusion to the famous Ismaili treatise.[68]

The *Rasa 'il Ikhwan al-Safa* is an early medieval encyclopedia that was composed by a group known as the *Ikhwan,* or "brethren," sometime between the ninth and the first half of the tenth centuries. Although scholars are not in agreement about whether or not the Ikhwan were working for the Fatimid Caliphate, the name "Ikhwan al-Safa," used by later Nizari Ismailis, became a famous and well-known reference to a secret *dawa* organization.[69]

The Freemason culture, it seems, served as one of the key institutions through which Afghani imparted his political strategies, but also the space in which he cultivated his esoteric religious ideas. This was the institution through which Afghani in fact initiated his most famous disciple, Muhammad ʿAbduh, as Rida, ʿAbduh's student, recounts:

> I asked him [ʿAbduh] once what masonry really was, and he said that its role—now ended—in the countries in which it is found was to resist the authority of the kings and popes who were fighting against knowledge and freedom and that this was a great achievement and one of the pillars of European progress.[70]

The Freemason lodges in Egypt were spaces in which political dissidents were able to work out their ideas that were in conflict with ruling regime. For ʿAbduh, the appeal of Freemason lodges was not simply political; these were places that also imparted values of "knowledge and freedom." What exactly was the "knowledge" that was transmitted from Afghani to ʿAbduh beyond politics? The kinds of relationships that Afghani developed with students, ʿAbduh in particular, went beyond the standard teacher/student connection. One of ʿAbduh's students recounted that when ʿAbduh mentioned Afghani, ʿAbduh would be seized with "strong trembling" and tears, and that ʿAbduh told this student that Afghani's relationship to him was not just one of brother to brother or disciple to master but a "relation of love that had overwhelmed the heart."[71] ʿAbduh also writes in his short essay, *Risalat al-Waridat*, or *Treatise of Mystical Inspirations*, that as a student he was discouraged by his teachers to pursue the study of science, since it was western. He found their mentality "limiting" and was generally despondent about this state of affairs until he met Afghani. He notes:

> While I found myself in this state, the arrival of the perfect Sage, of Truth personified, of our venerated master Sayyid Jamal al-Din al-Afghani who does not cease to garner the fruits of science, made the sun of truths rise for us which illuminated the most complicated problems.[72]

This quasi-divine status that ʿAbduh attributes to Afghani is further corroborated in a letter that ʿAbduh writes to Afghani in Paris while ʿAbduh is in exile in Beirut in 1883. In the letter, ʿAbduh says to Afghani: "You know what is in my soul, as you know what is in yours. You have made us with your hand, invested our matter with its perfect form and created us in the best shape. Through you . . . have we known the whole universe." After having attributed to Afghani powers of creation as well as omniscience, ʿAbduh then explains what Afghani had passed on to him:

> I have been endowed by you with a wisdom which enables me to change inclinations, impart rationality to reason, overcome great obstacles, and control the innermost thoughts of men. I have been given by you a will so powerful as to move the immovable, deal blows to the greatest of obstacles, and remain firm in the right (*haqq*) until truth (*haqq*) is satisfied.[73]

What were the ideas and beliefs about leadership that Afghani claimed that led intelligent reform-minded individuals such as ʿAbduh to revere Afghani as a "perfect Sage" and "Truth personified?" One source, I suspect, was the Bahai tradition, in particular its earlier form that Afghani was exposed to in Iran. Afghani came of age in mid-nineteenth century Iran within a religious climate shaped by Twelver Shiism, and more significantly for this discussion, the Twelver offshoot schools of Shaikhi and Babi thought. The Shaikhi school was founded in the late eighteenth century and spread throughout the Shii areas of Ottoman Iraq and Iran. It has been described as a "combination of rationalist philosophy and mysticism typical of Iranian philosophers and also a stronger messianic tension than the usual Twelver Shiʾi doctrine."[74] According to Nikki Keddie, in the 1860s, Afghani carried with him Shaikhi treatises, one of which was written by the founder of Shaikhi thought, Shaikh Ahmad Ahsai (1753–1826), whom some Twelver *mujtahid*s had excommunicated, and another was written by his successor Hajji Muhammad Karim Khan Qajar Kirmani (1809–1870). The texts discuss philosophical and mystical aspects of Shiism and the multiple levels of meaning in the words and suras of the Quran. One of the most significant of these Shaikhi ideas was the "Fourth Pillar"—"the idea that there is always in the world a perfect Shii who can guide men in right ideas and action during the absence of the Twelfth Imam."[75] Whereas the Twelvers believe that in the absence of the Twelfth Imam the *mujtahids* serve as the fallible guides, the Shaikhis believe that each epoch had its own guide that was more perfect and exalted than the *mujtahid*. This particular Shaikhi idea was one possible theory of leadership that Afghani adopted as he cultivated his role as mystic and teacher in Egypt.

Another religious tradition from which it is possible that Afghani discursively shaped his role as a charismatic leader is Ismailism. Turning back to the discussion of the *Rasa 'il Ikhwan al-Safa*, the Ismaili treatise he refers to in his application to the Freemasons in 1875, the parallels between the political context of its composition and Afghani's use of the idea in his application to the masonic lodge are noteworthy: Both were underground movements in which the language of religious secrecy was inextricably tied to the language of political dissidence. The *Ikhwan* were the learned people commissioned with the task of promoting their ideas (*dawa*). They represented a special class of people (of wise men and philosophers as well as of prophets, successors of prophets, and imams) who described themselves as the "elect," and "sincere Friends of God [His] faithful servants."[76] Similarly, the nineteenth century Egyptian masonic lodges were spaces in which Afghani participated in the exchange of secret religious ideas and political agitation.

The "Refutation" has been interpreted as defense of orthodoxy. However, as I conveyed in my reading of the text, it would be difficult to make such a claim when the piece offers very little by way of theological argument and/or reference to the Quran. Second, the "Refutation" has been understood, from another perspective, as a political disagreement between Afghani and Sayyid Ahmad Khan about British rule. In this view, Sayyid Ahmad Khan represents a pro-British position, and Afghani, anti-British. This interpretation too seems inadequate, as Afghani and Sayyid Ahmad Khan were both "pro-European" insofar as they both were intellectually shaped by colonial ideas of progress and rationality and made explicit their positions as proponents of western science and education. Furthermore, they agreed that Islam was a civilization that was once unified but spiraled into decline. Both Afghani and Sayyid Ahmad Khan were concerned with the problem of a lagging Islamic civilization and found in western education a possible corrective to the matter of decline. Education was the most important solution for both, but for Afghani, education necessitated proper leadership to disseminate knowledge to the masses. As he explained in "Commentary on the Commentator," the Muslim community needed a "sage," and in *L'Intransigeant* he described the ideal guide for the people as the "Mahdi."

Neither the orthodoxy perspective nor the pro-British versus anti-British argument can explain why Afghani would denounce Sayyid Ahmad Khan in the derogatory manner he did. I argue that Afghani wrote three pieces maligning Sayyid Ahmad Khan because he saw in him competition—a leader who was in fact successful in guiding Indian Muslims along modernist lines in ways that Afghani had hoped to do. What allowed Sayyid Ahmad Khan to make inroads in leadership with the Indian Muslim community was his elite formation, pedigree, and commitment to establishing institutions of education (such as Aligarh). Afghani didn't have anything similar to offer. However, he was politically savvy and established himself as a charismatic leader over the course of his life. It was through his experience with teaching, political agitation, and leadership that he was able to cultivate a network of disciples such as ʿAbduh in the Egyptian Freemasonic communities. Ismaili and Babist/Shaikhi ideas provided the discursive language of religious authority that allowed him to assert that he was qualified to serve in a leadership role for the Muslim community of the time, especially Indian Muslims.

2

Muhammad ʿAbduh, Rashid Rida, and Bahai "Esotericists"

JAMAL AL-DIN AL-AFGHANI (1838–1897), Muhammad ʿAbduh (1849–1905), and Rashid Rida (1865–1935) are widely regarded as the collective founders of Islamic modernism. Muhammad ʿAbduh's perspectives about Islam were configured through ideas of civilizational rise and decline similar to Afghani's view—and, like Afghani, ʿAbduh's formulation of *tawhid* as Muslim political unity made explicit demarcations between insiders and outsiders. In his classical treatise *The Theology of Unity*, ʿAbduh offers an extensive reading of Islam's rise and gradual decline to the contemporaneous present, in which interpretations of decline are expressed through the temporally bifurcated idea of *tawhid*. That is to say, ʿAbduh represents the Muslim community as once unified but gradually weakening over the course of Islam's history. This logic of *tawhid* as temporal bifurcation exhibits possibilities of return in the future, similar to Afghani's understanding. *Tawhid* serves not only as the conceptual structure through which he conveys this decline and aspiration for future unity but also as the framework through which he identifies and denounces specific communities—in this case the Shia—as deviant. Whereas Afghani branded Ismailis, Bahais, and the followers of Sayyid Ahmad Khan as *neicheri*, ʿAbduh isolated and accused the Shia, specifically the *batiniyya* (those who seek a hidden truth), of creating divisive fissures within a once cohesive community of Muslims.

As standard accounts of modernism have all noted, Afghani was integral to the intellectual formation of Muhammad ʿAbduh and ʿAbduh was crucial in mentoring Rashid Rida. These accounts tend to represent the three canonical reformers as sharing somewhat uniform positions on the relationship between Islam and modernity. However, there are many significant differences in these figures' intellectual formations and interventions that are put into sharp relief when it comes to the subject of perceived outsiders/transgressors. For example, Afghani, ʿAbduh, and Rida all take very different positions on Bahai ideas and leadership. Afghani made public proclamations against the Bahais though he was influenced by early Bahai thought. ʿAbduh's student, Rashid Rida, vehemently opposed Bahai beliefs and practices unlike his mentor ʿAbduh, who was sympathetic to Bahai ideas and went to great lengths to defend the work and life of ʿAbdul Baha, the leader of the Bahai community at the time.

The chapter begins with a discussion of key components of ʿAbduh's religious and intellectual formation that have been recounted in the secondary scholarship, followed by an analysis of his interpretations of Islam's rise and decline in *The Theology of Unity*. From there, the chapter turns to Rida's account of a dialogue between ʿAbduh and Rida about Bahai beliefs, practices, and leadership, pointing to ʿAbduh and Rida's opposing positions. The conversation between Rida and ʿAbduh reveals ʿAbduh's fondness and respect for ʿAbdul Baha and endorsement of Bahai beliefs and reforms. The exchange makes it apparent that ʿAbduh is also quite sympathetic to aspects of Sufi and Ismaili practices as well. Rida, however, explicitly denounced the legitimacy of the Bahais, as well as Ismailis and Sufis, branding them all as "propagandists." The chapter concludes with Rida's writings about reform and examines how he, like Afghani, condemned the successful leadership of Ismaili, Bahai, and Sufi groups on the basis of a Sunni normative logic. Moreover, Rida, like Afghani, made statements about how it was time for a new reformer to guide the Muslim community. In Rida's famous speech "Renewing, Renewal, and Renewer," he refers, more than once, to the famous hadith about *tajdid* and the periodic arrival of a *mujaddid*. He explicates his position on the subject of *tajdid* in opposition to what he sometimes calls "false renewers" and at other times "heretics," thereby asserting the exclusive legitimacy of *his* interpretations of reform. Although he does not make an explicit case for self-appointment, he argues that reform ought to be undertaken by someone who falls in line with the Afghani/'Abduh pedigree, thereby discursively validating the possibility of his credentials as leader.

Scholarly accounts of 'Abduh's biography are for the most part in agreement about the following figures and moments that were integral to 'Abduh's intellectual formation: his traditional Quranic learning from an early age that continued in Cairo at al-Azhar; his early exposure to Sufism; 'Abduh's relationship with his mentor Afghani; and European ideas of history and science that were brought to Egypt in the nineteenth century. The most comprehensive narrative of Muhammad 'Abduh's life comes from his biography that was constructed by his Syrian student, Muhammad Rashid Rida (1865–1935). When 'Abduh died, Rida published a number of articles in his journal *Al-Manar* in 1905 about 'Abduh that would later become the standard account of 'Abduh's life. They were later assembled into a biography, *Tarikh al-Ustadh al-Imam al-Shaykh Muhammad 'Abduh*, which consists of three volumes: the actual biography; writings by 'Abduh; and a selection of newspaper articles, poems, and eulogies about 'Abduh.

According to this standard biography, 'Abduh grew up in a village in Lower Egypt. He began his studies of the Quran at age ten, at home. His father was keen to cultivate his skills in Quranic recitation, and so he sent him to a madrasa in Tanta. After a couple of years, he began studying Arabic grammar and jurisprudence but found this experience frustrating, both for the technical nature of the texts as well as the inadequate explanations from the teachers.

He therefore left the school and returned home, at which point his father instructed him to go back. Instead, 'Abduh escaped to a nearby village where he met his paternal great-uncle, Shaykh Darwish al-Khadir, who introduced 'Abduh to Sufism.[1] This Sufism was of the reformist kind that originated in North African orders such as the Sanusiyya and Tijaniyya. The traditions' teachings consisted of the rejection of *taqlid* and emphasis on direct access to prophetic inspirations via the Sufi sheikh, ideas that would become significant to 'Abduh later in life. Shaykh Darwish allegedly encouraged 'Abduh to read the Quran as a religious and scholarly endeavor, and to slowly attempt to understand its meaning. This method and experience were refreshing and new to 'Abduh and gave him an opening to a world that was religious but not inflected by the traditionalist perspectives of the *'ulama*.[2]

In 1866, 'Abduh arrived in Cairo and joined the famous center of Islamic learning, al-Azhar Mosque, also known as al-Azhar University, where he studied Muslim religious sciences. Here he found many of the same problems he had encountered in his youth, namely the limited range of pedagogy as well as the narrow focus of traditional learning. It was for this reason, it seems, that 'Abduh was drawn to Afghani, who arrived with fresh ideas—both religious and political—that were different from those of the *'ulama* as well as traditional Sufism. Rida makes the argument that most of 'Abduh's ideas were influenced by the teachings of Jamal al-Din al-Afghani, pointing to the period when both were exiled after an unsuccessful revolt against the British in Egypt as the time in which the close relationship between the two developed. Later biographies build on his lineage story: One of the main proponents of the argument that 'Abduh's intellectual thought was mostly influenced by Afghani is C.C. Adams, the most well-known European biographer of 'Abduh.

Afghani's influence in 'Abduh's life was certainly monumental, as Afghani brought fresh perspectives on religion and philosophy into the traditional cultural milieu in which 'Abduh studied in Cairo. Afghani also led 'Abduh down a path of political engagement—in action and in writing—that was made possible, it seems, by Afghani's personality as a charismatic leader (this was demonstrated in the previous chapter's account of 'Abduh's perceptions of Afghani as a quasi-divine guide). Although Afghani was instrumental to 'Abduh's political and intellectual formation, it is also important to keep in mind conditions outside the Afghani lineage, such as the Egyptian political context, which shaped 'Abduh's views of reform. During his life, a new kind of Egyptian public sphere emerged, specifically with educational reforms undertaken during the rule of Muhammad Ali in 1805. In the first half of the nineteenth century, the commercial ties between Europe and Egypt grew stronger with the expansion of the European market in Egypt and the Anglo-Turkish Commercial Convention of 1838, both of which came together in the British occupation in 1882.[3] As a way to stand up to Europeans, Muhammad Ali built up a large army, initiated a state capitalist system that established monopolies over produce, and created modern technical schools and new industries. The Anglo-Turkish convention of 1838 outlawed state monopolies, which eventually led to the disintegration of the land system built by Muhammad Ali. During the rule of his successors, Khedives Said (1854–1863) and Ismail (1863–1879), landed proprietors were created as a class and Egypt was fully incorporated into the world market as a producer of cotton. The modern bureaucratic structure of the Egyptian state and army was financed by foreign loans, which, after its going bankrupt (1875–1882), eventually led to the establishment of British colonial rule. It was these two developments of state formation and incorporation into the world capitalist market that led to the rise of an Egyptian public sphere. With the emergence of the new class of landed proprietors arose a new class of Muslim intellectuals who were graduates of either new state schools or foreign schools. This group of intellectuals was keen to incorporate and respond to western forms of knowledge and modern forms of education.[4]

Muhammad Ali commissioned one key figure, Rifa al-Tahtawi, an Azharite scholar, to Paris for five years. When Tahtawi returned to Cairo, he initiated a series of educational reforms in the university and decided to make the press a forum for civic public discussions on topics such as government policies, *sharia*, Islamic reform, and Egyptian identity.[5] Muhammad ʿAbduh was born in the post Muhammad Ali period and educated in the 1850s and 1860s in two major traditional forms of Islamic education— *ʿilm* and *tasawwuf*— followed by training in a *madrasa*, and at al-Azhar in the traditional transmitted sciences of *hadith*, jurisprudence (*naqli*) as well as Sufism. ʿAbduh also drew inspiration from Tahtawi and included modern methods of instruction in history and natural sciences into the curriculum when he taught at Dar al-Ulum, one of the first teachers' training colleges in Egypt. It was at this time that he also began to publish his ideas about educational reform and science in the press.

It is necessary to situate ʿAbduh's thinking in relation to both changes in the Egyptian public sphere as well as Afghani's tutelage. Despite the fact that ʿAbduh was a Sunni Arab and Egyptian and Afghani a Shii Iranian, they both wrote about their concerns about Islamic societies through the same language of civilizational progress and decline. However, the key difference between ʿAbduh and Afghani was how each figure applied his concerns about the specific problem of West versus East.[6] Afghani was untethered to family, uprooted from his homeland, and participated in political intrigues that took him across the globe, often as a fugitive. ʿAbduh, on the other hand, was shaped by the specific land of Egypt and was invested in the country's religious, political, and cultural reforms. ʿAbduh's intellectual and political campaigns were thus directed to the Egyptian sociopolitical context and were a product of the Egyptian educational system and changes of the post-Muhammad Ali period.

ʿAbduh was trained in both traditional as well as modern western forms of learning. For example, in his early career, ʿAbduh began teaching in a school called Dar al-Ulum, which was founded under the rule of Khedive Ismail in 1873 with the premise of training *ʿulama* "in a modern way"—that is to say, by teaching modern sciences and traditional sciences together, alongside lectures on the history of civilizations, drawing from Arabic translations of Guizot's *History of Civilization* in Europe and France as well as the *Prolegomena* of Ibn Khaldun.[7] Afghani too was influenced by Guizot and so it is likely that ʿAbduh was taught many of these ideas of civilizational rise and decline by Afghani as well, as civilizational progress was no doubt at the center of Afghani's thought. Turning back to Afghani's response to Renan, it is important to remember how crucial theories of civilizational rise were to Afghani's argument. He conceded that conditions in the Islamic world presented obstacles to the development of modern science and progress, but he was not resigned to this state of affairs. He believed that just as the West was gradually transformed into a "civilized" society despite its Christian past, the same would eventually be the case with Muslims:

> If it is true that the Muslim religion is an obstacle to the development of sciences, can one affirm that this obstacle will not disappear someday? How does the Muslim religion differ on this point from other religions? All religions are intolerant, each one in its way. The Christian religion ... seems to advance rapidly on the road of progress and science, whereas Muslim society has not yet freed itself from the tutelage of religion. Realizing, however, that the Christian religion preceded the Muslim religion in the world by many centuries, I cannot keep from hoping that Muhammadan society will succeed someday in breaking its bonds and marching resolutely in the path of civilization after the manner of Western society, for which the Christian faith, despite its rigors and intolerance, was not at all an invincible obstacle. No, I cannot admit that this hope be denied to Islam.[8]

Afghani narrates his view of Islam as a discrete religious civilization through the framework of European Enlightenment values of science and progress. This totalizing idea of Islam that he invokes speaks neither to any specific historical moment nor to any geographic region. "Muhammadan" society has no connection to any particular society; rather, it functions as a synecdoche for an Islamic civilization that is a counterpart to the West. 'Abduh's view of Islam is similarly totalizing and civilizational, and he too was very much informed by Guizot's *History of Civilization in Europe*.[9] The period in which Afghani began mentoring 'Abduh was the time that Khedive Ismail landed into debt, which was followed by European control over Egyptian finances. Neither Khedive Ismail nor his successor were popular, and the national opposition of different groups coalesced into a revolt led by Urabi Pasha. 'Abduh followed Afghani in his support of Urabi Pasha against the British, which led to his imprisonment, maltreatment by the British, and exile to Beirut, where he taught for three years. Afghani returned to Egypt in 1888, with the hopes of returning to teach, but instead was made judge of native tribunals and eventually became Grand Mufti of Egypt in 1899.

'Abduh's *Risalah al-Tawhid*, or *The Theology of Unity*, was based on his lectures in Beirut. The overarching premise of the treatise is that Islamic societies have fallen into a state of decay, and the principal question that drives his argument in the piece is "how to bridge the gap between what Islamic society should be and what it had become."[10] This is the same bifurcation that we find in Afghani's writings about Islam and Islamic civilization. What differentiates 'Abduh's thinking from Afghani's, however, is his specific formation as an Egyptian and concern for Egyptian political unity. His diagnosis of the state of decay and prescription for reform is directed not to the Muslim world at large but to the people who share the same country, even minorities.[11] Below, I offer, one, an analysis of selections from *The Theology of Unity*, with attention to the temporal bifurcation about Islamic unity—the ideal Islam of the past and aspiration for that same ideal in the future—that is at the center of modernist thinking, and, two, an examination of which Muslim groups are perceived as having undermined the unity of Islam.

'Abduh states at the opening of the piece that the original meaning of *tawhid* is the belief that "God is one in inalienable divinity."[12] However, this theological idea is quickly sidelined as soon as the argument unfolds. As his opening discussion of *The Theology of Unity* develops, it becomes apparent that it is not theology that he is interested in interrogating but rather the history of how a once-unified Muslim community during the time of the Prophet became divided. The focus is on the growing *dis*unification of Muslim community rather than on the unity of God. The essay also reflects on the possibility for unity again—which can only be made possible through a renewed understanding of the Quran. As for Afghani, temporal bifurcation is the primary epistemological function of *tawhid* in ʿAbduh's writings.

After a brief statement about the theological meaning of *tawhid* in the Quran, ʿAbduh offers his reading of the significance of the Quran, which he interprets as the singular and fundamental source of Islam that is both coherent and transparent:

> The Quran came and took religion by a new road, untrodden by the previous Scriptures. . . . The Book gives us all that God permits us, or is essential for us, to know about His attributes. But it does not require our acceptance of its contents simply on the ground of its own statement of them. On the contrary, it offers arguments and evidence. . . . It spoke to the rational mind and alerted the intelligence. It sent out the order in the universe, the principles and certitudes within it, and required a lively scrutiny of them that the mind might thus be sure of the validity of its claims and message.[13]

What ʿAbduh sees as the Quran's essential rationality is important for his narrative of Islamic civilization, which unfolds in a specific trajectory: a golden period, the long period of decline, and finally, the possibility of a return. The period of the Quranic revelation was, as ʿAbduh recounts in the statements above, a unique time in which the text operated seamlessly with the life of the Prophet and early community, so much so, as he later explains, that that there was no need for "either excessive abstraction or over-rigorous definition" of the revealed text. After the death of the Prophet, the first three caliphs worked to keep the community together through the "literal meaning of the words," thereby holding to the integrity of the original Quranic message.

According to ʿAbduh, the unraveling of this harmonious relationship between text and community arose at one particular historical juncture: the death of the third caliph ʿUthman. This event "did irreparable damage to the structure of the caliphate and brutally diverted Islam and the Muslim people from their right and proper course." Interestingly, however, ʿAbduh states directly thereafter: "Only the Quran remained unimpaired in its continuity." This is significant because, in his view, there was a break between the Quran and the community in terms of the Quran's rationality and capacity to speak to the people. From ʿAbduh's perspective, it was possible to extract the Quran from these historical forces. This is relevant for his later prescription for the contemporaneous Muslim community: despite the fact that the community has been divided by various sects, schools, and interpretations, a return to the Quran remains a salvific possibility for this disunity of history.[14]

This separation between the community and text begins with the death of ʿUthman, the last of the Sunni *Rashidun* caliphs. Thereafter, the unity of the community spiraled into decline. By the time of the Ummayyads,

> the community had been sundered and its unity broken. Rival schools of thought about the caliphate developed and were propagated in partisanship, each striving by word and act to gain the better over its adversary. This is turn gave rise to forgeries of traditions and interpretation, and the sectarian excess brought sharp divisions.[15]

When he moves to a discussion of the Abbasid period, he brings the same kind of criticism to bear on various sectarian groups. He explains that during this period, due to the influence of Manichees, Yazidis, and other "Persian persuasions," atheism was popular. It was a moment in which views "inimical to belief in God" arose. In particular, he focuses on what he calls the "esoteric" groups of the Batiniyya and the Ismailiyya. He explains: "Their schools of thought had a disastrous influence on the faith and undermined conviction."[16] He describes at length an overall climate in which "progress of knowledge was arrested" and "obscurantists who got the upper hand destroyed the remained traces of rational temper which had its source in the Islamic faith." 'Abduh concludes this discussion of religious schools and groups until the Abbasid period with the following point: "The foregoing is a summary of the history of theology, indicating how it was founded on the Quran and how at length partisanship sadly distorted its true goal and quality." 'Abduh laments this loss with what appears as a counterintuitive response: "We must believe however, that the Islamic religion is a religion of unity throughout. It is not a religion of conflicting principles but is built squarely on reason, while divine revelation is its surest pillar."[17] He brings up this subject of unity again at the end of *The Theology of Unity*, but this time alongside a question of the current state of disunity. He writes:

> It is said by some that if Islam truly came to call diverse peoples into one common unity . . . how does it come about that the Islamic community has been sundered into sectarian movements and broken up into groups and schools? . . . If Islam is a faith that unifies, why this numerous diversity among Muslims?[18]

What we find here is the same vision of a temporally bifurcated conception of Islam similar to what Afghani outlined in his "Refutation." Both Afghani and 'Abduh invoke *tawhid* as a condition of the past as well as a "call" for unity. Afghani doesn't specify when exactly this *tawhid* existed, whereas 'Abduh identifies *tawhid* as the sociopolitical condition of the time of the Prophet until the rule of 'Ali, the fourth caliph. For both, however, this unity is retrievable, but only through an individualistic rationalist interpretation of the Quran. Everything in between the past and present is both irrelevant and superfluous, having undermined the original message of the Quran, as 'Abduh himself contends: "What are all these accretions to their religion, when all the time Muslims have

the very Book of God as a balance in which to weigh and discrimi-
nate all their conjectures, and yet its very injunctions they abandon and forsake?"[19] In the closing of *The Theology of Unity*, ʿAbduh
writes: "A glimmer of Islam, it is said, illuminated the west, but its
full light is in the east. Yet precisely there its own people lie in the
deepest gloom and cannot see."[20] This is of course the modernist
practice of *ijtihad* that ʿAbduh applies in his *Theology of Unity*,
whereby the solution for a compromised *tawhid* can be found
through a renewed return to the fundamental source of Islam, the
Quran.

ʿAbduh's account of Islamic history relies on many of the same
ideas and rhetorical devices as Afghani's. For example, Afghani
concludes his "Refutation" with a discussion of *tawhid*, which he
claims is unique to Islam. For Afghani, *tawhid* represents the social
unity of Muslims rather than the Quranic or theological unity of
God. This unity is what distinguishes Islam from "the Christian,
Brahman and Zoroastrian" religions. The problem, however, lies
with the people who have failed to sustain this unity of the past.
Afghani's concluding point in the "Refutation" mirrors ʿAbduh's
statements about the incapacity of Muslims to "see." Afghani writes:

> If someone says: If the Islamic religion is as you say, then why
> are the Muslims in such a sad condition? I will answer: When
> they were [truly] Muslims, they were what they were and world
> bears witness to their excellence. As for the present, I will con-
> tent myself with this holy text: 'Verily, God does not change the
> state of the people until they change themselves inwardly.'[21]

Both Afghani and ʿAbduh blame the Muslim people for making
divisive a religion that was once held together by unity—which
for both is conveyed through a sociopolitical reinterpretation of
tawhid. And both turn to the Quran as a solution to the prevailing
state of affairs, claiming that the only recourse available to change
this condition is the proper reading and incorporation of the fundamentals of the Quran. Furthermore, both of their arguments
about *tawhid* rely on the rhetoric of boundaries: there are insiders

and outsiders. That is to say, there are people and ideas that facilitate the possibility of unity on the one hand, and people and ideas that undermine the same possibility. In the "Refutation," Afghani blames the *neicheris*—the catchall term for any group Afghani believes is a political deviant or threat to unity—whereas 'Abduh casts blame specifically on the Shia.

'Abduh's condemnation of the Shia is further corroborated with what Rashid Rida writes in his account of his conversation with 'Abduh about the Shia and their connection to the Bahais. In this dialogue, the two discuss a Bahai scholar, Gulpayagani, whom 'Abduh describes as the key figure who proved to 'Abduh that the Bahai tradition was founded on the idea of reforming Shiism. In the dialogue, Rida recounts that 'Abduh stated that the "Shi'ite school is ___. They are the sect most in need of reform." Rida leaves a blank purposely, and in the note to explain the blank he offers the following information: "Here he said something he did not allow me to take down during his lifetime, and I see the wisdom in leaving it out now that he passed away. But I will say that his judgment on them is more severe than that of Ibn Taymiyyah."[22]

Although 'Abduh takes a strong anti-Shia position in *The Theology of Unity*, which is supported by Rida's statements above, 'Abduh offers sympathetic arguments in support of the Bahais, as recounted in the conversation between 'Abduh and Rida recorded by Rida. Rida is extremely critical of the Bahais, and as the dialogue unfolds, he formulates arguments against their teachings and practices. 'Abduh, however, does not share the same antipathy toward the group. Yet as we see from his outline of sectarianism in *The Theology of Unity* as well as his comments about the Shia that Rida recalls, he is just as intolerant of the Shia as Rida is of the Bahais. Turning back to Afghani's statements in the "Refutation," he identifies both the Ismaili Shia and the Bahais as *neicheris*. With Afghani, I have shown that he in fact drew on the language of Ismailism as well as Shii messianism more broadly to assert his religiopolitical authority. For 'Abduh, this is not the case. His message is equally salvific in tone and claims to provide a solution to the decay of Islam, but he does not try to assert a leadership role for himself (something I had suggested of Afghani). Despite the fact that ʿAbduh was anti-Shia, he was in fact open to the line of thinking and reform that the Bahais were promulgating in the late nineteenth century. It is Rida's antipathy to the Bahais, as well as to the Ismailis and Sufis, that is worth probing further.

Before I turn to the Bahai teachings that ʿAbduh endorsed, first let us turn to some background on the historical and religious development of this community. Mirza Husayn Ali Nuri or "Bahaʾuʾllah" (1817–1892) was the head of the Babi movement based in Baghdad. Bahaʾuʾllah was exiled to Istanbul in 1863, and shortly thereafter (sometime between 1863 and 1868) he founded a new movement called the Bahai faith. Whereas the earlier Babi religion—founded in 1844 in Shiraz by Sayyid ʿAli Muhammad Shirazi (1819–1850)—was shaped by ideas of eschatology and protest, the later Bahai faith as outlined by Bahaʾuʾllah transformed into a religion directed at reforming society in response to the changes brought on by western social, political, and economic modernity. Bahaʾuʾllah's writings focused on the importance of implementing parliamentarian forms of government, stabilizing nationalist state systems, and the state responsibility to help the poor.[23] In 1875, Bahaʾuʾllah's son ʿAbduʾl Baha ʿAbbas (1844–1921) wrote a book directed to the Iranian government in which he made the case that they adopt reforms based on the Bahai sociopolitical vision.[24] The modernist reform propagated by ʿAbdul Baha put his ideas in line with reformers at the time who were concerned with similar issues, such as Muhammad ʿAbduh.

Despite this turn of the Bahai faith from millenarianism to modernism, there was often a mixed reception to their arrival in Egypt. The Iranian Bahais came to Egypt starting in the late 1860s, and by the 1890s there was a small but intellectually vibrant community in both Alexandria and Cairo. One of the key figures to have emerged on the scene at this time was Mirza Abul-Fadl Gulpaygani (1844–1914), a Bahai convert and trained ʿalim sent to Egypt by ʿAbdul Baha. Gulpaygani established himself amongst a small group of students at al-Azhar, where he taught history, geography, and theology (*kalam*). It was through Gulpaygani that Bahai ideas were introduced into intellectual life in Cairo. Around this time, in 1898, a follower of Afghani assassinated Iran's Nasir ud-Din Shah, and many people in Cairo believed that Bahais conducted the assassination. Consequently, many Egyptians held to the view that Bahais should be massacred in Egypt.[25] The leader of this movement against the Bahais was Mirza Mihdi Khan Zaʾimud-Dawlih. Although his call to persecute the Bahais was arrested, he openly accused Gulpaygani of being a Bahai, which the latter did not deny. In fact, Gulpaygani took it upon himself to write about the Bahai faith in the secular periodical *al-Muqtataf*, which introduced Bahai ideas to intellectuals throughout the Arab world. For example, when Rida was a student in Tripoli, he read the article and wrote, along with a group of students, a response in protest of the ideas, which he found to violate the norms of Sunni Islam. In particular, he took issue with the fact that Bahaʾuʾllah could modify the law. This led him to believe that the Bahai faith was a completely new religion with a new set of laws that accepted the divinity of Bahaʾuʾllah. When Rida arrived in Cairo he engaged Gulpaygani about these ideas and in particular the issue of theophany (*zuhurullah*). He accused the Bahais of theological extremism, especially in relation to the issue of the appearance of a prophet after Muhammad. ʿAbduh, however, did not share these same views. It is interesting to note that ʿAbduh draws a very clear distinction between the Bahais and the Shia, despite their shared history.[26]

The Middle East historian Juan Cole has translated the conversation about the Bahais between Rida and ʿAbduh recorded in Rida's diary. According to Cole, this discussion between the two came right at the start of their relationship, when Rida arrived in Cairo.[27] In this piece, Rida begins by saying that he had grown interested in the Bahai faith while studying Islamic Sciences in Tripoli, Syria (now Lebanon). He met with Gulpaygani in Cairo in 1897 and thereafter debated with him repeatedly. On the basis of those conversations, he developed his critical positions on the Bahais, and as the piece demonstrates, on Sufis and Ismailis as well. At the start of the conversation, Rida introduces the Bahais by identifying their religious beliefs and practices with both those of the Sufis and what he labels "extremist" Shiism:

> *Rida:* (The first conversation that took place between us concerning them [the Bahais] occurred at the end of a discussion of jurisprudents and Sufis. When I noted the similarity between Sufism and extremist Shi'ism (*al-batiniyyah*) in the use of esoteric interpretation (*ta'wil*) [of the Qur'an], I asked him his opinion of the Babi [Bahai] Faith).

> *Abduh:* "This sect is the only one that strives so that sciences and arts might be acquired by the Muslims. There are learned and wise men among its adherents, but I do not know the truth of their school, nor do I know if the incarnationism and the like which is attributed to them is attributed rightly so or not. Rather, I find it exceedingly strange."[28]

'Abduh's response illustrates his reluctance to accept the parallel that Rida draws between the Bahais and the Sufis/"extremist" Shia (*al-batiniyyah*). Rather, he switches the focus of the conversation to underscore the Bahai emphasis on education—as advocates of arts and sciences—as well as the salubrious consequences of these undertakings on their followers whom he describes as "learned and wise . . . adherents." Furthermore, 'Abduh claims an agnostic position with regard to the controversial subject of continuous prophecy. Thereafter, Rida asks specifically about Gulpaygani, to which 'Abduh replies that he is "an historian and man of refinement." Rida explains his reservations about what Gulpaygani had to say about the Bahai religion, starting with the point that the Bahais are essentially propagandists. 'Abduh refutes this point with the argument that proof of Bahai truth is the fact that their message has endured:

> As for that which possesses life, such as the call to a religion or school, it will neither preserve nor endure save if the call be intrinsically true, even if some degree of falsehood encompasses it in

some of its phases. For this is an accidental quality that cannot prevent its endurance and continuance, unlike a call that is false in foundation.[29]

'Abduh's logic equates success—the endurance of a religion—with truth and failure of a religion to persevere with its inherent falsity. He makes the point that the Bahais had a message to communicate, and because the religion spread, the validity of its fundamental message of truth was proven. Rida, on the other hand, takes issue with this equation. Rida claims that the success of a religion is not determined by its message, but rather its messenger, and the messenger's "miraculous rational faculty." This was the case, he argues, with Bahai leadership:

> Rida: "The followers of the Báb and Bahá' were attracted by them when they saw a miraculous rational faculty in them ... It has been well-known in nature for some individuals to possess a miraculous rational faculty (such as the late Czar of Russia). Thus at sometimes [sic] persons exist with miraculous rational faculties, and if any of them arises with a call to something such as a religion, school (madhhab), or a Sufí order (tariqah), many people follow him. They are attracted by him and admire his impressive thought, perceptions, and words, even though his call is to something unreasonable, and even though he cannot establish a proof for it."[30]

According to Rida there have always been, throughout history, individuals who possess this "miraculous rational faculty" and announce a new religion, school (madhhab), or Sufi order (tariqah). People become attracted to these new beliefs because they are impressed by their ideas and ways of speaking.[31] In Rida's view, this "miraculous rational faculty" is "unreasonable" because it is unsupported by "proof." 'Abduh, surprisingly, comes out with a strong argument in support of what Rida dismissively denounces—the miraculous rational faculty of the Bahais as well as Sufis. He responds to Rida with the following:

'Abduh: "I believe that when someone with a miraculous rational faculty calls people to good things and has success in this he must be supported by a Spirit from God. For God does not bring this rational faculty into existence on a whim."[32]

Rida then asks 'Abduh whether he has "rational evidence" for this statement and 'Abduh says: "History from beginning to end witnesses to it and gives evidence for it. Indeed the Prophets and founders of the true schools were all of this sort." Rida thereafter takes 'Abduh to task on a contradiction—namely, that on the one hand 'Abduh agrees that the basic laws and principles of Islam cannot be changed and that humans must turn to personal endeavor (*ijtihad*), but then, on the other hand, endorses the role of Bahai intermediary authority as an agent and renewer of the law.[33]

Rida proceeds from the subject of the "miraculous rational faculty" to his second concern, namely what he sees as Bahai "propagandist" methods. In his view, the Bahai "propagandist" first asserts to the potential convert the possibility for a renewer of the law, and after the recipient of this message accepts this idea, he then raises the prospect of the renewer bringing a new law. This two-step induction method that he claims the Bahais adopted is not new, according to Rida.

[T]heir way of making propaganda and interpreting Qur'an verses and prophetic Traditions according to their base desires is like the way of their forbears among the esotericists, such as the Ismailis, etc. They say that the objective of their religion, or its principles and intentions (*maqasid*) is the unification of religions."[34]

He elaborates further that after having read about the Bahais, he and his fellow students learned that "the Bahai faith is a new religion and that they propagandize for it secretly, like the propaganda of the esotericists before them."[35] Rida thus identifies the Bahai claims of continuous prophecy and new revelation as a fundamental exercise in deception that "esotericists" such as the Ismailis adopted at an earlier point in history.[36] In this regard, there is a direct parallel with Afghani's argument, whereby Ismailis and Bahais are linked through the framework of "*neicheri*." For Rida, Ismailis and Bahais share a common set of beliefs and practices as "propagandists."

ʿAbduh does not concede to any of these points that Rida makes about deception, false prophecy, and new revelations. In fact, ʿAbduh provides a response that acknowledges the validity of Bahai, and in turn, Ismaili teaching practices, and implicitly endorses both traditions. ʿAbduh says:

> Yes, there is nothing wrong with extremism in speech or address for the sake of influencing or attracting people, or frightening and deterring them. But not everything that is said is to be written down and acted upon. I often say things in study or preaching sessions that I do not wish to be written down and transmitted from me. Their only value is their immediate effect on the soul of the one who is addressed."[37]

ʿAbduh does not agree with what Rida sees as a "propagandist" tendency in the Bahai religion, and he in fact believes that people have different needs and often require different methods of instruction. If there is a valid message to be taught, there is nothing wrong in taking an "extreme" position if necessary for the specific context.

Juan Cole has argued that by 1897, ʿAbduh thought the Bahai movement was the most progressive and creative Muslim community. In this way, Cole sees the sympathy ʿAbduh has for the Bahais in modernist terms—that is, concerned with progress and reform. ʿAbduh specifically defended Bahai reform projects, especially their legal mandate that limited the number of wives to two rather than four. ʿAbduh makes the case, in the dialogue recounted by Rida, that this modification was important and necessary for reform because Muslims had deviated from the law and engaged in excess with regard to polygamy and concubinage over the course of history.[38] It is no doubt the case that there was some kind of alignment between ʿAbduh's positions on modernist reform with the Bahai movement, but I think that it is not just the reform piece that was attractive to Abduh. His statements in the dialogue with Rida reveal that he was drawn to Bahai beliefs and practices and approved of many components of Ismaili and Sufi esoteric traditions. ʿAbduh's refutation of Rida's arguments about the deceptive nature of esotericists' "miraculous rational faculty" and their methods of instruction indicates his sympathetic view of charismatic leadership. ʿAbduh's defense of esoteric beliefs of the Bahais is further corroborated by his positions on theological unity and progressive revelation. The closing exchange between Rida and ʿAbduh demonstrates ʿAbduh's complete acceptance of the idea of the equality of religions:

> Rida: "They assert the soundness of all the religions and religious scriptures and call all peoples of all religious communities to their religion, that the word of mankind may become one thereby. They give as evidence, in calling the people of each religion to their faith, what is in the scriptures of the former, particularly the Pentateuch, the Gospel, and the Qurʾan. It has become apparent to me that their way is wiser than that of the Masons. The Masons found it advisable not to differentiate between the religions in membership in their association, claiming that it does not touch on religion, even though their objective is the destruction of all the religions. . . . The Bahaʾis assert the soundness of each religion in itself and seek evidence within it for their own religion, which abrogates whatever preceded it."

> ʿAbduh: "Drawing the religions closer together is among the things which the Islamic faith brought: 'Say: O people of the Book! Come now to a word common between us and you.'"[39]

ʿAbduh sees the value of theological equality and unity, specifically how it is tied to the notion of progressive revelation, which he explains to Rida:

> The entire human race is like a single member of it, whose father and trainer speaks to him in every phase of his life according to

the level of his intellect and the needs of his age. . . . He addressed the people of every Messenger according to their intellectual level and the condition of their society at that time. As man progressed, God ordained more advanced religious laws for him, until He sealed them with the mission of the Seal of the Prophets, which is the religion for mankind's maturity.[40]

He makes this same point about progressive revelation in *The Theology of Unity*:

> There are, of course, types of worship and diversities of pattern in the true religions, ancient and modern, and also varieties of precepts, new and old. But these we trace to the mercy of God and his gentleness in shape to each people and time according to his knowledge of what is best for them. . . . God's way . . . is to proceed by stages in the nurture of a man, from the time he is born, knowing nothing, to a ripe intelligence and a mature personality capable of penetrating the veiled mysteries of existence by his reason and attaining a knowledge of them.[41]

As I mentioned at the start, Afghani, ʿAbduh, and Rida all shared the same desire for Muslim political unity.[42] However, their logics and arguments were shaped by very different questions and concerns. ʿAbduh and Rida's positions on the Bahais, for example, could not be more divergent: ʿAbduh endorsed Bahai ideas of religious unity and progressive revelation, whereas Rida saw Bahai teachings as fractious and fraudulent. Rida published extensively about the Bahai religion in his journal, *al-Manar*. He wrote his first argument against the Bahais in response to Abuʾl Fadl Gulpayagni's theory of persistence—that the intrinsic truth of the Bahai faith was corroborated by the fact that the movement persisted and grew. Rida provided a response to this specific argument in his article "Propaganda Is the Life of Religions," in which he refuted the argument that religious sects were successful in spreading because of their message of truth. To make his case, he gives the examples of "pagan religions like those of Buddha, Brahma, and

Zoroaster" that have spread and persisted, even though they do not convey religious truth. Inherent truth cannot serve as a valid reason why religions are successful, in his view.

According to Rida, the reason why the Bahai religion was successful was because of its missionary impulse.[43] He built on this particular argument in a subsequent article, "Religious Propaganda: Its Rules and Methodology." In it, he offers an analysis of how religious propaganda is disseminated. The first criterion of missionary success is leadership. With the examples of the Sanusiyya movement in Libya and the Ahmadiyyah movement in India he makes the point that the successful leader speaks to the elite with "philosophical proofs" and provides "sermons on morality for the masses." The missionary leader, he argues, ought to be well-versed in the local language and customs, must be convinced by the message himself, and "must evince great patience and a never-failing hope of success."[44] In short, the truth of a message is irrelevant to understanding the growth of a religion. One must instead interpret the skills of the "propagandist." Furthermore, this rise of sects—the Sanusiyyah, Sudanese Mahdism, Babi/Bahai, and Ahmadi—demonstrates the poor state of Muslims and their inability to fully grasp the basic tenets of their religion. Rida saw in the Bahai religion a fundamental denial of reason in particular with the Babi doctrine of theophany. In his view, the theophany idea demanded that devotees submit to leadership, a line of thinking that he traced to Shii ideas of taqlid (or the following of traditional authorities). For Rida, the Quran required people to use reason and ask for proof, whereas Babism demanded that its followers accept all that Bab taught, without question.[45]

Rida also attributed Bahai success to the ignorance of the masses. He claimed that Muslims had insufficient understanding of the Quran, the biography of the Prophet, and the Arabic language, and that they had become dependent on the authority of the 'ulama. Muslims' reliance on religious authority predisposed them to belief in mystical figures and their ideas. Rida was fundamentally elitist in his outlook with regard to the reasons why people were drawn to these new religious movements. He believed that the Bahai movement contravened the fundamental principles of Islam and thought that it could be curtailed with literacy and education of the masses.[46] Rida shared with 'Abduh a distrust of Shiism, but Rida was particularly critical of charismatic leaders of Shiism, whom he branded as propagandists and manipulators of the uneducated.

It is important to think about why Rida had such a strong reaction to the Bahais, especially when he was a devoted student of 'Abduh. Rida was no doubt deeply shaped by the thought of 'Abduh and Afghani. He became 'Abduh's biographer and was in fact the person who defended and promulgated 'Abduh's ideas. Despite this close connection to his mentor, he took much more strident and conservative positions, likely due to his very different intellectual and social formation.[47] Rida was a Syrian who grew up in a cultural milieu surrounded by Christian communities, as well as several Shii groups such as the 'Alawites, Druze, and Ismailis. One possibility, as Cole has argued, is that his "orthodoxy" (that is, his conservatism and reaction to these groups) was not exclusively theological; rather, it was a response to the ways in which sectarian groups aligned themselves politically.[48] Rida was formally trained in Arabic and the traditions of Islamic learning at a Quranic school, and thereafter attended a Turkish government school in Tripoli. Later, he attended a "National Islamic school" founded by Shaykh Husayn al-Jisr of Tripoli (1845–1909). The curriculum included Arabic, French, and Turkish languages, logic, mathematics, and religious sciences, as well as European sciences. It was in this latter institution that Rida became deeply influenced by al-Ghazali's *Ihya 'ulum al-din* (*Revival of the Religious Sciences*).[49] He approved of intellectual Sufism and was drawn to the importance of inner devotion and reflection. However, he explicitly denounced any kind of mystical practices. In fact, Rida found the practices of Sufi orders abhorrent. It seems that Rida had decided to join the Naqshabandi order since he followed their teachings over a long period of time. One day he attended a session of a different order, the Mevlevis, and thereafter was completely put off by and denounced all forms of Sufi mystical practices:

> They said to me "Won't you come and attend the meeting of the Mawlawis in their monastery—it is like the heavenly paradise." . . . I agreed and went with those who were going after the Friday prayers. . . . There were handsome beardless youths among them, dressed in snow white gowns like brides' dresses, dancing to the moving sound of the reed-pipe, turning swiftly and skillfully so that their robes flew out and formed circles. . . . They stretched out their arms and inclined their necks and passed in turn before their shaykh and bowed to him. . . .
>
> I could not control myself, and stood up in the center of the hall and shouted something like this, "O people, or can I call you Muslims! These are forbidden acts, which one has no right to look at or to pass over in silence, for to do so is to accept them. To those who commit them God's word applies 'They have made their religion a joke and plaything.' . . . Then I left the place and retraced my footsteps quickly to the city.[50]

Rida, unlike his mentors, was deeply critical of mysticism. He drew a distinction between true and false mysticism. He believed that it was necessary for Muslims to be reflective in their doctrines as related to the *sharia* and that submission to a *shaykh* would undermine the relationship between the individual and God.[51] His position on Sufism was tied to the anxiety about (the lack of) progress among Muslims.

Rida, like Afghani and ʿAbduh, was preoccupied with what he considered the backwardness of Muslim countries, which he attributed to Muslim society's abandonment of the fundamental beliefs and practices of Islam. However, unlike his mentors, he thought that these fundamental principles could be found in the early teachings of Prophet Muhammad and in the practices of the first generation of Muslims. It is interesting to note that both ʿAbduh and Rida are considered "*salafi*" in their approaches to Islam. According to this designation, they both emphasize the important role of the earliest Muslims, who are considered the exemplary upholders of Islamic practices. There is, however, an important difference between the ways in which each of these figures understands the significance of the first three generations of Muslims. For ʿAbduh, it was a general reference to the early Islamic centuries whereas for Rida it referred to the first Muslims and Companions of Prophet, whose example needed to be emulated.[52] Rida's position was thus more anti-western and more emphatic in its prescription to follow the traditions of the early ancestors. Rida carried out the Afghani-ʿAbduh legacy, calling for reinterpretation of Islam and the implementation of Islamic law, and claiming that the ʿulama were backward and ill-equipped to understand the modern world. However, because he was not as exposed to the West and western forms of learning compared to ʿAbduh and Afghani, Rida was wary of modernists' western aspirations. He cast his reformism in the idiom of a defense of Islam against the dangers of the West, which was to become influential to the thought and politics of Hasan al-Banna (1906–1949), the founder of Egypt's Muslim Brotherhood.

The overlaps and points of difference between the modernism of Afghani/ʿAbduh and Rida are illustrated in a speech he gave late in his life, "Renewal, Renewing, and Renewers," published in al-Manar in 1931. In the opening, he explains that renewal is necessary in all aspects of life because it is a time that is afflicted by political turmoil, as with the case of the Communist and Bolshevik revolutions, and social upheaval in which the "women's revolution" is threatening the family with "heresy and unfettered promiscuity." Because of these conditions, there is a "dire need" for renewal as well as renewers. From the onset, Rida makes it clear that the renewal he calls for should not model itself on the Europeans. He writes how it is necessary to embark on an "independent renewal like that of Japan." That is the only way, he notes, that "we shall become a strong state, while preserving our nation's religion, culture, laws, and language, and national character." This independent renewal is opposed to the "imitative renewal like that of the Ottoman state," which culminated in the disintegration of the sultanate. According to Rida, the state started out strong and independent under the reign of Muhammad Ali, but then turned to imitation, became vulnerable to occupation, and finally lost all independence. In the speech, Rida identifies the need for great "renewers of civilization" such as Muhammad Ali and "renewers of knowledge" such as ʿAbduh and Afghani. In terms of the latter two, he explains how they have left their legacy of reformist and scientific thinking amongst a group of followers, but "nonetheless, destructive individuals have assumed the leadership of renewal . . . they urge the nation to abandon the guidance of religion, take off the apparel of virtue . . . allow the mixture of women and men in dancing halls . . . permit drinking and all types of sinfulness that follows." In Rida's view, the heretics are not the Shia or any particular religious group but rather the secularists. These are the false renewers, as he writes: "a horde of heretics in this great country are at present attempting to assume this honorable title [of renewer]." And later, "the false renewers here do not consider existing conditions because they imitate the heretics in their hostility to religious scholars."[53]

It is interesting to note that the titles he ascribes to those threatening unity—heretics and false renewers—are similar to terms his mentors invoked against leaders who posed some kind of threat. What distinguishes Rida's modernism from that of ʿAbduh and Afghani, however, is its strident anti-western position that is concerned with the question of the nation-state. It would be incorrect to say that Rida was anti-imperial because he too benefited and learned from European thought and cultural mores. Late in life, however, he grew disdainful of those cultural mores, scholars, and leaders who attempted to renew and reform in European terms. Rida writes about renewal as it relates to the nation-state under the section "The Alleged Renewal of the Heretics Constitutes a New Division of the Nation":

This so-called renewal is almost becoming a real renewal of divisive strife. This could be worse than the divisions of ethnic and national extremisms and of political parties. . . . [This party] in imitation of the heretics of Europe and its liberals, is hostile to religion and despise the devout, who constitute the majority of the nation. Ulama, orators, and writers urge people to respond to this party to declare their resistance to it.[54]

Similarly to 'Abduh, Rida is concerned with what he calls "divisive strife"; however, the target here is not any specific Muslim community but people who emulate Europeans and are hostile to religion. In his discussion with 'Abduh, the "heretics" are Bahais as well as other religious groups—such as the Ismailis, Ahmadis, and Sufis—that center on a charismatic leader. Here, the heretics are those who attempt to reform, but on western secular terms.

What exactly does Rida see as a solution to this problem? What is the proper form of renewal? In the same piece on renewal, he writes: "Some of the means for this renewal include the revival of the Arabic language in vocabulary, writing and speech; the writing of books in easy modern styles; the spread of education and socialization, according to scientific methods; and the spread of Islamic teachings in the world."[55] Interestingly, he closes the piece "Renewal, Renewing, and Renewers" with a quote from a well-known hadith—"God sends to this nation at the beginning of every century, someone who renews its religion," with the explanation that "the objective of this hadith focuses on the return to the simplicity and guidance of religion as it was at the beginning; to reunify the Muslims around their commonality, prior to disunity and discord . . . following the doctrine or the scholar whose knowledge they trust, without divisive extremism that turns the nation into factions and mutually hostile groups."[56]

Rida interprets this hadith in relation to the Egyptian Muslim community, which he sees as having been unified in the past but later divided in history. Similarly to his modernist predecessors, Rida calls for a return to the classical age, the "beginning," a time of "simplicity" when there was no "disunity and discord—a sentiment which echoes his mentor 'Abduh's argument that "sectarian divisions" and "movements broken up into groups and schools" have damaged the Muslim community. Rida attributes hostility within the Muslim community to "divisive extremism" within religion and no doubt implies there should be *someone* to conduct renewal. When piecing together Rida's language about "propagandists" with his lecture on the need for renewal with specific reference to the famous hadith about periodic renewal and renewers in the history of Islam, it is evident that the successful renewer (or *mujaddid*) could not be a leader from any of the "propagandist" group, nor any member of the secular elite he describes as "heretics" in his famous speech. He makes explicit reference to Afghani and 'Abduh as paradigmatic reformers, gesturing that the renewer ought to be someone from this particular intellectual lineage.

To conclude, there are three accounts of 'Abduh's life in Beirut (where he was exiled after the unsuccessful 'Urabi Revolt in 1883, until 1888)—the first by Rashid Rida, and the latter two by his students in Beirut, Sayyid 'Abd al-Basit and Shakib Arslan. Among these three versions, there is not much difference, except for the subject of 'Abdul Baha.[57] It is only Arslan's account that makes a reference to the mutual respect between 'Abdul Baha and 'Abduh:

> None of the notables or his acquaintances journeyed to Beirut without coming to greet him ['Abduh]. He honored and exalted each one and even if he disagreed with him in belief, he did not cease to respect him. Foremost among those he honored was Abbas Effendi al-Baha, leader of the Babis, even though the Babi way is different from what the Shaykh believes and is the creed that Sayyid Jamal ad-Din refuted so strongly. But he revered Abbas Effendi's knowledge, refinement, distinction, and high moral standards and 'Abbas Effendi similarly honored 'Abduh.[58]

Rida, however, was not satisfied with Arslan's account. He adds in a footnote that 'Abdul Baha practiced *taqiyyah*, or "dissimulation," and falsely depicted himself as a Shii reformer to 'Abduh. Rida states that he will later clarify the relationship between 'Abduh and 'Abdul Baha at the end of the biography, which is the dialogue discussed above. In both the footnote explaining the encounter and in the dialogue itself, Rida makes it a point to convey that 'Abduh was unable to fully comprehend 'Abdul Baha's teachings, rather than, say, that if he did, he would have denounced them. As recounted above, 'Abduh in fact makes his understanding of Bahai teaching methods and beliefs such as progressive revelation sufficiently clear.

Although 'Abduh made critical comments about the Shia and other "sectarians" in *The Theology of Unity*, his conversation with Rida demonstrates his unambiguous support not only for Bahai reform and ideas but also for the authoritative leadership of 'Abdul Baha himself. During 'Abduh's first period of exile in Beirut in 1883, he began to translate Afghani's "Refutation of the Materialists" from Persian to Arabic for the followers of Bab and Baha'u'llah. In the piece, Afghani identifies the early Bahai community, the Babis, as one of the many *neicheri* groups in the following manner:

> Let it be noted that the Babis who recently appeared in Iran and iniquitously spilled the blood of thousands of God's servants were apprentices of those same neicheris of Alamut . . . and their teachings are an example of batini teachings.[59]

'Abduh's translation of the Persian text, however, removes the "Babis" altogether:

> It is clear that a group (*fi'ah*) has appeared in recent days in some of the Eastern countries that has shed abundant blood and murdered noble souls. It appears under a name that is not far removed from the names of similar movements that preceded it. They picked up the remnants of the materialists (*dahriyyu*) of Alamut and the naturalists (*Tabi'iyyu*) of Kardku and its teachings are like the teachings of the Batinis. We must see what the effect is of its innovations (*bida*) in the community in which it appeared[60]

Although Rida writes that ʿAbduh was deceived or uninformed about the movement, ʿAbduh's published translation in which he removes the explicit reference to the Babis suggests that he sought to protect the group from ill-repute. Perhaps it was because of the respect he had for ʿAbdul Baha, which was in many ways parallel to his sentiments toward Afghani.[61] ʿAbduh wrote about both Afghani and ʿAbdul Baha in similar Sufi idioms of love and longing for a great teacher.

In the dialogue recounted above, Rida attempts to rewrite ʿAbduh in a way that aligns with Rida's Sunni normative bias. It is quite mysterious why Rida would take such a vehement position against the Bahais, especially when, as a community, they shared a similar commitment to unity and the idea of reform. Herein, the differences between ʿAbduh and Rida could not be more divergent: Rida denounced Bahais and Ismailis as propagandists and criticized Sufi ecstatic practices. ʿAbduh, on the other hand, accepted esoteric ideas and beliefs of continuous prophecy. As recounted in the first chapter, he found in Afghani divine inspiration, and as discussed here he recognized the same in ʿAbdul Baha. Moreover, he even endorsed Bahai methods of instruction and theological ideas of progressive revelation.

It is important to keep in mind the context of Rida's anti-western statements. Rida gave the renewal lecture toward the end of his life, when Egyptian nationalism was very much on the rise—so it is possible that his conservative positions against esoteric groups were in part a response to homogenize and unify Islam under nationalist pressure. To conclude, I would argue, like Juan Cole and William McCants, that Rida rewrote many parts of ʿAbduh's biography, and as a result the important connections between the different kinds of modernists—canonical and esoteric—have been occluded and the frame of who is (and is not) included in studies of modernism has narrowed. Furthermore, it seems that Rida's Sunni chauvinism laid the groundwork for later reactionary tendencies in the Muslim Brotherhood—an issue I will address in Chapter 4.

3

Muhammad Iqbal on the Question of Ahmadi Exclusion and Ismaili Inclusion

MUHAMMAD IQBAL (1873–1938) WAS THE most renowned Muslim intellectual in British India, after Sayyid Ahmad Khan. He was born in Sialkot, Punjab, and studied at Government College at Lahore, from where he graduated in 1899 and taught philosophy. He received a scholarship to Trinity College in Cambridge, obtained a Bachelor of Arts in 1906, and shortly thereafter qualified as a barrister. In 1907, Iqbal moved to Germany to pursue a Ph.D. and completed his doctorate in 1908, which was later published as *The Development of Metaphysics in Persia*. He returned to Lahore in 1908, where he taught, practiced law, and eventually grew more involved in politics. In 1930, he was elected President of the All Indian Muslim League.

What distinguished Iqbal from Sayyid Ahmad Khan, as well as contemporaneous Muslim elites, was his European intellectual training. Afghani, Sayyid Ahmad Khan, ʿAbduh, and Rida were all exposed to western ideas of history and philosophy, but none of them had studied abroad in European universities. Iqbal was unique not only in terms of his European intellectual formation and mastery of traditional Islamic literature, but in his involvement with formal politics as well, as he was the only one in the above-mentioned group to occupy an official state position as president of a political party. For Iqbal, the perspectives of Nietzsche and Bergson were just as informative as traditional scholarly approaches to the Quran. In his famous speech as president of the Muslim League he spoke passionately about the need for a separate territory for Muslims because of the ethically distinctive and dynamic nature of Islam.

Although there were clear divergences in thought between Iqbal and earlier modernists, there were also continuities which I explore here. Iqbal too shared the same concern about a fractured *tawhid*, and like his predecessors and contemporaries he articulated its challenges through theories of civilizational rise and decline. At one level, Iqbal's *tawhid* functioned in a similar register as that of his modernist counterparts. Like Afghani and ʿAbduh, Iqbal argued that *tawhid* was complete and pure at the start of Islam and gradually weakened throughout history. He believed that *tawhid* was one of the fundamental principles of Islam that Muslims needed to comprehend in order to begin the process of reunification, or reconstruction, to use the title of his famous collection of essays. *Tawhid* was critical to Iqbal's civilizational logic: it served an emancipatory role, representing the Enlightenment principles of freedom and equality. Thus, *tawhid* became more expansive and layered in Iqbal's writings compared to earlier modernist interpretations.

Just as Iqbal's views on *tawhid* were arguably more robust than those of previous modernists, so too was his position on "transgressors" of *tawhid*—in this case the Ahmadis. The Ahmadis were not simply part of a larger story of *tawhid*'s decline as were the *neicheri* for Afghani and the Shia for ʿAbduh. His criticisms were much more detailed, sharply articulated, and strident. In the 1930s, he wrote an extended polemic accusing the Ahmadis of heresy, which had longstanding repercussions for the community later in history.

The chapter begins with an analysis of *tawhid* in Iqbal's *Reconstruction of Religious Thought in Islam*, followed by an extensive reading of his piece *Islam and Ahmadism*, in which he formulates a sustained case against the Ahmadis as heretics. Although he makes an argument that is purportedly theological—namely, that Ahmadis violate the Muslim fundamental belief in the finality of prophecy—I argue that his main target was Mirza Ghulam Ahmad, whose charismatic leadership threatened Iqbal's authority as representative of Muslim unity, defined by values of freedom, equality, and progress. In his view, Ahmadi belief in the prophecy of Mirza Ghulam Ahmad kept the community in a "backward" state and contravened Iqbal's understanding of what it meant to be modern. This chapter explores the contours of Iqbal's accusations against Ahmadi heresy through theories of the "heretic" outlined by sociologists such as Zimmel, Zito, and Bourdieu. Finally, this analysis of Iqbal's punitive stance against the Ahmadis concludes with the unexpected contrast Iqbal draws to the Ismailis, in which he claims the Ismailis adopted and adhered to progressive beliefs aligned with the modern Muslim community in ways the Ahmadis refused to do.

Tawhid in *Reconstruction of Religious Thought in Islam*

"Humanity needs three things today—a spiritual interpretation of the universe, spiritual emancipation of the individual, and basic principles of a universal import directing the evolution of human society on a spiritual basis. . . . Believe me, Europe today is the greatest hindrance in the way of man's ethical advancement. The Muslim, on the other hand, is in possession of these ultimate ideas on the basis of a revelation, which speaking from the inmost depths of life, internalizes its own apparent externality. . . . Let the Muslim of today appreciate his position, reconstruct his social life in the light of ultimate principles, and evolve out of the hitherto partially revealed purpose of Islam, that spiritual democracy which is the ultimate aim of Islam."

—Muhammad Iqbal, "The Principle of Movement in the Structure of Islam" [1]

This quote from Muhammad Iqbal's "The Principle of Movement in the Structure of Islam" essay illustrates in microcosm the central questions and arguments that animate *The Reconstruction of Religious Thought in Islam*, the larger volume of which this essay is a part. *Reconstruction* is a collection of writings most of which were based on lectures Iqbal gave at Madras, Hyderabad, and Aligarh that were published for the first time in 1930 and later in 1934. Iqbal's reformulation and redefinition of Islam is at the center of the project outlined in the volume. The above selection is noteworthy in that it illustrates, first, Iqbal's position on Islam—configured through possibilities of progress, rooted in the Quran, and fundamentally opposed to "Europe"—and second, his call for Muslims to "reconstruct" themselves in light of what he sees as Islam's "ultimate principles." Iqbal's use of the imperative makes it clear that these fundamental principles are available to Muslims but are nonexistent in the present day. What are these principles exactly? At what period were Muslims governed by these principles? Why do they not exist in the present?

Iqbal begins the "Principle of Movement in Islam" with his interpretation of Islam's rise as a great civilization. He starts with a quote from a "modern historian of civilization," J. H. Denison, who, according to Iqbal, made the following statements about the decline of the Christian civilization and the rise of Islam:

> the civilization of Christianity, which was built up over the course of a thousand years . . . stood like a gigantic tree . . . rotted to the core, riven by storms of war, and held together only by the cords of ancient customs and laws that might snap at any moment. Was there any emotional culture that could be brought in, to gather mankind once more into unity and to save civilization?[2]

Iqbal then states that Denison argued how "the world stood in need of a new culture to take the place of the culture of the throne, and the systems of unification which were based on blood-relationship."

Islam was this new "dynamic" culture that emerged in response and in opposition to the "earth-rootedness" of Christianity.[3]

Iqbal calls attention to what he sees as the culturally superior aspects of Islam.[4] For instance, Islam, in his view, was explicitly "non-territorial" in character and therefore had built into it the capacity for unification unlike Christianity:

> Islam . . . flashed across the consciousness of a simple people untouched by any of the ancient cultures, occupying a geographical position where three continents meet together. The new culture finds the foundation of world-unity in the principle of Tawhid. Islam as a polity is only a practical means of making this principle a living factor in the intellectual and emotional life of mankind. It demands loyalty to God, not to thrones. And since God is the ultimate spiritual basis of all life, loyalty to God virtually amounts to man's loyalty to his own ideal nature. The ultimate spiritual basis of all life, as conceived by Islam[,] is eternal and reveals itself in variety and change. A society based on such a conception of Reality must reconcile, in its life, the categories of permanence and change. It must possess eternal principles to regulate its collective life, for the eternal gives us a foothold in the world of perpetual change.[5]

This "new culture" of Islam is set against Christianity in a series of oppositions. While Christian civilization is defined by allegiances to blood, land, and thrones, Islam, according to Iqbal, rejects blood ties, is unbound geographically, and emphasizes exclusive focus on God. Moreover, in contrast to Christianity, Islam offers the possibility of a new kind of individual and society, precisely because of the primacy given to God. Moreover, in Islam devotion to God is in fact the means to reflect on one's individual self, as he explains—"Loyalty to God in Islam virtually amounts to man's loyalty to his own ideal nature."[6]

What further distinguishes Islam from the Christian civilization is that it is both eternal and mutable, unlike Christianity, which reached its peak and then declined. The Quran is, on the one hand, unchanging and timeless, but on the other hand it operates in history, specifically to regulate collective life and thus provides a "foothold in the world of perpetual change." How is it possible to configure a society that is at once eternal and changing? The starting point for understanding the eternal and timeless components in Islam is the idea of *tawhid*. In the Quran, *tawhid* refers to a theological idea, namely God's unity. For Iqbal, however, the term serves both a socially unifying as well as an emancipatory function. He introduces this first understanding of *tawhid* in the above passage, whereby he argues that this "new culture of Islam "finds the foundation of world-unity in the principle of tauhid."[7] And later Iqbal describes "the essence of tauhid," as "equality, solidarity, and freedom."[8]

Both the social unity and ethical equality/freedom components of *tawhid* are nonexistent in the present. Take for example his discussion of society in the above passage, which operates in a similar syntactical manner as "social life" in the passage I introduced at the opening. In the first passage cited, Iqbal states: "Let the Muslim of today appreciate his position, reconstruct his social life in the light of ultimate principles." In the second one, Iqbal writes: "society based on such a conception of Reality must reconcile, in its life, the categories of permanence and change. It must possess eternal principles to regulate its collective life." In both instances, it is the ideal social order, not the present social condition, that is the subject of discussion. The second passage is clearly more emphatic, opting for "must" rather than the "Let the Muslim . . . reconstruct his social life" formulation of the first example. Both examples, however, make it clear that this newly envisioned society based on a reconstructed spiritual Islam does not exist in the contemporaneous context. It is something that *ought* to be implemented.

Tawhid is the universal given in Iqbal's worldview, but it is not static. Rather, this freedom and/or unity is activated in a dynamic form—that is to say, it must respond to changing conditions, which is made possible through *ijtihad*:

> But eternal principles when they are understood to exclude all possibilities of change, which, according to the Quran, is one of the greatest "signs" of God, tend to immobilize what is essentially mobile in its nature. . . . What then is the principle of movement in the structure of Islam? This is known as ijtihad.[9]

Iqbal defines *ijtihad* as the process "to exert with a view to form an independent judgment on a legal question." His interest in the idea stems from a concern about why Islamic law, which is based mainly on the fundamentals provided by the Quran, has come to assume a "stationary character." It is for this reason, he explains, it is necessary to undergo an examination of its application in Islamic history. Iqbal begins this discussion of *ijtihad* with the argument that the conceptual possibilities of *ijtihad* were closed off because of three specific developments in the history of Islam: first, the rise of the Rationalist movement during the Abbasid period; second, the growth of "otherworldliness" in Sufism; and third, the anxiety that arose in the aftermath of the destruction of Baghdad. As a response to these developments within the tradition, Iqbal argues, conservative thinkers found it necessary to preserve social order through the mechanisms of Islamic law. He explains further that while he was partially sympathetic to their response, this tendency toward "over-organization" was not the most befitting solution, as it directly contradicted the "impulse of Islam."[10]

Thereafter, he states that despite the fact that the legal schools became quite stringent, there were key people who were able to work against this conservative response, tap into this dynamic nature of Islam, and activate the original spirit inherent to *ijtihad* that became too restrictive within the legal schools. Ibn Taymiyya was one example. Iqbal explains that Ibn Taymiyya was trained in the Hanbalite school of law but broke with its tradition of interpretation because he found it too limiting, opting to return instead "to the first principles in order to make a fresh start." It was this kind of renewed perspective that proved critical for the larger Islamic tradition, as he inspired the reformer Muhammad Ibn ʿAbd al-Wahhab and conservative movements in Asia and Africa thereafter in the eighteenth century. Iqbal explains that although these movements were sometimes inward looking, they were remarkable for the "spirit of freedom" they embodied, which Iqbal traces to the revolt initiated by Ibn Taymiyya against the confines of the legal schools.[11] What Iqbal finds in *ijtihad* are possibilities for freedom of interpretation. But what does this have to with the new reconstructed Islam that he is calling for? Before turning to his analysis of where he sees the application of *ijtihad* successful, let us turn to Reinhart Schulze's discussion of Muslim elites of the colonial period.

One of the points Schulze makes about the new public of Muslim intellectuals is that they were keen to demand the reestablishment of *ijtihad*. By dismissing *taqlid* (the strict adherence to authority), it was their hope that their positions would be heard. According to Schulze, Muslim elites were successful at breaking the traditional scholars' monopoly without relinquishing the Islamic tradition. He writes, "Outwardly the new public represented by the 'secularized' elites still remained Islamic. They argued in an Islamic manner, propagated Islam as an ideology, and regarded Islam as a suitable response to imperialism."[12]

Schulze's understanding of Muslim elites' propagation of *ijtihad* fully accords with Iqbal's invocation of the concept in the "Principle of Movement" essay. *Ijtihad* is a source of inspiration that Iqbal finds necessary to activate and apply to history. It is apparent that Iqbal's use of *ijtihad* is framed within the language of Islam—but the question is, to what extent does this idea of *ijtihad* operate within the parameters of tradition? Although Shulze argues that these secularized elites remained Islamic—arguing in an Islamic manner, etc.—Iqbal's discussions of *tawhid* and *ijtihad* in the essay are rarely analyzed in relation to Islamic texts other than the Quran, and more importantly, discussion of these topics is never directed to any other Muslim scholar.[13]

Iqbal no doubt argues with reference to developments of the Islamic tradition in history, but his Islam is ideological rather than rooted in practice, and it is fundamentally grounded in a political vision. Take for example this thread of logic about *ijtihad* and *tawhid*. As I outlined above, Iqbal locates the dynamism of Islam in its ur-text, the Quran, and the practices that sustain that dynamism in the idea of *ijtihad*. What connects the text to practice is the specific concepts that Iqbal invokes throughout the essay as the "the spirit of freedom"—*tawhid*. *Tawhid*, for Iqbal, is at once physical ("world-unity") and ethical. These two aspects of *tawhid*—as the physical force of unification, as well as the possibilities of freedom, solidarity, and equality—come together later in his discussion of *ijtihad* in the modern period. It is noteworthy that he directs his analysis of the modern state of *ijtihad* not to India, but to Turkey. Iqbal explains that *ijtihad* was broadened and reinforced in the modern Turkish context, where two political groups emerged—the Nationalist Party and the Party of Religious Reform.[14] The Nationalist party advocated the separation of Church and State (thereby operating under a dualism which does not exist in Islam, according to Iqbal), while the Reform party claimed the opposite, namely that Islam could not be divided into these two realms. Iqbal is supportive of the latter, and provides evidence with a discussion of *tawhid* to support his point. His reading of the situation is based on the statements of Said Halim Pasha, the Grand Vizier of the Ottoman Empire from 1913–1917 and leader of the Religious Reform Party. Iqbal cites Pasha's alleged statements about the unity of Islam to underscore his own position.[15] He quotes Said Halim Pasha further to explicate this point about Islam as fundamentally a unified tradition:

As there is no English Mathematics, German Astronomy, or French Chemistry . . . so there is no Turkish, Arabian, Persian, or Indian Islam. Just as the universal character of scientific truths engenders varieties of scientific national cultures which in their totality represent human knowledge, much in the same way the universal character of Islam verities creates varieties of nation, moral, and social ideals.[16]

According to the above statements, Iqbal/Pasha's position conveys that Islam is essentially and fundamentally a coherent tradition, despite variegated and national cultures. From this standpoint, there are no differences between the various linguistic and cultural expressions of Islam. Turkish, Indian, and Arabian Islam are presumably all the same "Islam" but with different names. Islam in this instance is made equivalent to "science," which, too, in this analogy, is universal, but just happens to have different names and subdivisions. For science as well as Islam, the universal character supersedes all differences.

Despite this axiomatic assertion that Islam is fundamentally indivisible, there is also, on Iqbal's part, an acknowledgment that the forces of history have worked counter to this principle, which he reiterates, again citing Pasha:

> He [Pasha] however deplores that during the course of history the moral and social ideals of Islam have been gradually deislamized through the influence of local character.... The pure brow of the principle of *Tawhid* has received more or less an impress of heathenism, and the universal and impersonal character of the ethical ideals of Islam has been lost through a process of localization. The only alternative open to us, then, is to tear off from Islam the hard crust which has immobilized an essentially dynamic outlook on life, and to rediscover the original verities of freedom, equality, and solidarity with a view to rebuild our moral, social, and political ideals out of their original simplicity and universality. Such are the view of the Grand Vizier of Turkey.[17]

Iqbal argues that the Islamic tradition has lost sight of its fundamental principles. The purity of *tawhid*, he explains, has been mired by various forms of localization—what Iqbal describes as heathenism. If we take this point with the previous discussion about varieties of Turkish, Persian, or Indian Islam, it becomes clear that Iqbal believes that these different forms of religious expression have undermined the force and universality of *tawhid* in the physical as well as ethical interpretations of the idea Iqbal has outlined. First of all, *tawhid* is in a precarious state because geographic and cultural differences have led to the breakup of, or "de-islamized," ideals of Islam, of which *tawhid* is presumably at the center. And second, this geographic and cultural fracturing has weakened the dynamic spirit. It is for this reason, he contends, that it is necessary to unearth the power of *tawhid* and rebuild Islam through moral and political ideals based on the original impulse of unity and ethics of freedom and solidarity.

This discussion about Turkey is argued primarily in presentist terms. What is interesting in the above passage, however, is how the motif of decline is concomitant with the turn to a subjunctive mood—that which he desires/hopes to happen. In the above passage, it is the subject of *tawhid* upon which this decline is diagnosed: "The pure brow of the principle of Tawhid has received more or less an impress of heathenism. . . ." This is followed by the response of hope and aspiration to return to the fundamentals of *tawhid*: "The only alternative open to us, then, is to tear off from Islam the hard crust which has immobilized an essentially dynamic outlook on life, and the rediscover the original verities of freedom, equality, and solidarity."

He concludes that it is the Grand Vizier's intention to promote the "freedom of *Ijtihad* with a view to rebuild the laws of Shariah in the light of modern thought and experience." He follows this endorsement of Pasha's *ijtihad* with an analysis of the nationalist poet Ziya's *ijtihad,* whose words, Iqbal claims, "have done a great deal in shaping the present thought of Turkey." He quotes passages from Ziya's poetry that support the significance of political unity in Islam, women's rights, the role of science and its fundamental compatibility with religion, and a last point about the importance of the spiritualization of man's heart. All these points demonstrate for Iqbal that "among Muslims nations of today, Turkey alone has shaken off its dogmatic slumber, and attained to self-consciousness." He continues to explain:

> the Turk is on the way to creating new values. . . . The question which confronts him today, and which is likely to confront other Muslim countries in the near future, is whether the Law of Islam is capable of evolution—a question which will require great intellectual effort, and is sure to be answered in the affirmative.[18]

For Iqbal, the Reform Party's politics in Turkey of the 1930s represents a story of success because its political leaders and thinkers embraced the kind of *ijtihad* that was not restricted to the confines of legal schools and emphasized instead political unity. In short, this was an example of a reconstructed Islam that was fully aligned with Iqbal's idea of *tawhid*—as defined by social unity of people as well as freedom and solidarity. Turkey provided Iqbal with the assurance that Islamic law was indeed capable of evolution and fresh interpretation.

Tawhid and Sectarianism

Religious adventurers set up different sects and fraternities, ever quarreling with one another; and then there are castes and subcastes like the Hindus! Surely we have out-Hindued the Hindu himself; we are suffering from a double caste system— the religious caste system, sectarianism, and the social caste system, which we have either learned or inherited from the Hindus. This is one of the quiet ways in which conquered nations revenge themselves on their conquerors. I condemn this accursed religious and social sectarianism. I condemn it in the name of God, in the name of humanity, in the name of Moses, in the name of Jesus Christ, and in the name of him—a thrill of emotion passes through the very fibre of my soul when I think of that exalted name—yes, in the name of him who brought the final message of freedom and equality to mankind. Islam is one and indivisible: it brooks no distinctions in it. There are no Wah-habis, Shi'is, Mirza'is, or Sunnis in Islam.—Muhammad Iqbal, "Islam as Moral and Political Ideal"[19]

Iqbal's fervent denouncement of sectarianism in the above passage from his 1908 speech, "Islam as Moral and Political Ideal," came at a time when Muslim leaders were fighting hard to create and sustain a platform of representation that could contend with the increasing pressures and demands of the British and Congress in colonial India. The many speeches Iqbal gave to the Indian Muslim com-munity, as the one excerpted above, served as the medium through which he outlined his politics and vision for Indian Muslims. The plea for Muslim unity was no doubt a response to pressures the mi-nority group faced in colonial India, as well an expression of a new anxiety specific to the larger nineteenth and early twentieth century political context—a time when political leaders and intellectuals of the Muslim world were forced to redefine Muslim identity after the fall of the Mughal, Ottoman, and Safavid Empires.

The above passage intimates a fundamental contradiction at the center of Iqbal's campaign for Muslim unity: on the one hand, he recognized that Indian Muslims were a culturally and linguistically diverse community that identified with multiple theological orien-tations, but on the other hand, he insisted on speaking about and on behalf of Muslims as a single group. His impassioned tone in the above passage is meant, it seems, to invoke a feeling of communitas, as he states, "There are no Wahhabis, Shi'is, Mirza'is, or Sunnis in Islam"—thereby claiming the possibility of a unified Muslim com-munity despite the many theological schools. However, he describes internal differences within the Muslim community as "accursed religious and social sectarianism" and "the religious caste sys-tem." What serves as a rallying point for his audience—the call for unification—is undermined in the same discussion by his over-arching polemic against sectarian divisions within Islam.

Iqbal's definition of Islam as a world-unifying polity that could not be divided by race, nation, or ethnicity relied on a reformulation of *tawhid*, the Quranic idea of God's unity, as political unity of Muslims. Iqbal understood in the meaning of *tawhid* possibilities of "equality, solidarity, and freedom" of mankind.[20] These fundamentals, however, were mired by not only sectarianism, as described in the above passage, but also "heathenism," as he explains in *Reconstruction*: "The pure brow of the principle of Tauhid has received more or less an impress of heathenism, and the universal and impersonal character of the ethical ideals of Islam has been lost through a process of localization." This problem, he notes, can be resolved through a return to the original principles, as he explains further in the same piece:

> The only alternative open to us then, is to tear off from Islam the hard crust which has immobilized an essentially dynamic outlook on life, and to rediscover the original verities of freedom, equality, and solidarity with a view to rebuild our moral, social, and political ideals out of their original simplicity and universality.[21]

Some 25 years later, Muhammad Iqbal wrote "Qadianis and Orthodox Muslims" where he made the following request to the colonial state regarding the Qadianis (Ahmadis):

> The best course for the rulers of India is, in my opinion, to declare the Qadianis a separate community. This will be perfectly consistent with the policy of the Qadianis themselves, and the Indian Muslim will tolerate them just as he tolerates other religions.[22]

In 1908, the Ahmadis are invoked as one of several Muslim groups against whom he casts his polemic about sectarian divisions within Islam. In 1934, however, he singles out the Ahmadis and argues for their excommunication from the Muslim community. The reason, as he explains in *Islam and Ahmadism*—a piece that he wrote a year later in 1935—is that they contravene one of the two fundamental beliefs of Islam, the finality of prophecy:

> The simple faith of Muhammad is based on two propositions— that God is One, and that Muhammad is the last of the line of

those holy men who have appeared from time to time in all countries and in all ages to guide mankind to the right ways of living.[23]

Iqbal traces this specific violation to Mirza Ghulam Ahmad (1835–1908), the founder of the Ahmadis. Mirza Ghulam Ahmad of Qadian, Punjab, proclaimed himself as the *mujaddid* (renewer) of Islam, and over the course of his life he claimed to be also a *muhaddath* (a person spoken to by Allah or his angels), the *mahdi* (the messiah), and *masih-i-mawud* (promised Messiah). In 1888, he claimed to have received a command from God to establish a new community and thus called on Muslims to declare their *bay 'a*, or allegiance, to him. Iqbal too was born in the Punjab Province of British India, and his natal village, Sialkot, was part of the larger Ahmadi milieu. In fact, Muhammad Iqbal's father, Shaykh Nur Muhammad (d. 1929), took the *bay 'a* of Ghulam Ahmad, as did various members of Iqbal's family.[24]

Why then was Iqbal driven to write such an aggressive argument against the Ahmadis? According to Ayesha Jalal, Iqbal's anti-Ahmadi turn can be traced to Iqbal's personal and political grievances with Ahmadi leaders while serving on the All-India Kashmir Committee in the early 1930s. Iqbal Singh Sevea has argued that Iqbal's critique of the Ahmadis ought to be understood in light of Iqbal's conception of prophecy, which held that the chain of Prophethood culminated with Muhammad, who established the final revelation for spiritual development and a complete sociopolitical order as prophet. The Ahmadi conception of continuous prophecy would undermine the doctrine of *khatm-i-nabuwwat* (seal of prophecy) and, in turn, disempower both the individual and society.

Iqbal's political and personal disputes as well as his larger stakes in the finality of prophecy argument are certainly crucial factors to consider when reflecting on why Iqbal would mount such an accusation on the Ahmadis. In the following section, I build on this interrogation of Iqbal's accusation of heresy against the

Ahmadis with the claim that Iqbal's indictment of Mirza Ghulam Ahmad ought to be examined in relation to conflicting approaches to Muslim renewal in the nineteenth century Indian colonial context, which can be elucidated further through a theoretical interrogation of heresy. The argumentative reasoning Iqbal invokes against the Ahmadis is one of heresy. However, his explication of heresy—delineated as the violation of the finality of prophecy—calls into question the fundamental rationale of heresy as theological deviance. Drawing on the reconceptualization and theorization of heresy by sociologists such as George Zito, Georg Simmel, and Pierre Bourdieu, I argue that Iqbal's allegation of heresy must be considered in light of a nexus of sociopolitical factors that include Iqbal's familial and personal relationship to the Ahmadis, his anxiety about the minority Muslim community identity, the self-consciously public character of Mirza Ghulam Ahmad's declaration of prophethood, and Iqbal's belief that the Ahmadi leadership was "backward."

Iqbal and Mirza Ghulam Ahmad's Heresy

In 1935, Iqbal wrote *Islam and Ahmadism,* in which he explained that the reason the Qadianis (Ahmadis) ought to be excommunicated from the Muslim community is that they defy one of the two fundamental beliefs of Islam, the finality of prophecy.[25] *Islam and Ahmadism* was written as a response to Nehru, who had written a piece in *The Modern Review of Calcutta* questioning Iqbal's position that Ahmadis ought to be excommunicated from the larger Muslim community. Iqbal provided Nehru with a lengthy argument about why Ahmadi beliefs and practices are heretical, thereby explicating his position that they be considered a separate community. Iqbal's response starts by explaining his position on why Indian Muslim solidarity is undermined by both Nehru (whom he refers to as the "Pandit") and the Ahmadis ("Qadianis" in his words). He states that Nehru and the Ahmadis "inwardly resent, for different reasons, the prospects of Muslim political and religious solidarity, particularly in India." According to Iqbal, Nehru's nationalism demands a "total suppression of the cultural entities of the country," which for Iqbal undercuts the position of Muslim separatism and illustrates Nehru's resentment toward Indian Muslim solidarity. Similarly, in Iqbal's view, the Ahmadis are threatened by the cohesion of the Indian Muslim community: "It is equally obvious that the Qadianis, too, feel nervous by the political awakening of the Indian Muslims, because they feel that the rise in political prestige of the Indian Muslims is sure to defeat their designs to carve out from the Ummat of the Arabian Prophet a new Ummat for the Indian prophet."[26]

Iqbal thus begins his book with the point that Indian Muslim solidarity is under attack by Nehru's nationalism on the one hand and the Ahmadi movement on the other hand. Iqbal's interpretation of the Ahmadi response to Indian Muslim unity is the same as that of Nehru's—one of anxiety—but for different reasons, which he explains throughout the work. What is significant here is that from the onset, Iqbal's position is defensive; he formulates his entire argument in response to the alleged threat of Muslim unity. He begins his case with the point that Nehru as well as the Ahmadis both fundamentally misunderstand Islam and then proceeds with an extensive explanation of why the latter is considered heretical to Islam. Iqbal begins with a defense of Islam, refuting Nehru's assumption that declaring the Ahmadis heretical was part of a tradition of "inquisition" inherent to Islam:

> Pandit Jawahar Lal Nehru seems to think that a society founded on religious principles necessitates the institution of Inquisition. This is indeed true of the history of Christianity; but the history of Islam, contrary to the Pandit's logic, shows that during the last thirteen hundred years of the life of Islam, the institution of Inquisition has been absolutely unknown in Muslim countries. . . . The two propositions on which the conceptual structure of Islam is based are so simple that it makes heresy in the sense of turning the heretic outside the fold of Islam almost

impossible [:] ... that God is One, and that Muhammad is the last of the line of those holy men who have appeared from time to time in all countries and in all ages to guide mankind to the right ways of living.[27]

In Iqbal's view, heresy is not, as Nehru contends, intrinsic to the Islamic tradition. However, Iqbal believes that the practice of mandating groups as heretical can indeed be undertaken if the foundational doctrines of Islam are violated:

> The question of a heresy, which needs the verdict whether the author of it is within or outside the fold, can arise ... only when the heretic rejects both or either of these propositions. Such heresy must be and has been rare in the history of Islam which, while jealous of its frontiers, permits freedom of interpretation within these frontiers. And since the phenomenon of the kind of heresy which affects the boundaries of Islam has been rare in the history of Islam, the feeling of the average Muslim is naturally intense when a revolt of this kind arises. That is why the feeling of Muslim Persia was so intense against the Bahais. That is why the feeling of the Indian Muslims is so intense against the Qadianis.[28]

Iqbal traces the Ahmadi transgression specifically to the figure of Mirza Ghulam Ahmad, who, according to Iqbal, "avails himself of what he describes as the creative spirituality of the Holy Prophet of Islam, and at the same time, deprives the Holy Prophet of his 'finality' by limiting the creative capacity of his spirituality to the rearing of only one prophet, i.e. the founder of the Ahmadiyyah movement."[29] According to Iqbal, Mirza Ghulam Ahmad usurped the role of finality and, in doing so, undermined Muhammad's prophethood. In this way, the teachings and ideas of "Qadianism" violate what Iqbal outlines as one of the two basic principles of Islam, the finality of prophethood.

Further into his discussion, however, Iqbal acknowledges the fact that Mirza Ghulam Ahmad is no exception and that certain individuals in Islamic history have made similar kinds of claims to prophetic experience. The example he gives is of Ibn ʿArabi, who devoted his religious life to achieving the state of "prophetic consciousness." Regarding Ibn ʿArabi's Sufism, Iqbal explains:

> It is further claimed on the authority of the great Muslim mystic, Muhyuddin ibn Arabi of Spain, that it is possible for a Muslim saint to attain, in his spiritual evolution, to the kind of experience characteristic of the prophetic consciousness. I personally believe this view of Shaikh Muhyuddin ibn Arabi to be psychologically unsound; but assuming it to be correct the Qadiani argument is based on a complete misunderstanding of his exact position. The Shaikh regards it as a purely private achievement which does not, and in the nature of things, cannot, entitle such a saint to declare that all those who do not believe in him are outside the pale of Islam. Indeed from the Shaikh's point of view there may be more than one saint, living in the same age or country, who may attain to prophetic consciousness. The point to be seized is that, while it is psychologically possible for a saint to attain to prophetic experience, his experience will have no socio-political significance making him the center of a new Organization and entitling him to declare this Organization to be the criterion of the faith or disbelief of the followers of Muhammad.[30]

Iqbal states earlier in his piece that "heresy must be and has been rare in the history of Islam," and that Mirza Ghulam Ahmad was considered a heretic because he violated one of the two fundamental principles of Islam. Even though Mirza Ghulam Ahmad and Ibn ʿArabi both claimed some kind of special status through their achievement of "prophetic consciousness," only the former officially violated the basic tenets of Islam, in Iqbal's assessment. He dismisses Mirza Ghulam Ahmad's claims to prophethood quite categorically, but acknowledges and allows (although disagrees with) Ibn ʿArabi's claims to "prophetic consciousness." Iqbal's denouncement of the former and tolerance for Ibn ʿArabi necessitates the question of what exactly he finds so threatening about Mirza Ghulam Ahmad's teachings. Ibn Arabi was a Sufi, who, like other mystics, challenged and questioned the exoteric path of Islam through esoteric practices of devotion and reflection. Iqbal does not disavow this tradition, at least in the above statement, even though the practices associated with this tradition technically contravene what he has outlined as the core principles of Islam. It seems that his problem is not so much with those who have claimed some kind of prophetic consciousness—even though he finds this kind of assertion "psychologically unsound." In fact, Iqbal's discussion of Ibn ʿArabi demonstrates his tolerance for practices that do not necessarily fit into his vision of Islam as strictly defined by belief in God's unity and the finality of Muhammad's prophecy. According to the logic of this argument, it seems that the reason he is more charitable to Ibn ʿArabi than Mirza Ghulam Ahmad is: first, the latter created a new and public doctrinal statement on his prophetic status (as opposed to Ibn ʿArabi's "private" statements); and second, Mirza Ghulam Ahmad, according to Iqbal, asserted a new interpretation of Islam that denounced those who did not accept his prophetic status. For example, Iqbal makes the argument that the Ahmadis are heretical based on the fact that their understanding of their new revelation declares those who do not accept Ahmadi doctrine as infidels: "No revelation the denial of which entails heresy is possible after Muhammad. He who claims such a revelation is a traitor to Islam. Since the Qadianis believe the founder of the Ahmadiyya movement to be the bearer of such revelation, they declare the entire world of Islam is infidel."[31] Iqbal thus makes the point that it is the *Ahmadis* who are conducting decisions about heresy on the basis of whether or not the revelation of Mirza Ghulam Ahmad is accepted. In this instance, heresy is not the decision of those who represent the "orthodoxy" as would seem from Iqbal's initial statements, but rather a claim on the part of the new movement, directed to those who do not adhere to the new doctrine. How then are we to make sense of the point that Ahmadis are heretical on the one hand, but on the other hand that Ahmadis are the ones who declare all non-Ahmadis as heretical? How can the group accused of heresy be accused of declaring heresy? What then does "orthodoxy" come to mean here?

In order to answer these questions about heresy and orthodoxy, it would be helpful to reflect on what scholars have discussed on the topic of heresy. It is important to remember that the original religious meaning of heresy as a negative social phenomenon started in the medieval period, with its origins in Christianity. Although religion was no doubt the dominant institution through which heresy was defined, sociologists like George Simmel have argued that it would be misguided to think that heresy could be understood on the basis of the theological or doctrinal beliefs of the heretic. Simmel argues:

> That which arrays great masses of people in hatred and moral condemnation of heretics is certainly not the difference in the dogmatic content of the teaching; in most instances, this content really is not understood at all. Rather, it is the fact of the *opposition* of the one against the many. The persecution of heretics and dissenters springs from the instinct for the necessity of group unity. . . . Nonconformity therefore seems to threaten the unity—that is to say, the very life form—of the group as it is and as people visualize it.[32]

This secular and social significance of heresy is echoed in the work of George Zito, who has explained that what once was referred to as "difference of opinion" in relation to the Catholic Church expanded to a new and wider arena of "profane discourses." Zito defines heresy as "an attack, veiled or quite open, upon an institutionalized way of speaking about the world. It is therefore a thing of a distinctly social kind, directly related to social deviance. . . . In heresy the speaker employs *the same language* as the parent group, retains its values, but attempts to order its discourse to some other end."[33] According to Zito, the social, rather than the religious, aspect of heresy is significant, and for him the significance of the relationship between the heretic and what he calls the "parent group" is paramount. The heretic is not an outsider, but actually speaks and acts from within the group; he acknowledges the same values and ideas but interprets the shared idioms against the grain.

Aspects of Muhammad Iqbal's personal biography are relevant to this point that Zito makes about the "parent group." Muhammad Iqbal's father, Shaykh Nur Muhammad (d. 1929), entered into the path of allegiance to Ghulam Ahmad in 1891, and when Muhammad Iqbal and his brother were young, they were members of the Ahmadi community. In 1906, a *maulavi* from Ludhiana attacked Ahmad when Iqbal was a student in Sialkot, and apparently, Iqbal wrote a defense of him as *aftab sidq* (sun of truth) as well as several pieces describing Ahmad as "the greatest religious thinker among modern Indian Muslims." According to Ahmadis, he remained active in the movement until 1913, after which he broke away because of tensions within the movement. Although many of these details of Iqbal's life are disputed, they certainly reveal the complex ways in which he was imbricated within the same cultural and religious fabric as Ghulam Ahmad. Iqbal's criticisms of the Ahmadis must be seen therefore in light of some kind of familial and intimate connection.[34]

Iqbal claimed that Ghulam Ahmad was a heretic. However, from Iqbal's discussion, we see that Ibn ʿArabi, in theory, violated the same doctrine, with his claims to prophetic consciousness. How then are we to understand this inconsistency? According to the arguments of both Simmel and Zito, the social rather than the theological or doctrinal difference must be analyzed in order to understand the thoughts and actions of the heretic. The heretic is an individual who has made a choice that threatens group solidarity.[35] Iqbal's concern, as he outlined in the opening of his letter, is with Indian Muslim solidarity. Ibn ʿArabi did not threaten group unity as Mirza Ghulam Ahmad did. Ibn ʿArabi's practices were not considered threatening to an idea of group unity because, as Iqbal explains, they were circumscribed to the "private" domain.

Of course, it is also important to keep in mind here that Iqbal is addressing two totally different figures in completely different contexts—the first in the twelfth century and the second in the twentieth century. The term heresy cannot be uniformly applied across different temporal contexts, as Peter Berger has argued.[36] There are different social and cultural paradigms at work in the modern period. In the premodern context, it is possible that Ibn ʿArabi's ideas would have challenged Sunni jurists and theologians. However, official statements and declarations of heresy against Sufis were rare, because Sufis were always part of the larger theological and intellectual matrix of Islam.

With the onset of modernity, however, the social and cultural fabric transformed, whereby traditional structures were uprooted and replaced with new forms of religious authority. In this new modern context, Iqbal and Mirza Ghulam Ahmad emerged onto the colonial stage, speaking and defining Islam through opposing modernist perspectives. Iqbal argued that his definition of Islam was the correct "orthodox" position (claiming to speak on behalf of tradition, the preservation of God's unity, and the Prophet's finality), and condemned Mirza Ghulam Ahmad's movement as heretical. However, it is important to keep in mind that Mirza Ghulam Ahmad's conception of Islam was just as much of a new, independent, and secular (in terms of choosing a particular version over another) interpretation as Iqbal's. Mirza Ghulam Ahmad and Iqbal were making different kinds of arguments, but were equal players on the colonial modern platform of debate, where different Muslim leaders were defining and exercising their own choices and definitions of Islam.

Thus far, I have discussed the point that accusations of heresy are not exclusively motivated by theological or doctrinal violation, but also by social dynamics of a particular group, often amplified or complicated by the cultural and political terrain of modernity. How then are we to understand Iqbal's use of the term, now that we have opened up the idea beyond a religious or traditional framework of interpretation?

Bourdieu's discussion of heterodoxy helps elucidate further some of the issues and questions that are initiated in Iqbal's writings about heresy and Islam in the modern period. Bourdieu explains that the two concepts of heterodoxy and orthodoxy are inherently relational; they cannot be understood without one another and without the idea of doxa. Regarding these three terms, Bourdieu argues the following:

> Orthodoxy, straight, or rather *straightened* opinion, which aims without ever entirely succeeding, at restoring the primal state of innocence of doxa, exists only in the objective relationship which opposes it to heterodoxy, that is by reference to the choice—*hairesis*, heresy—made possible by the existence of *competing possibles* and to the explicit critique of the sum total of the alternatives not chosen that the established order implies. It is defined as a system of euphemisms, of acceptable ways of thinking and speaking the natural and social world, which rejects heretical remarks as blasphemies.[37]

Similarly to historians and theologians who engage this topic, Bourdieu confirms that heterodoxy and orthodoxy are conceptually dependent on one another. However, according to Bourdieu, these two concepts are divested of any theological or normative meaning because they lack any kind of inherent or ontological significance. For Bourdieu, heterodoxy and orthodoxy are located entirely in the realm of the discursive. Because orthodoxy does not exist in any stable or institutional form, heterodoxy cannot be understood as a kind of deviation from an established corporate center. In this way, the two ideas are a far cry from any Weberian understanding of church and sect. Orthodoxy, the claim of a "straightened" opinion, is an assertion of an authentic or correct practice; however, according to Bourdieu, this attempt to "straighten" is impossible because it is removed from the realm of actual practice, or *doxa*. Heterodoxy and orthodoxy are contrasted here to *doxa*, which exists in the everyday. *Doxa* represents "the world of tradition experienced as a 'natural world' and taken for granted." It is part of the "universe of the undiscussed and undisputed"—by contrast to orthodoxy and heterodoxy, which are part of the universe of discourse or argument.[38] Bourdieu argues that the assertion of orthodoxy is a response to a *hairesis*, the "choice" that is available in a field of possibilities but not sanctioned as an acceptable way of thinking and speaking about the world.

One way to think about how these three ideas operate in Iqbal's analysis is, again, through his comparison between Mirza Ghulam Ahmad and Ibn ʿArabi. Iqbal does not describe Ibn ʿArabi's Sufi practices as aberrant or exceptional in any way, nor does Iqbal criticize Ibn ʿArabi's religious practices devoted to the achievement of prophetic consciousness, despite his own strident position on preserving the two essential doctrines of Islam. In fact, Iqbal acknowledges the prevalence of this practice among like-minded individuals ("Indeed from the Shaikh's point of view there may be more than one saint, living in the same age or country, who may attain to prophetic consciousness"). In this regard, the practice is part of the "undiscussed and undisputed" realm of *doxa*. This type of doxic activity does not violate any normative code and thus does not enter into the discursive heterodox/orthodox realm because, in Iqbal's words, these practices are a "private matter." Iqbal accepts Ibn ʿArabi's practices, despite his own dogmatic stance against transgressing what he explains as the two fundamental doctrines of Islam. Iqbal himself states with the case of Ibn ʿArabi that it is not unusual for saints to allege that they have experienced prophecy or unity with God. Following this logic, Mirza Ghulam Ahmad's claim to prophetic status was in theory nothing new and something that was available in the field of practice. However, Ghulam Ahmad's choice, "hairesis," that was available in the realm of "competing possibles" was the pronouncement of his prophetic status. This declaration instigated a response from Indian Muslims, like Iqbal, that was "orthodox." That is to say, Iqbal responded with an attempt to correct and "straighten" out the definition of Islam, which he outlines as the unity of God and finality of Muhammad's prophecy.

According to the logic of Bourdieu's argument, there are no inherently heretical or heterodox sects. This is an important point for the study of Islam because there is a prevailing understanding that certain groups, such as Ahmadis and Sufis, are "sects," and with that, the assumption that they are theologically deviant from a center or norm. Again, Iqbal's comparison between Mirza Ghulam Ahmad and Ibn ʿArabi illustrates this point. Although Iqbal describes Ibn ʿArabi's practices as "private," it is important to remember that Sufi practices too were subjected to a similar kind of criticism that Iqbal imposes upon Mirza Ghulam Ahmad. Even though practices of Sufis were always integrated into the larger constellation of Muslim doxa, there were cases in which public declarations of prophetic consciousness by certain individuals were declared heretical. The ninth century mystic Al-Hallaj is one rather dramatic example of someone who was condemned because of beliefs and practices. It is possible to argue that he was condemned to death for purely political reasons because he spoke out against the state and the oppression of the caliph at the time. However, it is significant that he is remembered as a martyr because of his theologically transgressive pronouncements (in particular, "I am the Truth"). Al-Hallaj's statements were perceived as threatening the unity of God. The example of Hallaj would corroborate the sociological arguments of Zito and Simmel, as Hallaj made his practices public in a way that threatened group unity. The case of Hallaj also gives credence to Bourdieu's point that the orthodox position is a response to heterodox choices. That is to say, those in power who condemned and spoke about the ways in which Hallaj undermined Islam articulated an "orthodox" position *in reaction* to the specific actions and choices that Hallaj made, not on the basis of some preexistent structure or institution.[39]

In both cases, the ideas or "doctrines" associated with each figure are less relevant than the public nature of their ideas. This lends credence to Zito's and Simmel's point about the heretic as a threat to group unity, and Bourdieu's argument that orthodoxy, or correct practice, only becomes an issue when alternative choices are discursively articulated. Mirza Ghulam Ahmad presumably engaged in a similar type of exercise, but because his ideas and beliefs were consciously promulgated and debated in the public domain, they became branded as "heterodox."

To summarize, Iqbal claims that the Ahmadi beliefs and practices are theologically transgressive and thus heretical. What I demonstrate above is that "heresy" in this case is not a theological violation but rather a social violation of Muslim unity, conducted by an insider, who pronounced his controversial claims publicly. In the following section, I read Iqbal's closing statements in the same piece, in which he compares the Ahmadis to Ismailis to glean further insight into Iqbal's accusation of heresy against the Ahmadis. His comparison with the Ismailis opens up into a discussion of Zorastrianism and Magianism—traditions that he believes represent the retrograde elements in Islam's history. Iqbal argues that medieval Ismailism offered a crucial intervention and assertion of theological unity against Magian dualism, and the modern Ismaili community, under the leadership of the Aga Khan, supports the unity of the Indian Muslim community. By contrast, the Ahmadis adhere to beliefs similar to Magianism's, hold back the progress of Indian Muslims, and in turn, threaten the unity of the Muslim community.

Iqbal, the Aga Khan, and Ismaili Islam

Iqbal concludes in *Islam and Ahmadism* that the possibility for Islam to cohere as a political and religious entity is "shaken" in the current moment when Muslims rebel against the basic tenets of the faith and that in the interest of "eternal solidarity, Islam cannot tolerate any rebellious groups within its fold."[40] The didactic and explanatory tone of the Ahmadism piece ends here. Thereafter, he switches to a much more open-ended reflection about how Islam is passing through a period of transition, for he remarks—"as to what will be the attitude toward non-Muslims of a politically united Islam, if such a thing ever comes, is a question which history alone can answer."[41] This kind of question provides a natural closing point to the piece.

However, this penultimate statement is followed by a somewhat out-of-place afterthought about a topic he had not addressed at any previous point in the essay until the absolute end—the Ismailis and the Aga Khan:

> One word about His Highness the Aga Khan. What has led Pandit Jawahar Lal Nehru to attack the Aga Khan it is difficult for me to discover. Perhaps he thinks that the Qadianis and the Ismailis fall under the same category. He is obviously not aware that however the theological interpretation of the Ismailis may err, they believe in the basic principles of Islam. It is true that they believe in a perpetual Imamat; but the Imam according to them is not a recipient of Divine revelation. He is only an expounder of the Law. It is only the other day (*vide*, the Star of Allahabad, 12 March 1934) that his Highness the Aga Khan addressed his followers as follows:
>
>> "Bear witness that Allah is One. Muhammad is the Prophet of Allah. Quran is the Book of Allah. Ka'bah is the Qiblah of all. You are Muslims and should live with Muslims. Greet Muslims with Assalam-o-Alaikum. Give your children Islamic names. Pray with Muslim congregations in mosques. Keep fast regularly. Solemnise your marriages according to Islamic rules of Nikah. Treat all Muslims as your brothers."
>
> It is for the Pandit now to decide whether the Aga Khan represents the solidarity of Islam or not.[42]

To conclude the piece on Ahmadism with the Ismailis and the Aga Khan—neither of which is previously mentioned in any way—is a little surprising and strange. It is only when you turn to Nehru's piece that you see why Iqbal makes this reference to the Aga Khan. Nehru wrote from Almora Jail in 1935 a response to the question of the solidarity of Islam, as outlined by Iqbal's "Qadianis and

Orthodox Muslims" piece. Nehru begins by questioning Iqbal's argument about the ideal of Muslim solidarity:

> The Arabs of Syria and Palestine more or less follow Egyptian thought-currents and are partly influenced by Turkey's example. Iran is definitely looking for its cultural inspiration to pre-Islamic Magian days. In all these countries, indeed in every country of western and middle Asia, nationalist ideas are rapidly growing, usually at the expense of the pure and orthodox religious outlook . . . All this clearly shows that these nations have fallen away from the ideal of Islamic solidarity which Sir Muhammad lays down.[43]

Nehru concludes his summary of Iqbal's argument with the issue of Muslim leadership:

> He [Iqbal] stresses the need of a real leader to rise in the Punjab apparently to combat the 'Qadiani menace.' But what leader does he give in regard to the wider menace? The Aga Khan, we are told, is the leader of Indian Muslims. Does he stand for this solidarity of Islam as defined by Sir Muhammad Iqbal?[44]

Iqbal's brief reference to the Aga Khan and the Ismailis in the Ahmadism piece is no doubt a response to Nehru's question about whether the Aga Khan represents the solidarity of Islam. The answer for Iqbal, is a straightforward yes.

Here, I would like to examine why Ahmadi beliefs and leadership are completely dismissed and declared heretical whereas Ismaili beliefs and leadership are fully endorsed, to such an extent that Iqbal claims that the Aga Khan stands for the unity of Islam. What is surprising is that Iqbal's statements about the Aga Khan demonstrate an awareness of the *unorthodox* nature of Ismaili beliefs and practices. He illustrates this with two separate points that are directly related: first, "It is true that they believe in [the doctrine of the] Imamat," and second, that "theological interpretation of the Ismailis might err." He thus intimates that the Ismailis are not altogether aligned with his understanding of what are correct

Muslim beliefs. However, he resists any kind of elaboration on the skepticism he introduces, which is of course noteworthy considering theological deviance is the primary subject of the essay and the accusation he mounts against the Ahmadis. Instead, he is eager to disassociate the Ismailis from the Ahmadis and underscore the differences between the groups. He makes the point that divine leadership manifests differently with the figures of the Aga Khan and the Mirza: the Imam is only an "expounder of the law" compared to the Mirza who was a recipient of revelation. As I discuss below, Iqbal's earlier writings on Ismaili theology corroborate his support for the institution of the Imamate; Iqbal made the argument that Ismailism, through the figure of the Imam, offered a critical intervention in the history of Islam, recasting and redefining Islam through radically new progressive ideals. The Ahmadis and Mirza Ghulam Ahmad, by contrast, represent the opposite impulse: one of regression and division.

Although both Mirza Ghulam Ahmad and the Aga Khan were high profile modernist religious leaders whose authority rested on their charismatic and thus "prophetic" power, the Aga Khan's role as prophet was contained in the private sphere of Ismaili religiosity. Moreover, the political and public positions he assumed were fundamentally aligned with Iqbal's ideal of Islam and Muslim solidarity. Conversely, Mirza Ghulam Ahmad's religious leadership was not circumscribed in the same way. The basic presuppositions of Ahmadi thought relied on belief in the unmediated claim of Mirza Ghulam's authority as the new prophet of Islam. Iqbal saw in the continuous prophecy of the Mirza the revival of a devotional medieval mindset that undermined his progressive vision for the Indian Muslim community.

Nehru's response to Iqbal's "Qadianis and Orthodox Muslims" devotes a surprising amount of time probing the nature of the Aga Khan's political and religious authority. Nehru begins with pointing out how the Aga Khan is considered an outstanding leader by both Indian Muslims as well as the British. He then judiciously begins to question how exactly Iqbal could see in the figure of the Aga Khan someone who could represent the uniformity of Islam—

> I have long had a vague kind of idea, however, that he hardly belongs to the inner orthodox fold, and I have admired him for the truly wonderful way in which he manages to combine, and gracefully carry in his own person, the most contradictory qualities, and to take part in multifarious activities which appear to be mutually antagonistic and irreconcilable.

He describes the Aga Khan as a "modern of moderns highly cultured in western ways, a prince of the turf, most at home in London and Paris" on the one hand, and on the other hand, a divine leader who grants his devotees "spiritual favors and indulgences."[45]

Despite his respectful tone, it is obvious that Nehru is suspicious of what he sees as the Aga Khan's "double life": his capacity to inhabit the modern world and at the same time retain his divine status. It is not surprising why Nehru would be critical: he is writing from jail and observing Muslim leaders like the Aga Khan and Iqbal articulate positions on Muslim unity and separatism that undermine his own nationalist vision. Iqbal's take on the Aga Khan, however, is straightforward. The Aga Khan and the Ismailis represent the unity of Islam: they are part of the Indian Muslim community, in a way that the Ahmadis are not because they adhere to the same religious beliefs and practices of the five pillars.

But there is something slightly awry about the means through which Iqbal conveys his support for the Aga Khan. Iqbal invokes the Aga Khan's words about Islam that are focused on (four of the) five pillars of Islam to reinforce a Sunni orthodox position. Iqbal strategically selected the *farman* that is aligned with the orthodox conception of Islam that he promulgates in the course of his essay. To claim that the Aga Khan's idea of correct Islam can be encapsulated by this one particular *farman* is misleading. This is not to say that he misquoted the Aga Khan. The Aga Khan no doubt would have delivered *farmans*—his directives to the Ismaili community focused on proper social, religious, and political conduct—that would support a Sunni orthodox position: affirming the unity of God, Muhammad's prophecy, Mecca as the direction of prayer, the importance of praying in mosques, making sure children are given Islamic names, and following Islamic marriage rules. What is missing from Iqbal's account, however, is any kind of reference to his role as prophet in the Weberian sense. On the one hand, the Aga Khan publicly affirmed this kind of Sunni orthodoxy, but on the other hand he balanced this public endorsement of the five pillars with the beliefs of the primarily Gujarati-speaking Ismaili community whose devotion and practice were centered on reverence of imams, avatars of Vishnu, and most importantly devotion to the Aga Khan himself as the *hazar* imam of the time.[46]

Iqbal would most likely be aware of the specifically divine role the Aga Khan assumed, as well as the constellation of Ismaili religious ideas that are completely effaced in the Aga Khan's statements about following a Sunni path of Islam. However, because the Aga Khan publicly affirmed an ecumenical position that endorsed Sunni orthodoxy, it did not matter for Iqbal that "the theological interpretation of the Ismailis may err." Iqbal attributes the capacity to inhabit this dual role to the institution of the Imamate, the workings of which he outlined in his earliest work, *The Development of Metaphysics in Persia*.

Ismailism and Imamate Rationality

Iqbal extricates the Ismailis from any connection with the Ahmadis, but he never delves into Ismaili theology in the piece, nor does he explain why exactly Ismailis are off the hook in terms of religious transgression in a way that Ahmadis are not. If we turn to one of Iqbal's earliest writings, *The Development of Metaphysics in Persia* (1908), however, we see how and why Iqbal finds the Ismaili tradition compelling. He describes Ismailism as a new, creative, and intellectually expansive development in the history of Islam— similar to movements of religious and philosophical inquiry in eighteenth-century Europe when figures such as Fichte, Schleiermacher and Jacobi, and Comte emerged. He draws the specific parallel with De Maistre and Schlegel—both of whom believed in the "absolute infallible Pope," and argues that "The advocates of the doctrine of Imamat think in the same strain as De Maistre; but it is curious that the Ismailians, while making this doctrine the basis of their Church, permitted free play to all sorts of thinking."[47] He finds in the Ismaili tradition a structural parallel to the institution of the Church and in the figure of the Pope an equivalent to the Ismaili Imam, but in Iqbal's view, the Ismaili tradition is far superior to European Catholicism because the Ismaili imam, unlike the Pope we can infer, encouraged his followers to pursue free enquiry while holding office as leader. What he sees in the Ismaili tradition is what Faisal Devji has explained as "the simultaneity of belief in absolute authority and the assertion of absolute free thought."[48]

It is for this reason that Iqbal is completely sympathetic with and at times quite in awe of what he sees as a religious and intellectual cosmopolitanism of the Ismaili tradition. He illustrates the singularity of Ismaili theological intervention with the example of a ninth century Fatimid Ismaili leader, Abdullah ibn Maiman, whom Iqbal describes as having

> made an attempt under the pious cloak of the doctrine of Imamat (Authority), to synthesize all the dominating ideas of the time. Greek Philosophy, Christianity, Rationalism, Sufism, Manichaeism, Persian heresies, and above all the idea of reincarnation, all came forward to contribute their respective shares to the boldly conceived Ismailian whole, the various aspects of which were to be gradually revealed to the initiated, by the 'Leader' the ever Incarnating Universal Reason—according to the intellectual development of the age in which he incarnated himself.[49]

The Ismailis were, according to Iqbal, the great religious, scientific, and philosophical synthesizers of Islam. What is important for this comparison with the leadership of the Qadianis is that unlike the latter, Ismaili leadership is depicted as fundamentally rational. He describes the Imam as the embodiment of "Universal Reason," which, as I will discuss below, is the antithesis of what he sees in

Mirza Ghulam Ahmad. Moreover, he attributes significant historical and theological achievements to the Ismaili Imam, who not
only integrated multiple schools of thought, but who also, thereafter, imparted new ideas and teachings to his devotees in what
Iqbal sees as a rational and measured process.

This interpretation of the Ismailis is highly unusual for his time,
as it was commonplace thinking, especially by Sunni Muslims and
European scholars of Islam, to assume that Ismailis blindly followed the imam and were political rebels—a problem which Iqbal
himself addresses:

> The unfortunate connection, however, of this movement with the
> politics of the time, has misled many a scholar. They see in it
> (Macdonald for instance) nothing more than a powerful con-
> spiracy to uproot the political power of the Arab from Persia. They
> have denounced the Ismailian Church . . . as a mere clique of dark
> murderers who were ever watching for a possible victim.[50]

Iqbal was, in this regard, an intellectual pioneer, offering an insightful and generous perspective on this religious group that had
suffered a much-maligned reputation and whose intellectual and
philosophical interventions had yet to be understood. He explains
that the Ismailis were "a great religious movement that shook to
its very foundations the structure of a vast empire, and having successfully passed through the various ordeals of moral reproach,
calumny, and persecution, stood up for centuries as a champion
of Science and Philosophy."[51] Iqbal thus recognized the Ismailis as
having undertaken serious political struggle, on the one hand, and
having provided, at the same time, a crucial contribution to the
intellectual and philosophical thought of Islam.

Magianism: The Backward Past of Ahmadi Thought

This open mind he proffers to the Ismailis does not extend to all
Persian traditions. If Ismailism was the great rationalizer of intellectual thought in the history of Islam, the precursor to Ahmadism

was the exact opposite. Iqbal describes the "essence of Ahmadism" as a religious tradition "in which pre-Islamic Magian ideas have, through the channels of Islamic mysticism, worked on the mind of its author."[52] Iqbal outlines his problem with "magianism" further in *Reconstruction*. He describes Magianism as a culture associated with the religions of "Judaism, ancient Chaldean religion, early Christianity, Zorastrianism, and Islam." Magian culture, he explains, is characterized by "the perpetual attitude of expectation, a constant looking forward to the coming of Zoroaster's unborn sons, the Messiah, or the Paraclete of the fourth gospel." Iqbal further argues that, "a Magian crust has grown over Islam, I do not deny. Indeed my main purpose in these lectures has been to secure a vision of the spirit of Islam as emancipated from its Magian overlayings."[53]

For Iqbal, Magian beliefs are emblematic of a socially and religiously backward way of thinking, which he conveys in the following statement: "the modern man is spiritually far more emancipated than the Magian man. The result of the Magian attitude was the disintegration of old communities and the constant formation of new ones by all sorts of religious adventurers." When messianic expectation becomes the center of a particular community's belief system, it sets itself up for "religious adventurers"—that is to say, those who claim to represent some kind of continuity of revelation. This type of "Magian" thinking and religious community formation is not just part of the past. It finds expression in the present, as Iqbal explains. According to Iqbal, there are two forms of the modern Magian revival: Bahaism and Qadianism; Bahaism poses no direct problem because it "openly departs from Islam." Qadianism, however, is more complicated because it "retains some of the more important externals of Islam with an inwardness wholly inimical to the spirit and aspirations of Islam."[54]

Javed Majeed has shown that Iqbal's writings reflect an overall tendency to "marginalize the legacy of Persian Magianism in contemporary Islam and to refocus on its Arab legacy."[55] This is no doubt the case when it comes to the later writings in which nationalism is at the forefront of Iqbal's thinking, but it is important to keep in mind that the Ismailis are not part of this marginalization. Iqbal in fact sees in Ismailism a significant theological intervention in the history of Islam: the reformulation and reconciliation of dualism. He describes how Ismailis adopted their idea of divinity from the rationalists, claiming that God has no attributes and no contradictions. Most importantly, he states, the Ismailis resolved the question of plurality and specifically the problem of Zoroastrian dualism:

> The Ismaili doctrine is the first attempt to amalgamate contemporary Philosophy with a really Persian view of the universe, and to restate Islam, in reference to this synthesis, by allegorical interpretation of the Quran. . . . With them the Zoroastrian Ahriman (Devil) is not the malignant creator of evil things but it is a principle which violates the eternal unity, and breaks it up into visible diversity.[56]

For Iqbal, the most impressive contribution of the Ismailis is the way in which they reconciled and redefined the dualism of the Zoroastrians in terms of a monistic monotheism.[57]

In *Reconstruction*, Iqbal attempts to provide a corrective to Spengler's discussion of Islam in *The Decline of the West*. According to Iqbal, Spengler identifies the culture of Islam as "thoroughly Magian in spirit and character," which he describes as a synthesis of Judaism, ancient Chaldean religion, early Christianity, Zoroastrianism, and Islam." Iqbal's intention is to confute Spengler's assumptions about Islam's role in this Magian culture: "Indeed my main purpose in these lectures has been to secure a vision of the spirit of Islam as emancipated from its Magian overlayings, which, in my opinion, have misled Spengler." He turns to Ibn Khaldun as a conclusive authority on the influence of revelational thinking/ Magian thought on Islam. Iqbal explains how the argument that messianic, or what he calls revelational, thinking has shaped the contours of the Islamic tradition has been repudiated by Ibn Khaldun, who "finally demolished the alleged revelational basis in Islam of an idea similar, at least in its psychological effects, to the original Magian idea which had reappeared in Islam under the pressure of Magian thought." "Magian thought" and "Islam" figure in Iqbal's writings as two discrete, almost Manichean, entities that are willfully battling one another in the struggle to keep a progressive Islam distinct from the forces of Magianism.[58]

This discussion of Magian influence has specific relevance to Iqbal's views of the Ahmadis and Mirza Ghulam Ahmad, as outlined in the Ahmadism essay. In the opening and the closing of the Ahmadism essay, Iqbal describes Islam as a political and religious entity in crisis, and attributes this state of affairs to intra-community dissent. The community that is causing fissures and is responsible for the backward turn in Islam is the Ahmadis. What we find here, therefore, is the reemergence of messianic and revelatory thinking activated in the figure of Mirza Ghulam Ahmad, thus representing the modern manifestation of the same pre-Islamic Magian presence that Iqbal saw as debilitating the Islamic tradition in the past.

Iqbal explains that the "real nature of Ahmadism is hidden behind the mist of medieval mysticism and theology." He claims, however, that to go into the details of this particular tradition's theological formation is not his focus, although interesting from the standpoint of comparative religion. What he wants to address, instead, is Ahmadism in light of the history of Muslim thought, starting in 1799. In sum, he explains how starting in 1799, the year Tipu Sultan fell, there was a crisis. Indian Muslims started asking some basic questions, such as what their relationship to the Turkish Caliphate was, whether India could serve as the abode of Islam (*Dar al-Islam*) or not, the nature of *jihad*, and whether or not the hadith foretold the arrival of the Mahdi. Muslim politicians worked with sections of the 'ulama to provide theological arguments to these various questions. However, Iqbal claims, "it was not easy to conquer by mere logic the beliefs which had ruled for centuries the conscience of the masses of Islam in India." He then makes the assertion that "to the intensely religious masses of Islam, only one thing can make a conclusive appeal, and that is Divine Authority. . . . It was found necessary to find a revelational basis for a politically suitable orientation of theological doctrines involved in the questions mentioned above. This revelational basis is provided by Ahmadism."

Despite the fact that Iqbal provides a rational explanation of how and why Ahmadism appealed to the masses, he does not accept the legitimacy of Ahmadi Islam. Rather, he explains the desire and need for uneducated Muslims to seek out "revelational" and divine authority, but then takes the unequivocal position that the tradition ought to be understood as part of Islam's past. Modern Islam, in his view, has transcended this kind of revelational thinking: "Islam has already passed into the broad daylight of fresh thought and experience; and no saint or prophet can bring it back to the fogs of mediaeval mysticism." Here, he wants to believe that Islam has progressed and transcended its medieval past, but laments that Ahmadi revelational thinking provides a less than ideal solution to the "woes of India" as well as a rationale for "India's present political subjugation."[59]

Iqbal, interestingly, does not take specific issue with the Mirza's divine claims as such. In fact, Iqbal was quite interested in understanding the nature of prophetic experience and man's aspirations thereto. We also know from many of Iqbal's writings, in his poetry specifically, that he was sympathetic toward Sufism as a form of ethical self-cultivation.[60] The fact that the Mirza claimed a prophetic status was not therefore strictly the problem. Rather, what Iqbal takes issue with is the way in which this "new prophet quietly steals away 'the finality' of one whom he claims to be his spiritual progenitor."[61] Iqbal locates this problem further through the idea of *buruz*, or "re-appearance." He writes: "He [Ahmad]claims to be a *buruz* of the Holy Prophet of Islam, insinuating thereby that, being a *buruz* of him, his 'finality' is virtually the 'finality' of Muhammad."[62] He continues to take Ahmad to task for this claim. "In identifying the two finalities, his own and that of the Holy Prophet, he conveniently loses sight of the temporal meaning of the idea of finality."[63] More importantly, it is this idea of messianic continuity that is at the center of his critique against Mirza Ghulam Ahmad.

The issue for Iqbal is that "revelational" thinking leads to back-wardness as it keeps man in perpetual state of expectation.[64] Thus, Mirza Ghulam Ahmad's violation of prophecy stands in for the reappearance of "revelational" authority, which Iqbal finds socially detrimental: "To the intensely religious masses of Islam, only one thing can make a conclusive appeal, and that is Divine Authority."[65] He further claims that, "in the Punjab even an ill-woven net of vague theological expressions can easily capture the innocent peasant who has been for centuries exposed to all kinds of exploitation."[66]

Interestingly, Mirza Ghulam Ahmad makes his case about his religious authority from this specific idea of *buruz* that Iqbal criti-cizes. In "British Government and Jihad" (written in 1900), he invokes the idea of *buruz* to describe the character of his prophetic authority. He writes: "I have been granted two kinds of *buruz*: one is the *buruz* of Jesus, and the other is the *buruz* of Muhammad. In short, by way of *buruz*, my being is a blended compound of the personalities of both of these prophets."[67] His specific idea of *buruz* is used to justify his role as Mahdi, in the likeness of Jesus and Muhammad, and as the *mujaddid*, the reformer who arrives to bring peace and unity to Muslims:

> In the capacity of Jesus, the Messiah, I have been assigned the duty of stopping the Muslims from vicious attacks and blood-shed. It has been clearly mentioned in the hadith of the Holy Prophet (may peace and blessings of Allah be upon him) that the Messiah would end religious wars when he returns to the world. This is what is happening. . . . Each person who takes the *bai-ʿat* (pledge of allegiance) at my hand and believes in me as the Promised Messiah must accept that *jihad* is totally forbid-den in this age because the Messiah has come. . . . In the capac-ity of Muhammad Mahdi, my mission is to re-establish *Tauhid* in this world with the help of Divine signs. Our Lord and Mas-ter Hadrat Muhmmad (may peace and blessings of Allah be upon him) established the Grandeur, Might, and Power of God in the hearts of the idolaters of Arabia through heavenly signs

alone. I also have been given the help of the Holy Spirit. The same Mighty and Holy God who has descended upon me appeared to all Prophets. He appeared to Moses at Sinai, to Jesus at Mount Seir, and He shined forth on the Holy Prophet (may peace and blessings of Allah be upon him) at Mount Paran.[68]

This epistemic logic of the concept of *buruz* works within an entirely different structure of time from Iqbal's perspective of finality. Although Iqbal argues that Ahmad himself does not understand the temporal meaning of finality, it is apparent that the Mirza's use of the term *buruz* cannot be conceptualized within a linear framework of time, as his prophetic authority is in part a continuation of Jesus's as well as Muhammad's. As Ahmad explains, the reason why he has arrived is to establish the unity of God, similarly to the previous prophets. It is noteworthy that Iqbal and Mirza Ghulam Ahmad's arguments for and against Ghulam Ahmad's prophetic authority are drawn from the same two coordinates: the unity of God and the protection of the finality of Muhammad's prophecy. In the above passage, Mirza Ghulam Ahmad justifies his role as prophet of the time through the same two reasons as Iqbal: to unify the Muslim community, in the name of God's unity and Muhammad's prophecy. They are both concerned with the unity of the Muslim community in the context of colonial modernity—the point of contention being *continuous* prophecy versus final prophecy.

Throughout Mirza Ghulam Ahmad's career he was constantly defining and defending the position of his prophetic status— mostly in polemical settings of public debates and in his own writings. He was successful in preserving his charismatic power, a move that was threatening to Iqbal's ideal of Muslim unity. What Iqbal saw in the Mirza was a popular yet retrograde leader, as exemplified in his discussion of "magianism." Magianism represented the historical covering or "crust" that needed to be discarded from the Islamic tradition. Iqbal wanted to believe that Magianism was part of the past, as he writes—"Islam has already passed into the broad daylight of fresh thought and experience; and no saint or prophet can bring it back to the fogs of mediaeval mysticism."[69] However, the fact that Iqbal wrote this entire piece on Ahmadism makes it difficult to believe that the "fog of mysticism" had dissipated. In fact, it would be more appropriate to read *Islam and Ahmadism* not as a theological critique of the Ahmadis, but rather as a deep anxiety about "Magianism revival"—the prominence of prophet-types such as Mirza Ghulam Ahmad and the persistence of "backward" beliefs that precluded the rationalization of thought necessary for Muslim unity.

This point is illustrated further by "sectarian" comparison. The Aga Khan too, like the Mirza, was a prophet-type leader sustained by his charismatic authority; but what distinguished the Aga Khan from the Mirza was that the former assumed a public/private distinction (as Nehru noticed). He fully embraced the life of western progress and modernity and publicly accepted the form of Sunni normativity Iqbal promulgated. His charismatic role as messianic sovereign was relegated to the domain of private Ismaili religiosity, which did not interfere with his public ecumenical reform position. The Aga Khan publicly endorsed the type of orthodoxy that Iqbal advocates throughout his essay.

What is even more significant about this comparison between the Ismailis and Ahmadis is Iqbal's *longue durée* logic about the two groups. Iqbal's earlier writings on the Imamate demonstrate an equally sympathetic position to that of Aga Khan's leadership. The Imamate as an institution promoted both devotion to absolute authority as well as free thought, surpassing in Iqbal's mind any kind of western equivalent figure (such as the Pope). Moreover, Persian Ismailism intervened at a critical moment in Islamic history, resolving the problem of Zoroastrian dualism, which was for Iqbal a sign of progress, crucial to the development and history of Islam. In this regard, Ismaili leadership was exceptional and Ismaili theology integrative. Meanwhile, the religious and cultural predecessor of Ahmadism, what Iqbal explains as "Magianism," was what the Islamic tradition needed to extricate itself from, as it represented, for Iqbal, the backward mystical current of Islam that was necessary to excise. In the modern period, this regressive strain of Islam, Magianism, resurfaced with Mirza Ghulam Ahmad's public declaration as prophet and the community he built around this doctrine. This kind of practice of devotion and belief in Mirza Ghulam Ahmad's prophethood prevented the Ahmadis from effectively integrating into a community that could at least publicly participate, despite theological deviance, in the game of orthodoxy. The Ahmadis, in Iqbal's view, could not become the model minority Muslims like the Ismailis because they remained tethered to the backward, anti-intellectual, and devotional beliefs of Magianism.

Conclusion

During the late nineteenth and early twentieth centuries, political leaders and intellectuals defined Islam and what it meant to be Muslim against the backdrop of colonial modernity. Modernist reformers in India as well as in the larger Muslim world deemed it necessary for Muslims to unify as a community and formulated arguments on this topic through discussions of *tawhid*. It is within this context that Iqbal wrote about the heresy of the Mirza Ghulam Ahmad—also a modernist who wanted to unify and define Islam at the time. While their diagnoses of what needed renewal were similar—the reassertion of *tawhid*—their solutions were completely at odds. Iqbal claimed that sectarianism and continuous prophecy undermined *tawhid*, whereas the Mirza held to the view that continuous prophecy and a new movement were necessary to re-establish *tawhid* in the modern period.

Iqbal denounced Ahmadi ideas as heretical; however, as I argued above, this was not simply a theological accusation. Traditional theological indictments of heresy were premised on the idea of the heretic as an outsider to a religious community who confronts an established set of doctrines or beliefs. In this instance, however, the "heretic" Mirza Ghulam Ahmad was an intimate *insider*—someone from whom many members of Iqbal's family took an oath of allegiance. Second, Mirza Ghulam Ahmad threatened Iqbal's notion of group unity, which in this case was the minority Muslim community (in colonial India) that Iqbal sought to represent. Third, Mirza Ghulam Ahmad brought his practices and ideas into the public domain, at a time when protection of the status of Prophet Muhammad was integral to the ways in which Muslims defined themselves against other religious groups and against colonial interventions into the religious lives of Muslims. Mirza Ghulam Ahmad's ideas thus elicited a Sunni "orthodox" response from Iqbal, which led to his formal request that the British colonial state declare the Ahmadis a separate community.

Iqbal's statements about the Ismailis corroborate further the point that his theological arguments about Ahmadi violation of the finality of prophecy served as a smoke screen for a larger set of concerns about Ahmadi popularity and religious authority. It would be possible to make the argument that Ismaili leadership too violates the finality of prophecy, as the Aga Khan was no doubt understood as a prophetic figure by his devotees; however, Iqbal chose to deny any kind of prophetic component of the Aga Khan's leadership, disregarding all details of Ismaili religiosity and Shia devotion altogether. Iqbal claimed instead that the Aga Khan endorsed the five pillars of Islam, a position that distorts the true character of Ismaili beliefs and practices. Furthermore, Iqbal's comments about modern Ismailis as salutary for the broader Muslim community is further corroborated with his analysis of premodern Ismailis, whom he sees as having intervened in a critical moment of Muslim intellectual and philosophical thought. In both his modern and premodern accounts of Ismailism, Iqbal arrives at the conclusion that the group affirms *tawhid*—either as theological unity or that of the community.

The Ahmadis, by contrast, undermined *tawhid*. In many ways, they rhetorically feature in Iqbal's writings as the *neicheri* equivalent. As I argued in the first chapter, Afghani's *neicheri* figure functioned as a kind of dormant virus in the history of Islam. At one moment the *neicheris* were the Ismailis, at another the Bahais, and finally the followers of Sayyid Ahmad Khan. The *neicheri* for Iqbal was the premodern Magian who kept the Islamic tradition in a backward state. He explains in *Reconstruction* that one central aim in the project of reconstruction is "to secure a vision of the spirit of Islam as emancipated from its Magian overlayings." The Ahmadis exemplified the modern recurrence of this "backward" Magianism, compromising not only *tawhid* as civilizational progress of the Indian Muslim community but also *tawhid* as the freedom and dynamism fundamental to the Islamic tradition.

4

Abul Ala Mawdudi's Islamic State and Minority Ahmadis

SAYYID ABUL ALA MAWDUDI (1903–1979) is no doubt considered the foundational thinker of Islamist thought. Mawdudi was a philosopher, journalist, jurist, and politician whose reform efforts centered on Islamic law. In order to save Islam from contemporaneous political currents of secularism, nationalism, and socialism, he believed it was necessary to create a new system of governance, an Islamic state, in which God's sovereignty would be paramount. Mawdudi shared many approaches to reform with his modernist predecessors, but his ideas are reflective of a later phase of modernism and its transition to Islamism. Although Mawdudi is traditionally considered an Islamist rather than modernist thinker, this study situates many aspects of his writings as "late modernist" in order to illustrate conceptual connections between modernism and Islamism. Mawdudi echoed earlier modernists' concerns about Islam's civilizational progress, but diverged when it came to solutions. The earlier modernists sought ways to make Islam compatible with western modernity, which Mawdudi and later Islamists such as Sayyid Qutb eschewed. Islamist ideology was premised on the assumption that the Islamic tradition provided a complete system of cultural and political resources for Muslims. In short, Islamic sovereignty was possible because of Islam's inherent self-sufficiency.

The earliest modernists, such as Afghani, Sayyid Ahmad Khan, and Muhammad ʿAbduh, produced their ideas about reform squarely within the context of colonial empire. The contours of modernist thought changed slightly with figures such as Rida and Iqbal, both of whose definitions and conceptions of Islam were shaped by a growing awareness about nationalism among Muslims. Mawdudi wrote during both colonial and postcolonial periods; as a result, the nation-state was very much at the center of Mawdudi's thinking, with Pakistan, the first nation-state created in the name of Islam, established in 1947 in the middle of his political life. Mawdudi's theories of sovereignty and the Islamic state spread to Egypt and were seminal to the Islamist formation of Sayyid Qutb, who wrote at the transitional period from empire to nation as well.

This chapter examines modernist conceptions of Islam as political unity in the writings of Mawdudi and Qutb, in particular how the turn to Islamism opened up new interpretations of *tawhid*. The temporal bifurcation framework enjoined in the modernist idea of *tawhid* extended into Islamist thought. However, the end goal was not simply the unity of the community; it was God's sovereignty. According to the Islamists, God's sovereignty existed at the time of the Quranic revelation, was nonexistent in the present, but could be realized in the future. The chapter begins with a discussion of this new idea of *tawhid* as God's sovereignty and explores how it connects to the Islamic state Mawdudi envisions. Mawdudi makes the argument that his conception of the Islamic state refuses the framework of "majority" and "minority," and is therefore more egalitarian and just. However, Mawdudi invokes the language of "majority" and "minority" in his polemical treatise against the Ahmadis, "The Qadiani Problem." This appropriation of nation-state language demonstrates a profound shift from the earlier modernists. During the period of colonial empire, there was no equivalent apparatus through which Afghani, Rida, and Iqbal could officially denounce communities such as the Bahais or Ahmadis. The Pakistani nation-state provided a new structural idiom of Sunni chauvinism for the late modernist Mawdudi to denounce the Ahmadis.

This new form of Sunni chauvinism proved far more troubling for minority communities than its iteration espoused by the earlier modernists. It took concrete form with the persecution of the Ahmadis during the period of the 1950s. Mawdudi and his political organization, the Jamat-i-Islami, were actively involved in the campaign against the Ahmadis. Although Mawdudi did not explicitly endorse agitation and acts of violence against the community, he provided support for the movement to declare Ahmadis non-Muslim.

As part of this study's inquiry into patterns and continuities in modernist thought, the discussion of the Ahmadi issue in the 1950s is followed by an examination of the logic Mawdudi adopts from Iqbal in his condemnation of the Ahmadis and reflects on the parallels and differences between the two arguments. Thereafter, the chapter addresses a surprising contradiction at the heart of Mawdudi's argument about religious authority. At one level, he held to the idea that God was the only sovereign. However, his writings about the figure of the *mujaddid* kept open possibilities for religiopolitical leadership to emerge in this new context. Mawdudi, like Afghani, summons a Mahdi-type figure to guide the Muslim community but offers a distinct interpretation of the Mahdi's purpose and calling. Mawdudi explains that the Mahdi of the contemporaneous period will be a modern man who is equipped to lead, transform society, and establish the Islamic state. Finally, the chapter traces the wider impact of Mawdudi's Islamist ideas about the sovereignty of God and religious authority in the writings of Sayyid Qutb.

Background

Mawdudi was born in Aurangabad in 1903, into the family of Sayyid Ahmad Hasan Mawdudi, who was descended from the prominent line of the Chishti Sufis. Mawdudi traced his own lineage directly to Khwaja Qutbuddin Mawdud Chishti (d. 1133), from whom his family took their name. The Mawdudis were also related to Sayyid Ahmad Khan through Sayyid Ahmad Hasan's mother, and several members of the family, including Ahmad Hasan, were educated at the Anglo-Oriental College at Aligarh. However, the family was not supportive of the modernist program, and Ahmad Hasan's father summoned him to return home after hearing about his son adopting western cultural mores. Mawdudi's mother's family was of Turkish descent and became a family of nobility in Delhi and Hyderabad. Mawdudi's maternal grandfather was a poet who was active in the circles of Mirza Asadullah Khan Ghalib (1796–1869) and among the literary nobility in Hyderabad.[1]

Mawdudi was initially educated at home under the tutelage of his father who wanted him to become a theologian. He studied Persian, Urdu, Arabic, *fiqh*, and *hadith*. He became proficient in Arabic at a young age, so much so that apparently by age eleven he was able to translate the famous Egyptian modernist Qasim Amin's *Al-Mirah al-Jadida (Modern Women)* from Arabic to Urdu. At that same age he had begun studying at the Madrasa Fauquaniya of Aurangabad, which was connected with Osmania University in Hyderabad. Here he was introduced to western ideas and the work of modernists while continuing his studies in traditional Islamic subjects. He was unable to complete his formal education, however. His father fell ill in Bhopal, so he had to assume a caregiving role while still in his early teens. Despite his family responsibilities, he was encouraged by mentors to start a career as a writer, and in 1918, he moved to Bijnur in the United Provinces to write for the journal his brother edited there called *Madina*. This was short-lived, as two months later the two of them moved to Delhi.[2]

It was at this time that Mawdudi read closely the works of Ghalib, Iqbal, and Sayyid Ahmad Khan. He also learned English and read western thinkers like Plato, Aristotle, Marx, Lenin, Hegel, Nietzsche, and others. He grew interested in the question of how western ideas could relate to Islam, much like Sayyid Ahmad Khan. However, Mawdudi was interested in directly applying western ideas to Islamic thought rather than trying to find ways to make them compatible or synthesize them, as Sayyid Ahmad Khan did.

As he began writing, he also grew involved in politics, mostly directed against British rule. He helped found the Anjuman-i-Ianat-i-Nazarbandan-i-Islam, an organization that offered aid to Muslim political prisoners. During this period, he was a nationalist and supported famous Congress leaders, including Gandhi. He was interested in both the Swaraj and Khilafat anti-British movements. In 1921, Mawdudi met two prominent Deobandi *ulama* who were leaders of Jamiat Ulama-i-Hind (JUH). He worked as an editor for their publication *Muslim* and was inspired by them to continue his studies in *tafsir, hadith, fiqh,* and *kalam.* He then returned to writing and became the editor of *al-Jamiat,* a new newspaper of the JUH, while keeping up with his studies through the curriculum (*dars-i-nizami*) of Deoband. He also continued to read western works.[3]

During this period of his Deobandi studies and work for the JUH, he was active in the Khilafat movement, having become influenced by the leaders of the movement such as the Ali brothers, Ubaidullah Sindhi, and Abul-Kalam Azad. It was from this group that he learned about social mobilization and the importance of propaganda and religious symbology. After the collapse of the Khilafat movement, however, he grew disillusioned with nationalism and was convinced that Muslims would not be protected by it. In India, Congress was turning increasingly Hindu, and with the rise of communal tensions across India, instigated in large part by the Hindu Mahasaba and the Arya Samaj's Shuddhi campaign, he turned to Islamic revivalism as a political strategy.[4]

In 1928, he returned to Hyderabad, which marked his transformation from "journalist to scholar and later from scholar to reformer of Islam (*mujaddid*)."[5] He worked at 'Uthmaniyyah College's Translation Institute, where scholars translated European as well as Arabic and Persian works into Urdu—on the topics of theology, philosophy, and mysticism. In 1932, he bought and began editing the journal *Tarjuman al-Quran (Quranic Interpretation),* which relied largely on the local government for subscriptions. Mawdudi wrote most of the articles, and over time this journal became the vehicle through which Mawdudi offered his ideas and political visions shaped by events such as failure of the Khilafat movement, the Shuddhi campaign, the rise of 'Abd al-'Aziz ibn Saud's Wahhabi movement in the Hijaz, and the decline of Hyderabad as Muslim epicenter.[6]

Mawdudi did not offer a structure or outline to his revivalist program until 1937, when he returned to Delhi and was shocked to see changes such as "Hindu political ascendency, and secularization among Muslims . . . [including] decline in adherence to *purdah*."[7] After he traveled back to Hyderabad, he shifted his focus to writings that were specifically anti-Congress. He also took issue with the JUH, whose leader Mawlana Husain Ahmad Madani supported a nationalist position for Muslims in a pluralistic society. Mawdudi opposed the idea of pluralism and opposed Madani publicly.[8]

In 1941, Mawdudi took the organizational turn and created the Jamat-i-Islami in Lahore. He was opposed to the Muslim League as well as Congress and found no other viable solutions except to organize his own party for the renewal of Islam. He wrote, traveled, and gave lectures at universities and madrasas throughout India. Between 1933 and 1941, Mawdudi had completed all his works on religious doctrine and moved exclusively into the realm of politics.[9] His focus was on establishing Jamat-i-Islami as an organization premised on creating a Muslim state based on Islamic law that was to direct all areas of life and be governed by the entire Muslim community.

Tawhid as God's Sovereignty

In his book *The Islamic Law and Constitution*, Mawdudi discusses what he calls the "Fundamentals of Islam" in the chapter entitled "Political Theory in Islam." He begins with the point that "Islam is not a jumble of unrelated ideas and incoherent modes of conduct.

It is rather a well-ordered system, a consistent whole, resting on a definite set of clear-cut postulates. Its major tenets as well as detailed rules of conduct are all derived from and logically connected with its basic principles."[10] According to Mawdudi, the principal mission of Prophet Muhammad was to convey to humankind the necessity to acknowledge *tawhid*—the sovereignty of God. This declaration was in his words "revolutionary" not because it required the acknowledgment of God as the creator or because it required people to commit to a new kind of ritual or prayer, but because it demanded a new orientation toward God as *"rabb"* (Lord) and *"Ilah"* (Master and Law-giver) and necessitated complete and exclusive obedience to God alone.[11]

Mawdudi defines *tawhid* as both the "belief in unity" as well as the "sovereignty of Allah."[12] Like ʿAbduh, Mawdudi makes only brief reference to the theological aspects of this definition, namely that God cannot be divided or ascribed partners. The theological piece is ancillary to the much more significant aspect of his interpretation of *tawhid*, namely God as the exclusive sovereign.[13] For Mawdudi, *tawhid* functions as the essential principle, what he calls the "absolute postulate" of Islam, representing the foundation of the ideal political and social order.[14] To illustrate his point about this radically new understanding of God, he provides multiple references from the Quran that corroborate his argument that authority rests with God alone, and that God is the exclusive law-giver whose command the people must obey. For example, he cites Quran 16:102, Quran 3:64, and Quran 9:5 to demonstrate that God alone should be worshiped and that there should be no partners ascribed to him. However, as mentioned above, the significance for him does not lie in the new identity of God as undivided, but rather in an altogether new worldview established by the unique revolutionary message of God as exclusive sovereign. The consequences of this Quranic declaration were profound: He writes that "this was the proclamation that released the human soul from its fetters and set man's intellectual and material powers free from the bonds of slavery. . . . It relieved them of the

burden . . . that was breaking their backs. It gave them a real char-
ter of liberty and freedom."[15]

Until this point in his discussion, Mawdudi writes about the
Quran as part of a historical moment that has passed. Having cited
various passages from the Quran to illustrate his point that the
revolutionary message of the Quran gave humans liberty and freedom, he then turns to what he calls "the main characteristics of an
Islamic state," based on the passages he cites. He explains these
features as follows: first, no person or group of people can lay claim
to sovereignty, as God is the only sovereign; second, God is the
only law-giver; and third, "An Islamic state must, in all respects, be
founded upon the law laid down by God through His Prophet."[16]

What is noteworthy about this transition from the subject of
God's sovereignty in the Quran to the subject of the Islamic state is
that the temporal framework switches from the past, to the present,
to a possible future. First, he explains that God's sovereignty in the
Quranic revelation was "the proclamation that released the human
soul from its fetters. . . ." To this end, he invokes Quranic passages to
illustrate what had happened in the past. The Quranic idea of monotheism *gave* freedom and *released* the people from burden. On the
other hand, when he turns to an account of what constitutes the
Islamic state, the subject of God's sovereignty moves to the present:
he argues that the people cannot lay claim to sovereignty, and God
is the exclusive sovereign and law-giver. And finally, with regard to
the third condition of what is necessary for an Islamic state, he looks
to the future: an Islamic state *must* be founded on God's law. In this
regard, it is a state that has *yet* to happen. *Tawhid* as God's sovereignty
existed, remains possible in the current period as an abstraction,
and, if the necessary requirements are fulfilled, can take concrete
form in the future. There is, in short, a temporal ambiguity and elas-
ticity built into the idea of *tawhid* as God's sovereignty, as well as the
Islamic state. On the one hand, it appears that it happened already
in the Quranic period. On the other hand, there is hope that it will
take form in the future. There are, however, conditions that need to
be met before it can happen again.

His explication of this idea of God's sovereignty continues to move between the past and the present. Turning to his analysis of the existential human condition with regard to power and authority, he explains that the problem and root of all evil in the world is "the domination of man over man." Mawdudi notes:

> it is only man's excessive lust for power and desire for exploitation that prompts him to project himself on other people as a god and extract their obedience; force them to bow down before him in reverential awe, and make them instruments of his self-aggrandizement. The pleasure of posing as a god is more enchanting and appealing than anything else that man has yet been able to discover.

He explains further that there are two kinds of "aspirants" to godhood: first, there is the type who has power to impose their authority over subjects and make a direct claim to "godhood," such as the Pharaoh of Egypt and Nimrod; and then there is another less powerful group of those who are "cunning enough to cast a spell over the minds and hearts of the common people. By the use of sinister methods, they invest some spirit, god, idol, tomb, plant, or tree with the character 'ilah' and dupe the people." This group includes soothsayers, astrologers, fortune-tellers, and anyone who claims to be any kind of intermediary, insisting that rituals should be conducted through their mediation. He further describes them as ones who claim to be "bearers of the Book of God. . . . constituting themselves into mouthpieces of God, they start dictating [to] others what is lawful (halal) and what is unlawful (haram). In this way their word becomes law and they force people to obey their commands instead of those of God." Mawdudi explains that this latter form of thinking "is the source of Brahmanism and Papacy[,] which has appeared under various names and in diverse forms in all parts of the world from times immemorial down to the present day."[17]

His Quranic and Biblical accounts of the Pharoah and Nimrod serve as historical examples of what he sees as a universal condition of humans to dominate over other humans. However, when he speaks about fortune-tellers, soothsayers, and the like, he appears to be offering everyday examples of this condition in the present. Moreover, his explanation is not limited to people. He also cites religious phenomena more broadly—"papacy" and "Brahmanism"—thereby illustrating how entire religious institutional structures have taken shape as a consequence of this essential human desire to exercise power over others. In this way, what he sees as the human proclivity toward "domination of man over man" is not limited to any specific geographic, temporal, or religious context. In short, this was the case in the past and continues to the present and exists universally.

The prescription Mawdudi offers to this diagnosis of humankind is the Islamic state. This discussion operates at the level of abstraction and universalism as well. According to Mawdudi, the Islamic state is one in which God is the ultimate law-giver as no person, class, group, or population of the state as a whole can lay claim to sovereignty. In this regard, Mawdudi explains, Islam is the "very antithesis of secular Western democracy," as the latter is founded in the sovereignty of the people. Mawdudi provides an extensive explanation of the ways in which Islam fundamentally rejects the values of western democracy. He suggests that the more appropriate term to describe the Islamic state is "theo-democracy," drawing a distinction between democracy as a philosophy and democracy as a form of organization. The two philosophies are fundamentally opposed, but the democratic form of organization grafts onto his idea of the Islamic state. So, for example, "Every Muslim who is capable and qualified to give a sound opinion on matters of Islamic law is entitled to interpret the law of God when such interpretation becomes necessary. In this sense the Islamic politic is a democracy."[18]

God's law, according to Mawdudi, is rational and just, unlike western forms of law. It guarantees protection of the family order, and more importantly, what distinguishes the Islamic state from any western polity is the fact that it is universal and governs all aspects of human life. For example, in relation to his view of family life, he states:

> God has prohibited the unrestricted intermingling of the sexes and prescribed *purdah* . . . and clearly defined the rights and duties of husband, wife, and children. He has thus laid down limits which if observed by man would stabilize his family life and make it a haven of peace and happiness. There would remain neither that tyranny of male over female which makes family life an inferno of cruelty and oppression, nor that satanic flood of female liberty and license which threatens to destroy human civilization in the West.[19]

Similar to his modernist predecessors, Mawdudi invokes the language of civilizational progress, but unlike the earlier modernists he believes that the law of Islam as outlined by God provides the means to achieve that progress. According to Mawdudi, God's law, or *sharia*, is more just and balanced than that of the "West," as it refuses any kind domination of one sex over the other.[20] In this instance, the veiling of women and the refusal to accept western ideas of female liberty is one example of how the future Islamic state would protect Islamic society. Mawdudi, like his early modernist counterparts, views Islam in civilizational terms. However, what distinguishes his modernist concern with Islamic civilization from that of his predecessors is the turn to tradition. The position of women is key to this late modernist/Islamist worldview: in the above passage, it is evident that he wants to make sure Muslim society does not get corrupted by western ideas of female liberty. No early modernist—from Afghani, Sayyid Ahmad Khan, ʿAbduh, and even Iqbal—assumed the position that women ought to remain in purdah. In fact, ʿAbduh took it upon himself to reform marriage and inheritance laws such that women were given greater rights. This complete rejection of western forms of rights, in this case women's rights, is a fundamental component to the Islamist worldview that previous modernists did not endorse.

Although Mawdudi attempts to draw a clear distinction between western democracy and Islam, he cannot escape the language of democracy and the nation-state, which is demonstrated most clearly in his outline and conception of the Islamic state. With regard to the issue of rights of non-Muslims in the Islamic state, he asserts that there are five fundamentally opposing positions between the nation-state and the Islamic state. First, the Islamic state classifies people as believers and nonbelievers, whereas the nation-state uses the language of majority and minority defined by the dominant race. Second, the responsibility of running the state should reside with those who believe in the ideology of the Islamic state, whereas control of policy remains in the hands of the majority in the nation-state. The Islamic state, which draws a definitive distinction between Muslims and non-Muslims, is clear about the rights of non-Muslim citizens, whereas the nation-state claims all citizens are equal but draws an unfair discrimination between majority and minority. The Islamic state provides specific rights to non-Muslims, does not allow non-Muslims to be involved in affairs of the state, and always keeps open the possibility for non-Muslims to decide to embrace the Islamic principles and become full participants in matters of the state, whereas the nation-state either gradually destroys the minority community, exterminates them by genocide, or allows them to exists as untouchables. Finally, sharia confers basic rights onto non-Muslims that cannot be curtailed in any way, while minorities under a nation-state depend on the "whims and caprices of the majority," who at any point have the power to curtail the minority's fundamental human rights or even deprive them of it.[21]

According to this view, Ahmadis would be protected, whether classified as either Muslim or non-Muslim. However, Mawdudi himself made the argument that Ahmadis should be declared non-Muslim and encouraged a sustained political campaign against the group, making it difficult to reconcile his Islamist state position on protection of all communities with his anti-Ahmadi activism.

Anti-Ahmadi Campaign in the 1950s

The campaign against the Ahmadis in the 1950s involved several groups, each motivated by political and ideological agendas. Mawdudi and the *ulama* wanted Ahmadis designated as non-Muslim minorities and attempted to oust the Ahmadi leader, Sir Zafarullah Khan, from his high-level position in the government. This campaign led to mass riots in Lahore, the death of over 200 Ahmadis, and the declaration of martial law. Mawdudi was arrested and sentenced to death for his role in the agitation but eventually released after two years of imprisonment. The sociologist Sadia Saeed has analyzed how this particular group of key political figures was entangled in the buildup and outcome of the 1953 riots and declaration of martial law. Bureaucratic and military elites on the one hand and Islamists and *ulama* on the other hand were all struggling to advance their respective agendas regarding religion and the state during this period after Pakistan's formation. The first key player was the right-wing religious group based out of Punjab, Majlis-i-Ahrar al-Islam (Ahrar), which in 1949 first made the demand that Ahmadis be declared non-Muslim. Ahrar and some prominent *ulama* formed an organization called the Majlis-i-ʿAmal (Council of Action) that also called for the foreign minister of Pakistan Sir Zafarullah Khan, who was an Ahmadi, to be removed from his post, along with all Ahmadis in government positions. The Chief Minister of the Punjab, Mumtaz Daultana, began to use Ahrar's anti-Ahmadi rhetoric to win support from his constituents to detract from dire economic conditions of food shortage. In addition, Ahrar managed to draw the Jamat-i-Islami and Mawdudi into their campaign. Saeed notes that Mawdudi joined the Majlis-i-ʿAmal but "reluctantly," as his own Islamist project did not fully endorse the confrontational posture of Ahrar. Mawdudi pushed for the status of Ahmadis as non-Muslims but he held to the position that this change should happen through the constitution rather than through violence and riots. When Ahrar began agitation in 1952 and 1953, it became more directed at the state even when the Chief Minister and Prime Minister showed support for Ahrar and their inflammatory campaign in newspapers. Ultimately, under the direction of an influential bureaucrat, Ghulam Mohammad, it was mandated that the first martial law be implemented over Lahore. The arrests of prominent ʿulama and Islamists and the dissolution of the central government made it clear that "the march toward political authoritarianism" was underway.[22]

The official outcome to the Ahmadi issue was decided by two judges, Munir and Kayani, who were delegated with the task of figuring out what led to the need for martial law and who was responsible for the violence. According to what became known as the "Munir Report," the ʿulama claimed that their anti-Ahmadi position was motivated by their desire and promise for an Islamic state, but the report concluded that the ʿulama themselves were unable to agree upon the question of who was a Muslim. The report also criticized the Prime Minister Nazimuddin for his inability to confront the religious establishment, as well as the Punjab Chief Minister, Mumtaz Daultana. Saeed concludes, "In short, the Munir Report characterized political parties and leaders as exploiters of religion. In this narrative, Ahmadis emerge as the victims, the silent minority being used by corrupt political parties and victimized by religious bigots. The outcome was a policy of state accommodation of Ahmadis."[23]

Mawdudi wrote "The Qadiani Problem" in 1953 in support of 33 prominent members of the ʿulama who proposed an amendment to the constitution that followers of the Ahmadi community should be declared a non-Muslim minority, and that a seat in the Central Assembly should be allotted to them from the quota of Punjab. Mawdudi explains that he wrote his piece as an explanation and support for the proposal of the ʿulama since a solid majority of the intelligentsia as well as the masses had not accepted the statements of the ʿulama. Mawdudi begins his explication of his argument with a standard point about the Ahmadi reinterpretation of "*khatm-i-nabuwwat*," but with some exaggeration, arguing that "the Qadianis came forward with an open and unequivocal declaration that not one but thousands of prophets could come after the Holy Prophet." He then invokes another familiar contention—namely that Ahmadis believe that anyone who does not accept Mirza Ghulam Ahmad are *kafirs* and outside the pale of Islam. This is connected to another point, that the Ahmadis themselves have decided to sever ties with Muslims and created for themselves a separate *Ummat*. For these reasons, Mawdudi argues, the Qadianis ought to be "declared a separate minority quite apart from the Muslims." Mawdudi's reasons were not new. Most of these arguments were outlined by Iqbal in 1935. However, the language of "minority" was new. In 1935, Iqbal asked the British government to declare the Qadianis a separate religious community, whereas Mawdudi demanded that the Qadianis be declared a non-Muslim minority some fifteen years later. The key difference between the two positions is the context of colonial empire compared to that of the modern nation-state.[24]

Mawdudi followed and adopted the language of the ʿ*ulama,* whose statements were appended to the "Qadiani Problem." According to the document, "thirty-three accredited *Ulama* of various schools of thought" who assembled in Karachi for the Pakistan Constituent Assembly in 1953 proposed an amendment, that separate seats ought to be reserved for Qadianis in Punjab, along with two notes, one making clear that Qadianis of other areas (outside Punjab) should be eligible, and a second providing a definition of Qadiani as the following: "A Qadiani is a person who presses to believe in Mirza Ghulam Ahmad of Qadian as his religious leader." They then explain that it is incumbent upon the constitution-makers to understand "how delicate and tense their situation has become in areas where a considerable number of Qadianis are living side by side with Muslims," and that "They should not behave like our erstwhile rulers who did not care to take cognizance of the Hindu-Muslim problem until the whole of undivided India has become blood-stained on account of the Hindu-Muslim disturbances." The connection between the Hindu-Muslim problem of British India is then drawn to the "Qadiani-Muslim problem which needs an urgent solution. . . . The remedy even today lies in declaring them a minority altogether separate from the Muslims as had been proposed by the late Allama Iqbal twenty years back."[25]

If we return to Iqbal's statements we can see how Mawdudi's position on the Qadianis relies on Iqbal's argument but takes on a new form and significance with the question of the state front and center. First of all, Iqbal did not use the word "minority" to describe what he sees as the best outcome for the Ahmadi issue. He argued that the "Qadianis" ought to be declared a separate "community." Iqbal writes, "the best course for the rulers of India is, in my opinion, to declare the Qadianis a separate community. This will be perfectly consistent with the policy of the Qadianis themselves and the Indian Muslim will tolerate them just as he tolerates other religions."[26] As I noted at length in the previous chapter, he situates his argument against the Ahmadis in the framework of theological transgression, specifically, violation of the finality of prophecy doctrine. But what I did not discuss earlier is how he also conveys grievances toward the liberal state and, in particular, their support for religious tolerance. He writes:

> the encouragement in India of religious adventurers on the ground of modern liberalism tends to make people more and more indifferent to religion and will eventually completely eliminate the important factor of religion from the life of Indian communities.[27]

Iqbal finds liberalism an inadequate political structure when it comes to religion. He in fact directly attacks a foundational principle of liberalism—tolerance—when it comes to the question of the Ahmadis. He claims that the liberal government encourages "religious adventurers" such as Mirza Ghulam Ahmad:

> This liberal and indispensable policy in a country like India has led to most unfortunate results. In so far as Islam is concerned, it is no exaggeration to say that the solidarity of the Muslim community in India under the British is far less safe than the

solidarity of the Jewish community was in the days of Jesus under the Romans. Any religious adventurer in India can set up any claim and carve out a new community for his own exploitation. This liberal State of ours does not care a fig for the integrity of a parent community, provided the adventurer assures it of his loyalty and his followers are regular in the payment of taxes due to the State. [28]

Iqbal calls on the government to act—that is to say, to intervene with paternalistic hand on this religious issue. Although he makes the case for the Ahmadis to be declared a separate community, not a minority, he nevertheless sets a precedent for state intervention and forceful coercion in matters of religion and makes a strong case for endorsing religious intolerance.

Iqbal thus established a precedent for religious intolerance and state involvement with the Ahmadis—both of which Mawdudi deploys in his treatise. Mawdudi raises four theoretical objections to his own position and refutes each one. The first is that there have always been issues of heresy among Muslims, and so the Qadiani situation is no different. The second is why a "majority should be pressing for its separation from the minority in the face of the latter's opposition." And the third and fourth objections fall on the grounds that Qadianis have done important work defending Islam against Christians and Arya Samajis early on, and that Ahmadi leadership has strong ties in England and America. Mawdudi takes up the last first, claiming that Pakistan's relationships with England and America will not suffer on account of the eminence of "Qadiani Foreign Minister" Zafarullah Khan (it is not Pakistan who has gained importance because of Zafarullah Khan but vice versa). In terms of the heresy issue, he acknowledges that Muslims have been in the habit of mounting accusations of heresy upon one another, but the ʿulama (who are accused of heresy declarations upon one another) despite their differences "could sit together and accomplish what they did with complete unanimity" because they "do not hold one another as outside the pale of Islam." And unlike other sects of Muslims who differ from the majority who "merely isolated themselves form the general body of Muslims" and can thus be "tolerated," the Ahmadis "penetrate into the Muslim society posing as Muslims; they propagate their view in the name of Islam; start controversies everywhere, carry on proselytizing propaganda in an aggressive manner and continuously strive to swell their numbers" unlike "other passive sects." Furthermore, with regard to the "passive sects," Mawdudi explains, the problem of whether or not to include them in the "pale of Islam" is connected to their ideas:

> The problem of those sects is, after all, rather a theological problem, i.e. whether or not to include them in the pale of Islam in view of their specific creeds. Even if it is decided that they are outside the pale of Islam, their survival as a passive element of the Muslim society cannot do harm to the Muslims religiously, economically or politically.[29]

The above statements echo Iqbal's logic about the Ismailis, wherein he argued: "however the theological interpretation of the Ismailis may err, they believe in the basic principles of Islam."[30] Although Iqbal is explicit about his support for the Ismailis, and Mawdudi implicitly acknowledges tolerance for sectarian theological differences, for both Iqbal and Mawdudi it is necessary that the public statements of so-called "sects" align with the Sunni majority.

The biggest concern for Mawdudi that never figured for Iqbal is the issue of the state. For Mawdudi, the problem was twofold. First of all, he made the case that Ahmadis would never survive in an Islamic state. Mawdudi writes, "none but a non-Muslim and foreign Government can permit freely the growth of new prophethoods in Muslim Society. . . . An independent Muslim State is, so to say, a misfortune for them for it can never willingly tolerate the distinction of its own religion and the disintegration of its own social structure." Furthermore, Mawdudi explains, Ahmadis have aspirations for their own state: "They are planning to establish a Qadiani State within the State of Pakistan." Finally, he addresses the question of why separation, which is normally demanded by a minority, is in this instance demanded by a majority. Although he acknowledges the unusual nature of this case, he justifies it with the following: "In the present case, the demand for separation has been put forth by the majority because it is the majority that is the sufferer."[31]

In *The Islamic Law and Constitution*, he makes the argument that the language of the minority and majority enjoined in the nation-state is whimsical and oppressive, whereas the Islamic state would be clear in terms of its position on non-Muslims. But here, in "Qadiani Problem," he relies wholly and completely on the minority/majority framework of the nation-state and invokes its logic to make an official case about the status of the Ahmadis as non-Muslim.

Mawdudi and the Mahdi/*Mujaddid*

In the following section, I would like to explore another possible dimension to Mawdudi's anti-Ahmadi position that is not directly political, but one that can be read more in the line of competition, similarly to Afghani's relationship with Sayyid Ahmad Khan. Despite Mawdudi's dogmatic position for God's exclusive sovereignty over and against the "dominion of man over man," he supports the idea of a *Mahdi/mujaddid* to facilitate the creation of the Islamic state. This is of course ironic considering both his unyielding view about God as the only sovereign and his vociferous denouncement of Mirza Ghulam Ahmad.

Mawdudi wrote about this figure of the *mujaddid* most extensively in *A Short History of Revivalist Movements in Islam*. He begins with what he sees as a misunderstanding of the term. Invoking the same *hadith* as Rida did about the periodic arrival of a *mujaddid*, he contends that people have assumed that the *mujaddid* is one person who will arrive at the beginning of each century. However, this traditional view is misleading, as he explains:

in fact this task may be accomplished by a number of persons or groups of persons in the same century. Nor is it specified anywhere that the same *mujaddid* will suffice for the whole world of Islam. There may arise a number of persons in a number of countries contemporaneously and undertake [*sic*] the work of Islamic revival.[32]

He explains further that a *mujaddid* is not a Prophet, but he comes very close to the Prophet. Regarding the two he writes:

A Prophet is appointed to his mission by Allah. . . . He starts the work of his mission with a claim to prophethood; he has to invite people to himself; and the acceptance or rejection of his invitation by the people determines their being believers or unbelievers. On the contrary, a *mujaddid* . . . is not appointed. . . . Mostly he is not even aware of his being a *mujaddid*, but people recognize him to be a *mujaddid* after his passing away on account of the quality of the work accomplished by him. He may not be divinely inspired, but if he is, he may not necessarily be aware of it. However, as he starts his work all the good-natured people of the day gradually gather around him. . . . With these limitations and distinctions a *mujaddid* has to undertake and perform the same nature of work as is accomplished by a Prophet.[33]

According to Mawdudi, there has been important revivalist work done in the name of Islam. He offers a few names of figures he sees as having successfully performed this revivalist work: the Ummayad Caliph 'Umar Bin 'Abd al-'Aziz who created a just government, the four imams who created the four main schools of Islamic Fiqh (Imams Abu Hanifa, Malik, Shafi'i, Ahmad bin Hanbal), Imam Ghazali, Imam Ibn Taimiyyah, Shaikh Ahmad of Sirhind, and Shah Waliullah of Delhi. It is important to note, however, that in Mawdudi's view, the ideal *mujaddid* has not arrived yet:

History reveals that the Ideal Mujaddid is yet to be born. Caliph Umar bin Abdul Aziz might have attained this position but he did not get a chance to achieve it. All the *mujaddids* who appeared after him accomplished work in one particular or the other aspect only but none achieved the distinction of becoming the Ideal Mujaddid.[34]

This ideal *mujaddid* is the "Al-Imam-ul-Mehdi," whose arrival, he explains, has been foretold in the *hadith*. However, he makes it a point to say that there are many misconceptions around this idea. First, people who believe in the Mahdi

> seem to think that the Mehdi will be an old-fashioned man with the outdated appearance who will suddenly emerge, one day, rosary in hand, from some madrasa or monastery and will forthwith proclaim himself to be the Mehdi. At this the religious leaders and scholars will come out with their books and start checking and comparing his bodily features against the indications given therein and finally recognize him. Then *bai'at* will be performed.[35]

However, this view of the "common man" is erroneous and in fact, Mawdudi writes, "I have found the matter to be just the reverse." He explains further:

> In my opinion the coming one will be a most modern Leader of his age possessing an unusually deep insight in all the current branches of knowledge and all the major problems of life. As regards statesmanship, political sagacity and strategic skill in war he will take the whole world by surprise and provide himself to be the most modern of all the moderns.[36]

What distinguishes Mawdudi's view of the "Mahdi" from traditional interpretations is his argument about modernity. Mawdudi's Mahdi is a "modern of all moderns" whose work is practical and responsive to the conditions and needs of the time. This figure will not proclaim himself to be the Mahdi and "most probably he will not be aware of his being the promised Mehdi." This Mahdi will not perform any supernatural acts or ascetic or spiritual exercises. He will start revolution:

> I believe that the Mehdi, like any other revolutionary leaders, will have to struggle hard and encounter all the obstacles common in this way. He will create a new School of Thought on the

basis of pure Islam, change mental attitudes of the people and initiate a strong movement which will at once be political and cultural. Ignorance will muster all its forces and strength and come out to crush him, but he will eventually put it to rout and establish a powerful Islamic state.[37]

According to Mawdudi, the single task of the Mahdi is to establish the Islamic state. This Mahdi, as he explains, is not a religious traditionalist but rather a modern man whose purpose is to change the hearts and minds of the people, transforming both the cultural and political fabric of the society to a new vision. Although his *Mahdi/ mujaddid* idea is unequivocally an Islamist one, there are several connections here with Afghani's discussion of the Mahdi. The Mahdi role Afghani described was a parallel figure to the Sudanese Mahdi, whose mission was to undertake reform and provide guidance to Muslims during the period of empire, specifically colonial India. The Mahdi that Mawdudi writes about is a leader of a revolution whose goal is to establish an Islamic state. Despite the different contexts of colonial empire versus nation-state, Afghani and Mawdudi identify similar prognoses and prescriptions for the Muslim community: a vacuum in leadership and a remedy with the Mahdi. Moreover, just as Afghani condemned Sayyid Ahmad Khan and his community, Mawdudi did the same with Mirza Ghulam Ahmad and the Ahmadis. Afghani and Mawdudi both launched accusations of heresy/transgression against figures who were recognized as successful leaders while at the same time providing alternative visions of reform and leadership in the idiom of Shii messianism.

Qutb: *Tawhid* and Leadership

It is well known that Mawdudi's theories of the Islamic state— anchored in the idea of *tawhid* representing the sovereignty of God—came to shape Sayyid Qutb's political views, especially late in his life in the writings of *Milestones*. Sayyid Qutb (1906–1966) was an Egyptian government bureaucrat, author, literary critic, and Islamic political leader, but is most remembered as one of the most influential Islamist theoreticians. Qutb grew up in British-occupied Egypt and was imprisoned and executed in Nasser's independent Egypt. Though he came from a pious rural background, he studied Western literature extensively and wrote literary criticism, poetry, short stories, and journalistic articles when he moved to Cairo in the early 1930s. He was educated in the British system and began his career as a teacher in the Ministry of Public Instruction thereafter. It was at this time that he became particularly devoted to reading and writing literature. By the age of 25, he composed his first novel, translated as *The Mission of the Poet in Life and the Poetry of the Present Generation*.

Qutb spent two years, 1948–1950, in the United States on a scholarship, studying education at Teacher's College in Washington D.C. and the Colorado State College for Education in Greeley, Colorado. His first piece on the topic of religion, *Social Justice in Islam*, was published in 1949, during his stay in the U.S. After he returned, he wrote "The America that I Have Seen," where he commented critically and extensively about his negative perceptions of American life: materialism, racism, excessive individualism, mixing of the sexes, lack of faith in religion, and his disapproval of American women's sexuality. Shortly after returning to Egypt, he joined the Muslim Brotherhood and became one of the group's leading members.

Before I turn to Qutb's idea of *tawhid*, it is important to provide first some background on Islamism and the Muslim Brotherhood in Egypt, especially how it relates to this story of modernism. In Chapter Two, I discussed how Rida was ʿAbduh's primary biographer and carried on the legacy of modernism from his mentor, but how there were key differences between ʿAbduh and Rida: Rida took a much more conservative position against esoteric groups, such as Sufis, Bahais, and Shia. Moreover, later in life, Rida assumed a strident anti-western nationalist position ʿAbduh never adopted. I also mentioned at the beginning of this chapter that politically and historically, modernism developed within the context of empire, and Islamism began to take shape in the postcolonial period; that is, with the formation of the postcolonial nation-state. Furthermore, I noted that it was possible to think about the transition from modernism to Islamism as parallel to the political shift in colonial Egypt and India from the rule of empire to that of the nation-state. Modernism, I have argued, is typically understood as a movement that sought to make Islam compatible with western modernity. Islamism, on the other hand, explicitly rejected the values of western modernity and endorsed the idea of an Islamic state.

Rashid Rida was a transitional figure, occupying roles as both a modernist and an Islamist, in the period of late empire prior to the establishment of the nation-state. Hasan al-Banna (1906–1949), a student of Rida, founded the Muslim Brotherhood in 1928 during the period of British rule. The organization, which started out as focused on religion and social welfare, took a much more politically strident and Islamist turn in the 1950s, and by the time Egypt had become an independent nation-state in 1954, Sayyid Qutb was an active participant in the organization. In the early 1950s, the Muslim Brotherhood was in transition, as many of its participants shifted their focus from education as the way to bring about an Islamic revolution in Egypt to violence instead—Qutb included. In 1954, he and many other members of the Muslim Brotherhood were taken in by Nasser's regime, and Qutb was supposed to spend 10 years in prison. He was released in 1964 but rearrested in 1965 after members of the Muslim Brotherhood had attempted to assassinate Nasser. He was routinely tortured before being brought to trial and then hanged on August 29, 1966.

Although Mawdudi established the Jamat-i-Islam in 1941—some ten plus years later than the establishment of the Muslim Brotherhood in Egypt—there were many key similarities between the two organizations. Most notably, both political organizations combined religion with social activism and based their respective ideological structures on a reinterpretation of the early community of the Prophet.[38] Al-Banna studied in Cairo, where he encountered Rida and his *salafi* ideas and was very much influenced by Rida's conservative anti-Westernism. To put it simply, Islamism was a solution to the threat of the West. In order to combat the West, it was important not to emulate the West but, rather, to rely on the resources of the Islamic tradition. This self-sufficiency took on an explicit institutional form with the Muslim Brotherhood.[39] Both the Brotherhood and Jamat-i-Islami established communities of participants who were dedicated to the practice of *jihad*, which was interpreted as the commitment to transform society. Society was in need of transformation according to this Islamist worldview because it was marked by *jahiliyya*—a state of ignorance, disunity, and exploitation, comparable to the period of pre-Islamic Arabia— prior to the Quranic revelation. It is important remember that the Muslim Brotherhood and the Jamat-i-Islami were not formed as political parties. However, their vision for society and politics was holistic. That is to say, they believed that Islam should govern all aspects of life.

John Esposito has outlined four key components to the Islamist worldview enjoined in both the Jamat and the Brotherhood: first, Islamists believed that the Muslim world was taken over by factionalism, Sufi excess, and European institutions and practices that were both culturally alien and contrary to Islam. Second, they called for a return to the Sunna of the Prophet to establish the Islamic system of government. Third, similarly to modernists, Islamists rejected *taqlid* and upheld *ijtihad*. But unlike modernists who looked to the West and sought out ways to appropriate forms of Western learning, the Islamists emphasized the absolute perfection of Islam and were convinced that all solutions could be found in the Islamic tradition. And finally, rather than accept democracy, Islamists advocated traditional concepts of consultation and consensus and claimed that the people must always be subordinated to divine will.[40]

The above points provide a fairly comprehensive outline of key components of the Islamist worldview, especially as compared to modernism. All four of these points were addressed in some form in the previous discussion of Mawdudi and can be traced in the thought of Qutb as well. However, I would add one more component: the possibilities for religious leadership. Although both Mawdudi and Qutb were unequivocal about their position that any form of human subservience to another human undermines *tawhid* as God's complete sovereignty, the writings of both indicate that there are openings and possibilities of leadership for certain people. For Mawdudi, as I discussed above, this took form of a Mahdi figure. Qutb makes the argument that a select coterie of people, the vanguard, must lead the movement for an Islamic state to be established.

Milestones is in fact written for the vanguard, as he makes clear in the opening.[41] The vanguard is responsible for navigating the conditions of *jahiliyya* and implementing the Islamist vision of reform:

> How is it possible to start the task of reviving Islam? It is necessary that there should be a vanguard which sets out with this determination and then keeps walking on the path, marching through the vast ocean of *Jahiliyyah* which has encompassed the entire world. During its course, it should keep itself somewhat aloof from this all-encompassing *Jahiliyyah* and should also keep sometimes with it.[42]

I will return to this point about the *jahiliyyah* below, but first, it is important to note that the vanguard is in fact set apart from the masses and is required to lead the struggle to establish the sovereignty of God. It is distinguished as a group by its commitment to remain vigilant and exhibit special awareness about the process of revolutionizing people and society.[43] The vanguard, furthermore, is supposed to gradually invite participants into its movement and initiate a transformation of the mindsets of the people, especially with regard to the new idea of God's sovereignty:

> The callers to Islam should understand that when they invite people toward the revival of religion, they should invite them to accept Islam's fundamental belief—even through these people call themselves Muslims or their birth certificates register them

as Muslims. The people ought to know that Islam means to accept the creed "*La ilaha illa Allah*" in its deepest sense, which is this: that every aspect of life should be under the sovereignty of God, and those who rebel against God's sovereignty and usurp it for themselves should be opposed.[44]

Qutb adopts Mawdudi's idea of *tawhid* as the sovereignty of God, but also the temporal understanding of this idea, namely, that it has not yet been understood by the people. It is a condition of the future, and it is the task of the vanguard, the "callers" to Islam, to strive toward implementing. What he points to in the above passage as the "creed" of Islam, "*La ilaha illa Allah*" ("There is no god but God") is fundamental to his views of the state. This first component of what is normally understood as the profession of faith is separated from the second component ("and Muhammad is God's messenger") in his analysis of both the Islam of the past as well as the Islam of the future. That is to say, he disregards the subject of Muhammad's prophecy altogether in the above statement about what exactly the vanguard is supposed to impart to the people. This is precisely because Qutb's vanguard's project is not a theological but a political one. He is interested in having Muslims become better Muslims not through devotion but through participation in the revolution. Qutb himself makes the point that it is not enough that people call themselves Muslims or identify themselves as such at birth. It is necessary that they accept the new idea of God's sovereignty and reject any human claims to sovereignty. From this standpoint, Muhammad's prophecy does not play any kind of significant role for his project of *jihad*.

One place where it seems surprising that he does not make any reference whatsoever to the significance of prophecy is in the second chapter of *Milestones*, entitled "The Nature of the Quranic Method." Although he takes up the subject of the Quranic revelation, he only discusses the subject in relation to God's unity. Unlike Qutb's modernist predecessors, he does not invoke the time of the Prophet in civilizational terms, whereby the period of the prophet's life represents the golden age in Islamic history—as ʿAbduh, for instance, delineates in *The Theology of Unity*. Qutb gives primacy to the prophetic period, but not because the time of Muhmmad's prophecy exemplifies some kind of civilizational peak. Rather, Qutb is specifically interested in the early Meccan period of the Quranic revelation, because it signifies the critical moment in which the fundamental and unchanging message of the Quran was revealed to humankind, thereby establishing "the relationship between him and the Creator." Moreover, he emphasizes the importance of this period precisely because it was a difficult time for the early Muslims, who had to negotiate the widespread resistance to the Quranic message. The entire thirteen years in which the Quran was revealed in Mecca was crucial because it marked the time in which faith and belief were challenged and the fundamental Quranic message about the sovereignty of God was imparted to the first Muslim community:[45]

> They . . . knew the meaning of *Ilah* (God) and they also knew the meaning of "*La ilaha illa Allah*" (There is no deity except God). They knew that *Uluhiyah* means "sovereignty" and they also realized that ascribing sovereignty to only to God meant that authority would be taken away from the priests, the leaders of tribes, the wealthy and the rulers, and would revert to God. It meant that only God's authority would prevail in the heart and conscience in matters pertaining to religious observances and in the affairs of life, such as business, the distribution of wealth and the dispensation of justice.[46]

This Meccan period is symbolic for Qutb: it represents the moment in which the essential teaching of Islam, God's sovereignty, was first pronounced. It is interesting to note that at this juncture it would be appropriate to mention Muhammad's struggles in a political or theological capacity. However, for Qutb, there is only God and the people: "The Meccan period has this glorious attribute that it imprints 'There is no deity except God' on hearts and minds and teaches Muslims to adopt this method and no other—in spite of the fact that it appears difficult—and to persist in this method."[47]

The period of Meccan revelations calls attention to the struggle early Muslims confronted to accept the sovereignty of God. What is also interesting to note about his analysis of the Meccan period is its temporal location. On the one hand, Qutb refers to this period as a historical moment of the past in which the Quran was first revealed. However, it appears, simultaneously, transportable in time. It *has* the "glorious attribute" that it "imprints" God's unity upon the hearts and minds of Muslims. And more importantly, it continues to offer lessons in persistence.

The Quranic period that Qutb discusses thus moves between the past and the present, in a similar way to Mawdudi's discussion of the same topic. For example, when he addresses the Quranic period, he writes: "The Quran concentrated all its teaching on the question of faith alone, not mentioning the details of the system," and, shortly afterwards he states, "This aspect of the nature of Islam defines the way it is to be founded and organized: by implanting belief and strengthening it so that it seeps into the depths of the human soul."[48] In his view, the Quran operated with the direct aim of teaching faith during the Quranic period. Now, however, there is a need to replicate this same pedagogical function of the Quran, as presumably it does not exist. Tense here is important: this method of imparting faith in the people "defines the way it is *to be* [emphasis mine] founded and organized."

Qutb adopted from Mawdudi the view that the establishment of *tawhid* in the modern period necessitates a revolutionary struggle to transform the political as well as the cultural order. According to Qutb, God's sovereignty existed during the Quranic period, and will exist in the future after the vanguard has completed its mission. The current state, however, is one of *jahiliyya*, marked by disunity and the absence of Islam. In the introduction to *Milestones*, he writes:

> But as we have stated before, the beauty of this new system cannot be appreciated unless it takes a concrete form. Hence it is essential that a community arrange its affairs according to it and

show it to the world. In order to bring this about, we need to initiate the movement of Islamic revival in some Muslim country. Only such a revivalist movement will eventually attain to the status of world leadership, whether the distance is near or far. How is it possible to start the task of reviving Islam? It is necessary that there should be a vanguard which sets out with this determination and then keeps walking on the path, marching through the vast ocean of *Jahiliyyah* which has encompassed the entire world. During its course, it should keep itself somewhat aloof from this all-encompassing *Jahiliyyah* and should also keep sometimes with it.[49]

Jahiliyya is the present condition that is necessary to transform. The process required for this transformation is "*jihad.*" He explains: "the movement uses the methods of preaching and persuasion for reforming ideas and beliefs; and it uses physical power and *jihaad* for abolishing the organizations and authorities of the *jahili* system."[50] It is important to note that for Qutb, as for Mawdudi, the Islamic state is an ideal of the future. In fact, in Qutb's view, the Muslim community does not exist in the present. He notes:

> we can say that the Muslim community has been extinct for a few centuries, for this Muslim community does not denote the name of a land in which Islam resides, nor is it a people whose forefathers lived under the Islamic system at some earlier time. It is the name of a group of people whose manners, ideas and concepts, rules and regulations, values and criteria, are all derived from the Islamic source. The Muslim community with these characteristics vanished at the moment the laws of God became suspended on earth.[51]

According to Qutb, the Muslim community existed in the past, is nonexistent in the present, and has the possibility to exist in the future. In many respects, this is the same temporally bifurcated Islam of the early modernists. What is different for the Islamists, however, is the process of achieving unity and the new form it takes in the future. The process is the struggle, the *jihad* of the vanguard to transform the hearts and minds of the people steeped in *jahiliyya*, and the goal and culmination for the Islamists is an Islamic state.

With the idea of the Islamic state, we see both continuities and ruptures between modernist and Islamist thought. Modernists sought to delineate a path that was an alternative to secularism on the one hand and traditionalism on the other. They attempted to make Islam compatible with the values of secular modernity. They did so by blaming the loss of Muslim power and "backwardness" of Muslim society on the people, the masses. However, they stressed the dynamism and flexibility of Islam of the past, and believed that *ijtihad*, the reinterpretation of the Quran based on the exercise of individual reason, was the way to tap into the essentially dynamic spirit that had been lost in historical change.

Islamism, as represented in the thought of Mawdudi and later Qutb, also acknowledged the weakness of the Muslim community. However, unlike the modernists, who worked to find compatibility between Islam and the "West," the Islamists saw in western imperialism a fundamental threat and were far more sweeping in their denouncement of it. Although they acknowledged the value of western science and technology, they rejected western manners, thought, and cultural mores, which they claimed undermined the *shariah*, God's law. In turn, they upheld the view of Islam's self-sufficiency.

Conclusion

Mawdudi offered a radically new interpretation of *tawhid* as God's sovereignty, which, in tandem with his formulation of the Islamic state, shifted the intellectual project of modernism to an Islamist state-directed one. As I remarked at the start, this turn ought to be understood as part of a larger transformation in Muslim intellectual thought, responding to the transition from colonial empire to the modern nation-state. The modernists who wrote about Islam within the context of empire operated within a new modern definition of *tawhid* as social unity of the Muslim community—a concept that was temporally bifurcated and grafted upon theories of civilizational rise and decline: it existed at the time of the early Muslim community and gradually weakened. The modernist idea of *tawhid* was also marked by aspiration: in their writings, it signified a hope that the social and political unity of the first Muslim community will exist again in the future. This exact logic is enjoined in Mawdudi's writings on *tawhid*. He too locates *tawhid* in this temporal structure of a once unified past and aspirational future, but with one additional dimension: the Islamic state.

As I recounted in the above discussion, Mawdudi makes the argument that the Islamic state is qualitatively distinct and superior to the nation-state. However, he relies on the language and structure of the nation-state in his anti-Ahmadi polemical arguments. The Ahmadis thus continue to signify transgression of *tawhid*, a position implicitly addressed as such by Rida and explicitly by Iqbal. However, with Mawdudi, the Ahmadi question was much more than a problem of deviance, as was outlined in the earlier modernist intellectual and political vision. When Mawdudi wrote the "Qadiani Problem," the nation-state of Pakistan was established, along with the language of "minority" and "majority." The debate about Ahmadis thus shifted from the question of "community" to "minority." Mawdudi's polemical "Qadiani Problem" was not simply an intellectual argument about whether the Ahmadis ought to be included in the Muslim community, as was the case with Iqbal. It had direct impact on the political status of the Ahmadi community in the context of a Muslim majority nation-state. Mawdudi's anti-Ahmadi writings and positions must be understood as the confluence of several different yet convergent threads of Sunni chauvinism: earlier modernist ideas about unity and exclusion, Islamist conceptions of God's sovereignty, and nation-state majoritarianism.

Furthermore, Mawdudi, like modernists such as Afghani, envisioned a *Mahdi/mujaddid* who whose traits were not unlike his
own: a wise modern man capable of transforming society and
shepherding the revolution to establish an Islamic state. The seeds
of this particular idea of leadership were later planted in the
thought of Qutb, who outlined the crucial role of a vanguard. The
vanguard's purpose and goal were exactly what Mawdudi called
for: revolutionary transformation of society and the creation of an
Islamic State.

5

Postcolonial Legacies of
Modernist *Tawhid*

A QUEST FOR JUSTICE AND THE
NATION-STATE

THIS STUDY HAS TRACED THE CONCEPTUAL trajectory of *tawhid* as political unity from approximately 1870 to 1950 in the writings of key Muslim intellectuals, categorized into three distinct yet related phases of early, middle, and late modernism. The works of Afghani and ʿAbduh represented the first early stage of the modernist moment, whereby ideas and hopes for unity were shaped by the political climate of the colonial empire. The middle modernist period, exemplified in the writings of Rida and Iqbal, marked a shift in the significance of *tawhid*. For these two figures, Muslim political unity was envisioned in relation to a new awareness about nationalism. The late modernists, Mawdudi and Qutb, articulated their ideas about *tawhid* as political unity specifically in response to nation-state transitions. In all three phases, the concept of *tawhid* as political unity was both aspirational and abstract—albeit to varying degrees—when it came to the question of the state. That is to say, unity was imagined with various possibilities at the historical juncture where modern nation-states did not formally exist or were only starting to emerge. In this last chapter, I'd like to take a look at a few examples of the legacy of *tawhid* in the period after the 1950s when postcolonial nation-states were fully developed. While still aspirational, discussions about *tawhid* were formulated on the basis of new, concrete, and regionally specific nation-state issues.

This concluding chapter also examines continuities and breaks with earlier modernist concepts of *tawhid* and reflects on which components of this idea remained, which were discarded, and which transformed in the postcolonial period. I begin with a discussion of Fazlur Rahman (1919–1988), who was exiled from Pakistan to the U.S. in 1968. Rahman was a modernist scholar who devoted his intellectual and professional life to educational reform and the revival of *ijtihad*. Rahman was critical of the Islamists, especially Mawdudi, but also the *ulama*, both of whom he believed failed to recognize the underlying message and purpose of the Quran as a totalizing source of guidance and ethics. After analyzing the underlying assumptions about unity in Rahman's work *Islam and Modernity*, the discussion turns to the writings of Ali Shariati, whose Shii Marxism was a direct response to the failure of the Shah's imperial state. Next, I examine the concept of *tawhid* in South African liberation theology, as demonstrated in the work of Farid Esack, a key Muslim activist in the anti-apartheid struggle. In all three instances, *tawhid* as unity represents a fundamentally ethical response to injustices of the state. Finally, I turn to an exploration of the connections between Islamist aspirations of the unity of Muslim community and the ideas and structure of Al Qaeda. Here, I reflect on how Mawdudi and Qutb's concepts of the vanguard took form in Al Qaeda's call for global *jihad* against the West. Al Qaeda and the *mujahideen* saw themselves as the select group commissioned to rescue the Muslim community from weakness and division through *jihad*. The diverse group of intellectuals, political thinkers, and group leaders analyzed in this last chapter all frame their ideas about Islam and *tawhid* from a perspective of ethical practice. Unity serves as the idiom through which hopes and visions of justice are expressed, often as correctives to state failures.

Quran as the Source of Ethical Practice

Fazlur Rahman was born in the then North-West Frontier Province of British India, now the Khyber Pakhtunkhwa province in Pakistan. He studied Arabic at the University of the Punjab, completed a Ph.D. at Oxford, and thereafter taught Persian and Islamic philosophy at Durham University and Islamic Studies at McGill University. In 1961, he returned to Pakistan to head the Central Institute of Islamic Research in Karachi, founded by the Pakistani government, under the leadership of President Ayub Khan. During his leadership of the Institute, Rahman met resistance from the ʿulama, and ultimately they claimed Rahman was an apostate and called for his death. It was this heated political climate in Pakistan that led to Rahman's relocation to the U.S.—first as visiting professor at UCLA and thereafter to the University of Chicago, where he helped build a Near Eastern Studies Department and ultimately became the Harold H. Swift Distinguished Service Professor of Islamic Thought.

Rahman was a key figure in the shaping of modernism after 1950, especially in academic circles. There are certainly continuities with the early modernists in his writings, in particular the central role of *ijtihad*, but Rahman offers a new ethical perspective that the early as well as late modernists/Islamists never fully outlined. Rahman's primary focus was Muslim education. In particular, it was his hope to salvage "Islamic intellectualism" through Quranic interpretation. In Rahman's view, the Quran was not only the divine word revealed to Prophet Muhammad, but also came to represent "the most comprehensive guidance for man" that had both "practical and political implication" that was "geared toward the moral improvement of man in a concrete and communal sense, rather than toward the private and metaphysical."[1] According to Rahman, Muslims were never able to work out an effective and systematic method of interpretation because traditional institutions and methods of interpretation, such as *qiyas* (analogical reasoning), had adopted what he calls an "atomistic" approach that focused on interpreting specific words and/or verses in isolation. Traditional methods of Quranic exigesis resulted, in his words, in a "failure to understand the Quran as a deeper unity yielding a definite weltanschauung."[2]

From Rahman's perspective, the field of law was able to sustain itself though lacking the capacity to understand the Quran as a coherent text. Theology, in particular that of Asharite Sunni orthodoxy, suffered the most. Because theologians failed to develop an understanding of the unified nature of the Quranic worldview, they were unreceptive to Muslim philosophers whose ideas were shaped by Greek thought. As a consequence, the Sunni theological tradition "crushed the latter [philosophy] by its sheer weight. Subsequently philosophy took refuge and developed in a Shi'i intellectual-spiritual milieu or was transformed into intellectual Sufism." The philosophers and the Sufis came closest to understanding the Quran as a unity—however, he notes, from their perspective, unity was "imposed upon the Quran (and Islam in general) from without rather than derived from the study of the Quran itself." Rahman takes issue with this tendency to impose external frames of interpretation, and notes this problem with Sufism but also with examples in the modern period.[3]

This brings us to what exactly Rahman suggests as an approach to the Quran as unity from within. As he outlines it, this method involves two crucial steps:

> The first step . . . consists of understanding the meaning of the Quran as a whole as well as in terms of the specific tenets that constitute responses to specific situations. The second step is to generalize those specific answers and enunciate them as statements of general moral-social objectives that can be "distilled" from specific texts in light of the socio-historical background and the often-stated *rationes legis*. Indeed the first step—the understanding of the meaning of the specific text—itself implies the second step and will lead to it. Throughout this process due regard must be paid to the tenor of the teaching of

the Quran as a whole so that each given meaning understood, each law enunciated, and each objective formulated will cohere with the rest. The Quran as a whole does inculcate a definite attitude toward life and does have a concrete weltanschauung; it also claims that its teaching has 'no inner contradiction' but coheres as a whole.[4]

It is clear that Rahman proposes something new compared to his modernist predecessors: that is, a two-step interpretative process that turns back to the historical context of the Quran to understand personal and community ethical guidelines. This position is distinguished from that of the early modernists as well as the later modernists/Islamists, who saw in the early period of Islam an ideal golden age that spiraled into disunity thereafter. Rahman's approach to the study of Islam is not inflected with civilizational concerns, as was the case with modernist and Islamist interpretations of Islam. Despite this difference, there are indeed similarities. He too claims that the Quran is consistent, coherent, and can be accessed individually without mediation. Furthermore, he draws the same distinction between the Quran and the people, a line of thinking that developed as far back as Afghani. Rahman explains: "The Quran sets a very high value on knowledge, and the Prophet himself is ordered to pray to God: 'O Lord! Increase my knowledge' (20:114). . . . But by contrast, the Muslim attitude to knowledge in the later medieval times is so negative that if one puts it beside the Quran one cannot help being appalled."[5]

Rahman puts blame on many groups of people for not having understood the Quran in an adequate manner. Surprisingly, he takes modernists to task. He contends that even though the modernists endorsed *ijtihad*, a new line of thinking, this group "had no method except to treat ad hoc issues that seemed to . . . require solution for Muslim society but that were historically of Western inspiration."[6] He argues that modernists were too focused on western views of history and education, and that the only modernist who sought a distinctively Islamic method of interpreting the

Quran's metaphysical components was Muhammad Iqbal in his *Reconstruction of Religious Thought in Islam*. Iqbal offered certain important insights into the nature of Islam, but Rahman sees Iqbal's thought as more of a personal effort rather than a traditional systematic one that is based not on Quranic teaching but on contemporary philosophy and history.[7] The Islamists, whom he refers to as fundamentalists or "neo-revivalists," were no different in terms of their failure to understand the Quran. He argues that they had "no method worthy of name except to react, on certain important issues to the classical modernist."[8] The Islamists:

> reoriented the modern-educated lay Muslim emotionally toward Islam. But the greatest weakness of neorevivalism . . . is the almost total lack of positive effective Islamic thinking and scholarship within its ranks, its intellectual bankruptcy, and its substitution of cliché mongering for serious intellectual endeavor.[9]

Rahman blames the Islamists for having taken intellectualism out of Islamic scholarship. As a corrective, he proposes a method that examines the sociohistorical background of the Quran and the Prophet's life, as accounted for in the work of hadith collectors, historians, and Quran commentators, combined with a systematic attempt to study the Quran in the order in which it was revealed. This has never been done, he notes:

> It is only because the Quran was not treated as a coherent whole by many Muslim thinkers that the metaphysical part . . . received the wildest interpretations at the hands of the so-called esoteric school, be they Sufis, Batinis, philosophers . . . while the majority of the orthodox became dusty-dry literalists far removed from any genuine insight into the depths of the Quran.[10]

Whether Rahman offers a method that is more coherent and systematic and context-driven than any previous approach, as he argues, is not a claim I am interested in evaluating here. I am focused, rather, on examining the continuities and inheritances of modernism in the period after the modernist and Islamist movements discussed in previous chapters. One very clear line of thinking that can be traced from Afghani to Rahman, is the pressing need to view the Quran, and in turn Islam, as a coherent, legible, and unified tradition. Rahman does not frame this coherence of the Quran in civilizational terms, a position that the early modernists adopted. Nor does he deploy the logic of the Islamists who viewed the period of Quranic revelation as the establishment of God's sovereignty that gradually weakened throughout the course of history. He believes that the absolute unity of the Quranic message, when understood properly, can serve as a complete source for ethical life. In this line of argument, however, he blames various groups of people—Islamists, modernists, early Sufis, and Batiniyya—for having distorted the message of the Quran and in turn dividing and making divisive the community. That is to say, by ascribing "wildest interpretations" to the "esoteric" school, he makes it clear that these groups undermined the coherent unity of the Quran. This fundamental logic is no different from Afghani's *neicheris*, ʿAbduh's Shia, and Rida's "propagandists." In this regard, he exhibits the exact Sunni normative tendency to demarcate the boundaries of Muslim identity through accusations of transgression and deviation.[11]

Tawhid in Shii Modernist Marxism

All the figures I have discussed in previous chapters have explicitly or implicitly adopted what I call a Sunni normative bias. That is to say, they have all identified deviation and transgression from a Sunni orientation—and quite often the target groups were Muslim minorities, most often the Shia. It is therefore not surprising that Shii modernists articulated their approaches to unity in distinctive ways from the Sunni modernists. One of the most legendary Shia modernists, Ali Shariati, configured his modernism through a unique synthesis of Shii ideas, western sociology, Marxism, and the Third World anti-colonial thought of Fanon.[12] Shariati grew up as the son of a reform-minded cleric, and very early on joined a group of "God-Worshiping Socialists" in the 1940s with his father, where he was for the first time exposed to attempts to synthesize Shiism with European socialism. He studied Arabic and the Quran in college and Arabic and French at the Master's level at Mashhad University, and then won a scholarship to study Sociology and Islamic History at the Sorbonne for a Ph.D. This was the period in which the Cuban and Algerian revolutions exposed him to Third World anti-colonial revolutionary thought—at which time he read the works of Sartre, Fanon, and Che Guevara. He returned to Iran in 1965, where he taught in Tehran. His lectures were transcribed into over fifty pamphlets and booklets that were circulated to college and high school students. By 1972, the secret police grew suspicious of him and clerics were threatened by the growing popularity of Shariati's ideas. He was arrested, released in 1975, left for London in 1977, and suddenly died at age 43, shortly after his arrival.[13]

Shariati was the primary modernist ideologue of the Iranian revolution. He believed that Shiism was equipped to conduct a national and social revolution since it was built on ideas of justice and freedom from oppression. He corroborated many of his ideas about freedom and justice through his understanding of *tawhid* in early Islam. Shariati asserted that the Prophet's mission was to establish not simply a monotheistic religion but a *nizam-i-tawhid* (a unitary society) bound by a classless order, equality, and brotherhood.[14] In his essay, "The World-View of *Tauhid*," one of his many lectures collected into the series *On the Sociology of Islam*, Shariati writes:

> My world-view consists of *tauhid. Tauhid* in the sense of oneness of God is of course accepted by all monotheists. But tauhid as a world-view in the sense I intend in my theory means regarding the whole universe as a unity, instead of dividing it into this world and the hereafter, the natural and the supernatural, substance and meaning, spirit and body.... I regard *shirk* in a similar fashion; it is a world-view that regards the universe as a discordant assemblage full of disunity, contradiction, and heterogeneity,

possessing a variety of independent and clashing poles, conflicting tendencies. . . . *Tauhid* sees the world as empire; *shirk* as a feudal system.[15]

Here Shariati argues that *tawhid* conveys not only the ideal just political and social order, but it erases all "disunity, contradiction, and heterogeneity." Shariati's views of *tawhid* are formulated from the perspective of Marxist justice and in turn function in a pluralistic and inclusive manner, which was not the case for the Sunni modernists. What is interesting about Shariati's reading of *tawhid* is that he extends this idea of unity to the natural and supernatural ordering of the universe as well. In this regard, the political and social ideal is inextricably tied to the metaphysical ordering and understanding of the universe as outlined in the Quran. He explains further that the manifest world is composed of a series of signs (*ayat*) and norms (*sunan*)—the former he takes up further as subject of reflection. According to Shariati, signs designate "a natural phenomenon that bears profound meaning ("The oceans and trees, night and day, earth and sun, earthquakes and death, illness, vicissitude, law . . . all these are signs"). He continues:

> Among all the books of religion, science and philosophy, it is only the Quran that designates all of the objects, accidents and processes of nature as signs. . . . The Quran assigns positive scientific worth to the signs . . . and it is only by means of contemplating them in a serious and scientific fashion that one can attain the truth."[16]

What is apparent from this kind of reading of the Quran and *tawhid* is that Shariati, like ʿAbduh and Iqbal, alleged that the Quran was wholly transparent and intelligible to the human mind and fully aligned with the approach of modern science. In this regard, his logic operates in a similar fashion as ʿAbduh's: the individual can access the Quran through *ijtihad*, that is, without any form of mediation, and in doing so can arrive at a scientific and truthful understanding of the universe. This rationalist interpretation of the Quran is corroborated by

Shariati's explanation that the "structure of *tauhid*" does not allow for any kind of contradiction in human existence. This applies not only to the natural universe but also to the structuring of differences in society, as he explains, "nor can *tauhid* accept legal, class, social, political, racial, national, territorial, genetic, or even economic contradictions." And all social, political, and geographic differences—say between "black and white, noble and vile, clergy and laity, eastern and western . . . Arab and non-Arab . . . capitalist and proletarian, elite and mass . . . all these forms of contradiction are reconcilable only with the world view of shirk—dualism, trinitarianism or polytheism—but not with tauhid—monotheism."[17]

Neither ʿAbduh nor Iqbal extended their interpretations of *tawhid* to the social and natural ordering of the world as Shariati does. Shariati takes what he sees as the rational, structured, and transparent logic of *tawhid* that Iqbal and ʿAbduh invoked to another level of sociological application, thereby setting himself apart from his predecessors. Nevertheless, there is a similarity in the epistemic function of *tawhid*. For all three, *tawhid* is infinitely expansive and within this expansiveness lies the possibility of achieving the ideal, which had existed only in the past. And as with ʿAbduh, *tawhid* signifies a single unified tradition and community that leaves no room for internal theological, historical, and internal differences:

> In the world-view of *tauhid*, man fears only one power, and is answerable before only one judge. He turns to only one *qibla*, and directs his hopes and desires to only one source. And the corollary is that all else is false and pointless—all the diverse and variegated tendencies, strivings, fears, desires and hopes of man are vain and fruitless.[18]

The diversity that is built into the cumulative tradition of Islam is once again disregarded. These later modernists, such as Rahman and Shariati, assume a similar approach to that of the earlier modernists, who deny the heterogeneity of the tradition, but they do so for different reasons. The latter group is primarily concerned with the role of society and the question of ethics. For example,

Abdulaziz Sachedina has argued that for Shariati, inherent to the idea of *nizam-i-tawhid* is the ethical ideal of wisdom that the Prophet brought to bear in early Islam: "It is 'wisdom' that makes him the great moral reformer of the world; and it is precisely the moral and spiritual change that he brought about in society that makes him the great teacher and reformer."[19] Sachedina elaborates upon this ethical component as it relates to the individual's relationship to society: "In Islamic history, *tawhid* not only gives man certainty and a sense of inner tranquility; it also makes him responsible for the welfare of his own self and the society in which he lives, giving meaning and direction to his existence."[20] In this regard, Shariati's thinking reveals the influences of Iqbal.[21] In one of Ali Shariati's lectures, "Mohammad Iqbal: A Manifestation of Self-Reconstruction and Reformation," Shariati praises Iqbal as a "mystic" equivalent to figures like Ghazali, Ibn ʿArabi, and Rumi, a fighter more significant than Hasan Sabah or Salah al-din Ayyubi, and an intellectual who surpasses even Sayyid Ahmad Khan. Shariati describes Iqbal as having attained "the height of political awareness of his time . . . a contemporary thinker and philosopher of the same rank as Bergson in the West today or of the same level as Ghazzali in Islamic history . . . a reformer of Islamic society in which he himself lies and for which he performs the *jihad* for the salvation, awareness, and liberation of Muslim people."[22] Iqbal was the model Muslim because his commitment to the life of the mind as well as society signifies the paradigmatic orientation of the "reconstruction" process to which all Muslims must aspire:

> We wish for a school of thought and action which nurtures a human being who closely is aware of our culture and all of our good spiritual and religious assets, who is not alienated from the times, and who does not live in the 4th or 5th century. We long for it to develop a human being who can think, who has a scientific mind, yet does not remain negligent of the anguish, life, captivity, and hardships of his ummah. . . . All that we seek in these various domains can be seen in Iqbal.[23]

Furthermore, Shariati sees in Iqbal, as well as Afghani and ʿAbduh, a line of thinking that is fundamentally revolutionary:

> When we say Iqbal was a reformer or that the great thinkers after Seyyed Jamal are known as being the greatest reformers of the century in the world, it is not in the sense that they supported gradual and external change in society. No. They were supporters of a deep seeded revolution, a revolution in thought, in views, in feelings, an ideological and cultural revolution. Iqbal, Seyyed Jamal, Kawakebi, Muhammad Abduh . . . are great men who shook the East in the last one hundred years.[24]

Shariati valorizes this group of modernists for their work not simply as intellectual reformers but also as activists. He describes Iqbal, for example, as having a modern and scientific mind, and as a forward thinker capable of responding to exigencies of the contemporaneous time. In the above passage, he adds Afghani and ʿAbduh to this list, noting once again that their contributions were not limited to their propagation of gradual intellectual change. All three, in Shariati's view, sowed the seeds of revolutionary thinking, which, in his understanding, is tied to the establishment of *tawhid*. For Shariati, as for his modernist predecessors, *tawhid*, the ideal, existed in the period of early Islam and simultaneously can be realized in the future. However, it also serves a philosophical and ethical function as well. *Tawhid* bestows upon man a "wisdom" that perfects him and creates a worldview in which he acts rationally and responsibly, fully committed to the revolutionary transformation of society.

Tawhid in the Anti-Apartheid Struggle

Muslim activists in South Africa adopted this revolutionary and ethical interpretation of *tawhid* in the anti-apartheid struggle. This specific legacy of *tawhid* can be seen in the writings of Farid Esack, especially in his book *Qurʾan, Liberation, and Pluralism: An Islamic Perspective of Interreligious Solidarity against Oppression*. Farid Esack was born in 1959 in Cape Town, South Africa. He is a scholar, theologian, and political activist who was appointed by Nelson Mandela as gender equity commissioner. Esack's family was forced to relocate under the South African apartheid government's Group Areas Act, which assigned racial groups to specific areas. It was a law that effectively excluded non-Whites from living in the most developed areas of the city. Esack was a member of the reformist Tablighi Jamat in Cape Town and taught at a local madrasa. Esack left for Pakistan in 1974, where he specialized in Islamic studies in Karachi. He returned to South Africa in 1982 and became an active member of the organization Muslim Youth Movement of South Africa. Later he helped form an organization eventually named Call of Islam. The Call of Islam was part of a larger umbrella group, United Democratic Front, which was one of the largest anti-apartheid organizations of the 1980s that brought together student, civic, and church groups to combat, on nonracial grounds, the segregation laws and institutional racism of the apartheid regime.

In *Quran, Liberation, and Pluralism*, Esack outlines an approach that he and his fellow activists called a "theology of liberation." He describes this perspective as "a process that is participatory and liberatory.... An Islamic liberation theology derives its inspiration from the Quran and the struggles of all the prophets. It does so by engaging the Quran and the examples of the prophets in a process of shared and ongoing theological reflection for ever-increasing liberative praxis."[25] Two Quranic ideas that were particularly relevant to this revolutionary approach were *tawhid* and *mustad ʿafin fi ʾl-ʿard* (the oppressed in this world). Both of these concepts, he explains, were widely invoked in Iran but made their way into a specifically Islamic liberation discourse in South Africa.[26]

Esack notes how interpreting the Quran as a revolutionary text was something that was happening simultaneously in Iran and among South African Muslims, but what distinguished South African Islamic liberation theology as a discourse and approach to Islam was its focus on specific hermeneutical keys—such as *tawhid* and *mustad ʿafin fi ʾl-ʿard,* but also others such as *jihad* and *taqwa*—as a point of entry to both reflection and action. Esack makes it clear that the interpretation of these concepts was not mediated through the clerics. In this regard, the Muslim activists were modernists who adopted *ijtihad*, that is, they claimed that the text could be re-interpreted without recourse to the 'ulama, who were not activists in the same way as the group Esack was part of, the "progressive Islamists." Furthermore, he notes that the ideas the 'ulama found relevant, such as the abode of Islam (*dar al-Islam*) versus the abode of enmity (*dar al-harb*), did not speak to the pluralistic, nonracial, nonsectarian agenda of the Muslim activists participating in the anti-apartheid struggle. Most importantly, the Muslim activists identified with an approach of "liberating praxis," which Esack explicates further in the following passage from the Muslim Youth Movement (MYM) pamphlet literature:

> Liberating praxis, as opposed to practice, should be our major watchword. By praxis we mean doing and reflecting. The *halaqat* should be active circles of knowledge and practice (praxis) which integrate organic intellectuals (*alim/ulama*) with activists (*mujahids*) to fulfill the description of the early Muslim community: Gallant warriors by day and monks by night.[27]

The Islamists of South Africa worked with specific concepts to create what he calls a "Quranic hermeneutic of liberation" that entailed a continuous shift between text and context and active reflection on the connections between the two as applied to those who had been historically marginalized in 1980s South Africa. Esack begins his analysis of this process with *tawhid*, first acknowledging the prevalent Quranic understanding of this idea as One God without a partner. From there he argues that "*tawhid* has correctly been described as the 'foundation, the centre and the end of the entire [Islamic tradition].'"[28] Esack contends that Islam's comprehensiveness and holism is grounded in the central idea of *tawhid*.[29] He then cites Shariati's view on the liberatory potential built into the idea of *tawhid*.[30] The logical jumps that Esack makes with regard to *tawhid* are similar to those of the earlier modernists: that is, he introduces the concept first in a theological frame that foregrounds God's unity, but from there he makes the points that *tawhid* operates as the anchor of the entire religion, the foundation from which its social structure and community is built. What is new, however, is the liberatory potential that he sees in *tawhid*, drawing on Shariati.

At one level, Esack seems to invoke the Islamist perspectives of *tawhid*, namely the possibilities of this new holistic structure to emerge in the future. However, the key difference between the approach of the progressive Islamists and the more traditional Islamists, such as Mawdudi and Qutb, is that the former group deploys the idea from the location of the oppressed, those who have suffered under the racial and economic divisions established by apartheid ideology. Esack cites one particular passage from their pamphlet literature that reflects this particular position: "'Muslims are Muslims,' stated *Worldview*, the newsletter of the MSA, "because of their belief in the *tawhid* of God—a *tawhid* which goes beyond mere verbal acknowledgements and which necessarily demands that Muslims act in the face of injustice."[31] Explicating this position further, he quotes the leader of the MYM in 1986, who made the following point about how *tawhid* of the early Muslim community is relevant to the mission of the Muslim activists and their struggle in the present condition:

> He [Muhammad] spent 13 years in Makkah teaching . . . *tawhid* to the early Muslims. . . . He organized individual Muslims into a group and after the *hijrah* . . . he organized them into . . . an *ummah*. He then extended the *tawhid* from the individual and the group to the state. This is the most important mission of our beloved Nabi Muhammad (SAW); to destroy all false gods, [and] establish a *tawhidi* society on earth.[32]

"*Tawhidi*" society, Esack notes, had three primary markers: first, the affirmation of a "theological dogma," which is the unity of God; second, the rejection of a "dualistic conception of human existence whereby a distinction is made between the secular and the spiritual"; and third, the contrast to a "society that . . . divides people along the lines of ethnicity. Such division is regarded as tantamount to *shirk* (associating others with God), the antithesis of *tawhid*."[33]

Esack makes the point that apartheid represents a fundamental rejection of *tawhid*. According to the Muslim activists, apartheid epitomized the rejection of the unity of the nation, as it divided people along ethnic lines. In their view, race functioned as a form of *"shirk,"* or associationism that undermined the divine and sociopolitical holism the activists ascribed to *tawhid*.

Although the progressive Islamists of South Africa broke with the traditional Islamist views of *tawhid* in their appropriation of the term for the anti-apartheid struggle, there were, nevertheless, certain similarities between the ways in which the progressive Islamists and traditional Islamists approached *tawhid*. In the South African progressive view of *tawhid*, the implicit structure is that of the nation-state. That is to say, to struggle for *tawhid* had as its goal the inclusion of all South Africans as equal citizens of the state, without racial, religious, or ethnic division. Even though Mawdudi and Qutb's idea of the state is a Muslim state, its structure, as I outlined in the previous chapter, responds to and at times mirrors the nation-state. In this regard, the connection between the success of *tawhid* and the just nation-state is similar to the views of both Mawdudi and Qutb.[34] The second important parallel between the *tawhidi* state of the traditional Islamists and that of the progressive Islamists is the bifurcated temporal condition, in which the *tawhidi* state exemplifies the ideal state of the past as well as the future. As Esack describes in the MYM noted above, the progressive Islamist position is that Prophet Muhammad established a unified state, and the goal of the struggle was to destroy the divisions created by apartheid and return to an undivided society along the lines of that established by the Prophet. Esack's citation of another leader, Ebrahim Rasool, corroborates this point:

> Belief in tawhid with all its implications must have absolute hegemony in our consciousness and, until this has happened, we cannot convincingly say that we fully realize the meaning of 'Say indeed, God's guidance is the true guidance' [Qur'an 2:120].[35]

Looking to the model of the Prophet's early community as the ideal past and the hope for the future is, at one level, an inheritance of the Islamist worldview. However, it is important to bear in mind that the Muslim activists of South Africa did not see their goal to be the establishment of an Islamic state. Their aspiration for a society based on *tawhid* as unity without racial and ethnic divisions was aligned with the vision of the ANC, as Esack remarks in reference to ANC literature:

> A statement made by ANC cadres just prior to their being sentenced to death expands on this dream of a unitary South Africa build on the ashes of apartheid: 'The new South Africa must reflect our oneness, breaking down the destructive idea and practices of defining our people by race, colour or ethnic group' (Upfront, 1989, 21). Another ANC cadre, Ashraf Karriem, explaining in court why he had embarked on the path of armed struggle[,] said, 'Islam sees South Africa as oppressive and exploitative and believes in the oneness of God and oneness of the people' (*The Argus*, 10 November 1988, p.1)."[36]

It is important to note that, on the one hand, the bifurcated structure of *tawhid* remained part of the vision and worldview of the progressive Islamists. On the other hand, the goal of the just and *tawhidi* nation-state was premised on the idea of inclusion of all, despite racial, religious, and ethnic difference. In this regard, the Marxist inclinations of the South African progressive Islamists, informed and shaped by the Shii Marxism of Ali Shariati, diverged from both the early, middle, and late modernists in terms of the boundaries of *tawhid*. For the Marxist-inspired modernists, there was no outsider, since the ethical and political commitment was an inclusive and fundamentally pluralistic one.

Tawhid's Modern Vanguard: Al Qaeda

What I have yet to address is how modernist views on religious authority transformed post-1950. The early, middle, and late modernists had various proposals for leadership. Afghani and Mawdudi envisioned a Mahdi-figure to shepherd the Muslim community.

Rida suggested a *mujaddid* for the time. And Mawdudi and Qutb sought out a new role of the vanguard. In this concluding section, I would like to focus on how these ideas, especially Qutb's vanguard, took on the specific form of the *mujahideen* in the structure and organization of Al Qaeda in the 1980s.

The origins of Al Qaeda can be traced to the period of the Soviet-Afghan war (1979–1989), in which insurgent groups, known as the *mujahideen*, fought a guerrilla war against the Soviet Army and the government of Afghanistan during the period of the Cold War—the forty years of conflict, proxy wars, and competition between the Soviet Union and its allies, on the one hand, and the United States and its allies on the other hand. The United States, with the cooperation of Saudi Arabia and Pakistan, supported the *mujahideen* against the Soviets. The United States conducted this proxy war primarily through the CIA program called Operation Cyclone, designed to arm and finance the *mujahideen* in Afghanistan from 1979 to 1989—one of the longest and most expensive CIA operations in history. The funds were primarily channeled through Pakistan's Inter-Services Intelligence agency, the ISI, which ran training camps. The Islamist recruits came from all over the world—Algeria, Saudi Arabia, and Egypt. Two of the most well known of the CIA recruits were Sheik Abudullah Yusuf Azzam (1941–1989) and his student Osama bin Laden.

Al Qaeda ("the base") was founded in 1988 by Osama bin Laden and Abdullah Azzam. Osama bin Laden grew up in a prominent business family with close ties to the royal family in Saudi Arabia and studied engineering and business at King Abdulaziz University. Although bin Laden did not study religion formally at the university, he was introduced to radical Islamist ideas there, specifically to those of Qutb. In the last half of the twentieth century, when the Muslim Brotherhood operated underground, many members moved to Saudi Arabia where they were able to find jobs, either teaching at universities or working in government positions. After Sayyid Qutb's execution in 1966 and the suppression of the Brotherhood, Muhammad Qutb, Sayyid Qutb's brother, fled to Saudia Arabia and began teaching Islamic studies and actively publishing and promoting Sayyid Qutb's works.

Abdullah Azzam was a Palestinian who joined the Muslim Brotherhood in Palestine in the 1950s. He was involved in the operations against Israeli occupation but grew frustrated with the secular PLO, led by Arafat. Eventually, he became a founding figure in the creation of the Hamas movement in Palestine. Azzam was both politically active as well as drawn to work in Islamic studies, which he pursued further in Damascus and eventually at the Al-Azhar in Cairo, where he received a Ph.D. in Islamic jurisprudence. He tried to teach at the University of Jordan but was not welcome because of his radical ideas. Eventually, he secured a job at King Abdulaziz University in Jeddah, where he worked until 1979. It was at that time that Osama bin Laden met Azzam. When the Soviets invaded Afghanistan, Azzam moved to Islamabad and then Peshawar, where he began organizing in training camps and recruiting for the Afghani *jihad*. Azzam convinced Osama bin Laden to join him and help finance the training of recruits.

Both Osama bin Laden and Abdullah Azzam were shaped in part by Qutb's thought, what might be called "Qutbism." By "Qutbism" I mean the emphasis on an explicitly offensive *jihad*. The underlying assumption of Qutb's ideology is that the entire world, including the Muslim world, is overcome by *jahiliyya*, and that it is the responsibility of the vanguard to establish a righteous Muslim community that has been extinct, in Qutb's words, for centuries.[37] This call to combat *jahiliyya* through *jihad* was the primary mission of Al Qaeda. Furthermore, Al Qaeda's worldview was premised on the same binary as Qutb's: the believers and the infidels. Osama bin Laden's speeches and writings set up an opposition between believers and Kufr, or Islam and atheism, but the explicit target was the "West," often referred to as "the Crusader-Zionist alliance." In bin Laden's view, Muslims constitute one single group, and consequently, if any single Muslim is attacked, it is considered a violation against the entire group. Similarly, all non-Muslims and Muslims who do not adhere to Al Qaeda's views were considered legitimate targets for attack. What distinguishes bin Laden's use of *jihad* from Qutb's is the end goal. For Qutb, *jihad* was designed with the purpose of recreating the structure and order of the Egyptian nation-state, whereas for bin Laden the focus was not the transformation of the state or establishment of God's sovereignty but *jihad* itself. It is for this reason that bin Laden's thought has been described as "more episodic than systemic."[38]

Osama bin Laden's speech "Declaration of War against the Americans Occupying the Land of the Two Holy Places" refers to many of these key points. The speech begins with a diagnosis of the problem, which is that "the people of Islam have suffered from the aggression, iniquity, and injustice imposed on them by the Zionist-Crusader alliance and their collaborators." This is followed by an outline of regions—Palestine, Iraq, Lebanon, Tajikistan, Burma, Kashmir, Assam, Somalia, Eritrea, Chechnya, and Bosnia-Herzegovina—that bin Laden claims have been subject to the "aggression of the Zionist-Crusader alliance."[39] After an extensive discussion of the ways in which the Saudi government had not responded to the grievances of the people who have suffered at the expense of the western-Saudi alliance, he asserts: "Hence, it is essential to hit the main enemy who has divided the umma into small fragmented countries and pushed it into a state of confusion over the past few decades."[40] Since the "West" has weakened and divided the global Muslim community, it is necessary, he argues, to retaliate against this injustice. His solution is a call to arms:

> Today your brothers and sons, the sons of the Two Holy Places, have started their jihad in the cause of Allah to expel the occupying enemy from the Country of the Two Holy Places. . . . The mujahidin, your brothers and sons, request that you support them in every possible way by supplying them with the necessary information, material and arms.[41]

From the above passage, it is apparent that this work of the *mujahideen* was already underway, and what he requests from the global Muslim community is its further support. The *mujahideen* had been on active duty since their time in Afghanistan, as he explains later in the speech—"For more than a decade they carried arms on their shoulders in Afghanistan, and they have made vows to Allah that as long as they are alive, they will continue to carry arms against you until you are—God willing—expelled, defeated, and humiliated."[42] In this discussion of the *mujahideen*, there is no distinction drawn between their work conducted in Afghanistan, which was supported by the U.S., and the call to fight against the U.S. In bin Laden's view, the goal of the global *mujahideen* is simply to restore the unity of the community:

> My Muslim brothers of the world: your brothers in Palestine and in the Land of the Two Holy Places are calling for your help. . . . O you horses (soldiers) of Allah, ride and march on. This is the time of hardship, so be tough. And know that your gathering and cooperation to liberate the sanctuaries of Islam is the step toward unifying the word of the umma under the banner of 'No God but Allah.'[43]

The call for political and social unity is expressed in terms of the goal of God's sovereignty, "No God but Allah." As a statement on its own, it doesn't sound that different from the objective of the Islamists. However, this mandate is not motivated by concern for civilizational decline or the desire for an Islamic nation-state, as for the Islamists. Moreover, the agents who are implored to conduct this work are saddled with tasks much heavier and violent than that of cultural and state transformation, as Qutb outlined for the vanguard. The *mujahideen* that bin Laden calls upon were already radicalized soldiers who had been fully inducted into the ideology of destruction from the period of the Afghan War. In this regard, they represent the dark turn of the vanguard mission. The prophetic aspirations to enlighten the Muslim community and lead the Muslim community to a new Islamic state morphed into a bleak and broken project of destruction—destruction of the "West" but also destruction of the lives of the vanguard/*mujahideen* themselves.

Conclusion

The modernist definition of Islam as unity has left its mark in the post-1950 period as a call for an ethical corrective. Fazlur Rahman sought to salvage the Quran from what he saw as reductive Islamist and legalistic frameworks. He proposed a new understanding of the Quran as internally coherent. According to Rahman, it was possible to apply practical insights from the Quran—especially those pertaining to the Prophet's life—to present circumstances in a comprehensive manner. Although his position was not explicitly political or immediately nation-state-directed, it was no doubt a response to the political and legal state of affairs in the 1960s Pakistan—in particular the Islamist thought of Mawdudi and the legalistic interpretations of the Quran endorsed by clerics. Shariati too was a proponent of the Prophet's early life as a model ethical community, defined not in Islamist terms of God's sovereignty but in the form of an economically, socially, and racially equal society. His Marxist ideas about Islam travelled to South Africa in the 1970s, and by the time Muslims initiated anti-apartheid activism his writings were in full circulation. *Tawhid* in particular functioned as an anchoring concept for Muslim activists. As I discussed at some length above, *tawhid* served a twofold function for the Muslim minority community in apartheid South Africa: it represented the fundamental value of the early community of Islam, but also signified the goal and ideal toward which Muslim progressives orientated themselves in the anti-apartheid struggle.

It is possible to make the argument that Al Qaeda's mission was a deeply ethical project as well. Bin Laden certainly made a case about the suffering of Muslim people in Muslim lands at the hands of the West in terms of injustice and called on the *mujahideen* to fight on ethical grounds for the restoration of unity and God's sovereignty. This millenarian mission sharply broke from the beliefs, practices, and leadership protocols of modernists and Islamists. Mawdudi and Qutb proposed the role of the vanguard to undertake *intra*-Muslim transformation in the form of either the unity of the community or a possible Islamic state—both of which were ideas that were tied to an older history and lineage of modernism analyzed in this volume. Al Qaeda's *mujahideen*, by contrast, were not rooted in any specific region, nor were their beliefs and practices tied to any aspect of Islam's cumulative tradition. Though ungrounded in any specific territory, the nation-state was very much central to Al Qaeda's formation and its *jihadist* mission. Al Qaeda was the product of the Cold War, created through funding from a coalition of global forces who supported *jihad* against the Soviets. This *jihad*, initially targeted against the Soviets, was later redirected to the superpower nation-state of the U.S. on grounds of ethics, retribution, and justice.

NOTES

Introduction

1. In February 1989, *The New York Times* published an op-ed by S. Nomanul Haq, who was a tutor at Harvard at the time. The op-ed was a criticism of Salman Rushdie, in which the author argued that Rushdie should have known what the Muslim reaction to *The Satanic Verses* was going to be since "The Muslim nations have not gone through the turmoils of the Enlightenment and they have seen no scientific revolution; their sensibilities are different."—S. Nomanul Haq, "Salman Rushdie, Blame Yourself," *The New York Times* (23 February 1989), https://archive .nytimes.com/www.nytimes.com/books/99/04/18/specials/rushdie-haq.html, accessed on 15 February 2022. This debate about the need for Islam's reformation didn't begin with the *Charlie Hebdo* incident, but it did bring it into focus again, especially in the post-9/11 world.

2. Mehdi Hasan, "Why Islam doesn't need a reformation," *The Guardian* (17 May 2015), https://www.theguardian.com/commentisfree/2015/may/17/islam -reformation-extremism-muslim-martin-luther-europe, accessed on 28 January 2022.

3. Albert Hourani's *Arabic Thought in the Liberal Age, 1798–1939* (Cambridge: Cambridge University Press, 1983; first published in 1962), Malcolm Kerr's *Islamic Reform: The Political and Legal Theories of Muhammad 'Abduh and Rashid Rida* (Berkeley: University of California Press, 1966), Aziz Ahmad's *Islamic Modernism in India and Pakistan, 1857–1964* (Oxford: Oxford University Press, 1967), and most recently Muhammad Qasim Zaman's *Modern Islamic Thought in a Radical Age* (Cambridge: Cambridge University Press, 2012). Zaman's 2012 intervention provides a much-needed update to this older set of books on the topic. He opens up and deepens the debate about modern Muslim reform by including the contributions and scholarly activity of traditionally educated scholars, the *'ulama*. While my book overlaps with Zaman's in terms of the general time period, addresses some similar topics such as debates and critiques about reform among seminal political and intellectual figures, and raises similar questions about authority, my approach and subject of investigation are quite different.

4. Irfan Ahmad, *Religion as Critique: Islamic Critical Thinking from Mecca to the Marketplace* (Chapel Hill: UNC Press, 2017); Khurram Hussain, *Islam as Critique: Sayyid Ahmad Khan and the Challenge of Modernity* (London: Bloomsbury Academic, 2019).

5. In many ways, my line of argument about *tawhid* as political unity dovetails with what Cemil Aydin has argued in his recent publication, *The Idea of the Muslim World* (Cambridge: Harvard University Press, 2017). Herein Aydin contends that the idea of a unified Muslim community began to develop only in the nineteenth century—the height of European hegemony—and reached its peak on the eve of World War I and the ensuing abolition of the Ottoman Caliphate in 1924. It was in roughly this period from the 1870s to 1924 that Muslims began to write about Islam as a unified religious tradition in civilizational terms. Muslims only began to imagine themselves as a global political community in response to European representations of Muslim racial inferiority and European and Muslim theories of civilizational decline. As part of this campaign for Muslim unity, Muslim modernists wrote books that elevated the importance of certain texts they believed represented the essence of Islam and in turn denounced vernacular Muslim practices. They either ignored or wrote out the diverse practices in the history of Islam for the purpose of establishing an idea of unity that would allegedly empower them.

6. It is important to note that this preoccupation with unity is very much a modern concern. Thomas Bauer's recently published book, *A Culture of Ambiguity,* demonstrates how over many centuries, in classical and modern Islamic history, there was an active tension between the desire for uncontested truths on the one hand, and a tolerance for ambiguity and complexity, on the other hand. He explores this tension with reference to Quranic exegesis, law, various literary genres, and attitudes toward religious minorities. He argues that it was in fact the encounter with the modern West that led to the rise of both secular liberal and Islamist ideas—both of which rejected the historical and cultural ambiguity of the Islamic tradition. Thomas Bauer, *A Culture of Ambiguity: An Alternative History of Islam* (New York: Columbia University Press, 2021).

7. W. C. Smith, *The Meaning and End of Religion* (Minneapolis: Fortress Press, 1991).

8. Roxanne L. Euben and Muhammad Qasim Zaman, eds., *Princeton Readings in Islamist Thought: Texts and Contexts from al-Banna to Bin Laden* (Princeton: Princeton University Press, 2009), 6–7.

9. Seema Alavi, *Muslim Cosmopolitanism in the Age of Empire* (Cambridge: Harvard University Press, 2015), 33.

10. Spencer Lavan, *The Ahmadiyyah Movement: A History and Perspective* (New Delhi: Manohar Book Service, 1974).

11. Although Mirza Ghulam Ahmad made it clear that he was not a law-bearing prophet but a manifestation (*buruz*) of Muhammad's prophethood, his prophetic

claims were still contentious. For the specific terminology of the Mirza's prophe-thood, see Yohanan Friedmann, *Prophecy Continuous: Aspects of Ahmadi Religious Thought and Its Medieval Background* (Berkeley: University of California Press, 1989).

12. Hadrat Mirza Ghulam Ahmad, *The British Government and Jihad* (Islam International Publications, 2006), 36.

13. Teena Purohit, *The Aga Khan Case: Religion and Identity in Colonial India* (Cambridge: Harvard University Press, 2012).

14. The foundations of western esoteric thought—stoicism, Hermeticism, Gnosticism, and neoplatonism—can be traced to antiquity. However, the western esoteric tradition only developed as a new "semi autonomous domain" starting in the twelfth century, but most forcefully in the fourteenth century. It is important to remember that this break did not manifest itself as a clear dichotomy between the "secular" and the "religious"—but, rather, as a reordering or reconstitution of domains that were connected, especially so with the revival of Hermeticism that began in the fifteenth century. The point here is that in the European context the esoteric traditions of Hermeticism and Gnosticism were not supplanted or replaced with the discovery of science. Although enlightenment thinkers no longer acknowledged a continuity between the physical world and magical/esoteric worlds, the world of magic did not disappear. It became reconstituted as part of its own domain, still connected to the physical world. Antoine Faivre, cited in W. J. Hannegraff, *New Age Religion and Western Culture: Esotericism in the Mirror of Secular Thought* (New York: SUNY Press, 1997), 386–388.

Chapter 1: Jamal al-Din al-Afghani, Sayyid Ahmad Khan, and "Neicheri" Transgression

1. Albert Hourani, *Arabic Thought*, 125.

2. "The attack . . . was actually directed against Sayyid Ahmad Khan's belief in cooperation with the British . . . and against his [Sayyid Ahmad Khan's] willingness to borrow as much as possible from the British and to openly abandon much of the Indian Muslim heritage, thus ridding the Indian Muslims of a source of nationalist, anti-imperialist pride." Nikki R. Keddie, *An Islamic Response to Imperialism: Political and Religious Writings of Sayyid Jamal ad-Din "al-Afghani"* (Berkeley: University of California Press, 1968), 67.

3. Ibid., 5.

4. Ibid., 5–8.

5. Ibid., 14.

6. It is worthy to note that he adopted the language of Tanzimat reform even though he was never officially aligned with the Tanzimat reformers. Ibid, 16.

7. Ibid., 16–17.

8. Jamal al-Din al-Afghani, "The Truth about the *Neicheri* Sect and an Explanation of the *Neicheris*," in Keddie, *An Islamic Response to Imperialism*, 130.

9. Ibid., 131.

10. Ibid., 139–141.

11. Ibid., 142.

12. Ibid., 142.

13. Nikki Keddie has argued that Afghani's active campaigning for pan-Islam, that is, the unification of the Muslim world against the imperial West, was shaped by the political climate that motivated famous Young Ottomans such as Namik Kemal to defend Islam and pan-Islam in the 1870s, such as the increased British and French pressure on Egypt and North Africa, appeals to Ottomans from Central Asia during the Russian conquests in the 1860s, and Indian Muslims under British attack. Keddie, *An Islamic Response to Imperialism*, 22.

14. Abdulhamid was the most outspoken of the Ottoman leaders on this position of pan-Islamism, having made the explicit case that the Ottoman sultan was the caliph of Islam. Keddie writes: "With the growing of the pan-Islamic sentiment in the Muslim world form the late 1870's on, it was natural for Afghani to get the idea of attaching himself to the man who claimed to be Caliph and leader of all the Muslims." She explains further, "It was only in the 1880's that Afghani began to write pan-Islamic appeals and also to take care to present himself as an orthodox Muslim, and it may be posited that these two phenomena are closely connected." Nikki R. Keddie, "The Pan-Islamic Appeal: Afghani and Abdülhamid II," *Middle Eastern Studies* 3, no. 1 (1966): 48.

15. She outlines the specific aspects of this religiopolitical ideology, the most important being the anti-imperial "nascent nationalism": "Pan-Islam had several likely points of appeal for Afghani. It met his genuine concern over European and especially British attacks on Muslim countries. It provided a likely vehicle to ingratiate himself with the most powerful and independent Muslim ruler, Abdulhamid. Like Afghani's earlier use of the methods and arguments sanctioned by the Muslim philosophers, pan-Islam had the advantage of containing both a traditional element and an aspect which appealed to new needs. Calls for Holy War and a defense of Islam had a strong traditional basis, as did the notion of restoring a single Islamic state under a revived caliphate. Both ideas, however, appealed particularly to a newer feeling—a kind of nascent nationalism among the Muslims." She then explains that Italian and German nationalisms were certainly influential on pan-Islamic thinking, later quoting Bernard Lewis on the point that for Afghani, Islam was more of a civilization than a faith, and its basic demand was for loyalty rather than piety. Ibid., 50.

16. Afghani, "The Truth about the *Neicheri* Sect," 169–170.

17. Ibid., 170.

18. Ibid., 171.

19. Ibid., 172.

20. This specific historical connection allows him to make a separate but related argument about Islam's inherent rationality, which follows the Guizot reference: "The Islamic religion is the only religion that censures belief without proof and the following of conjectures; reproves blind submission; seeks to show proof of things to its followers; everywhere addresses itself to reason." Ibid., 172.

21. Ibid., 148.

22. Ibid., 148.

23. Ibid., 154–155.

24. Ibid., 155–156.

25. Ibid., 156.

26. Ibid., 158.

27. Ibid., 160. This group is the most out of place in his analysis. Whereas the previous bands of "*neicheris*" were tied in some way to religious beliefs that were considered heretical—Zorastrians, Ismailis, and Bahais—here the accusation of *neicheri* practices are defined as straightforwardly political acts that contravened the authority of the caliph, Abdulhamid. Keddie explains that Afghani is probably referring to Suleyman Pasha and Midhat Pasha, whom Abdulhamid accused of treason, forcing one to exile and the other to death. It is likely, as Keddie has explained elsewhere ("The Pan-Islamic Appeal"), that the ascription of "*neicheri*" to these military leaders whom Abdulhamid had exiled was one of the ways in which Afghani hoped to curry favor with the Sultan.

28. Afghani, "The Truth about the *Neicheri* Sect," 173.

29. Ibid., 155–156.

30. Jamal al-Din al-Afghani, "Answer of Jamal ad-Din to Renan," in Keddie, *An Islamic Response to Imperialism*, 183.

31. Ibid., 183.

32. Ibid., 187.

33. Jamal al-Din al-Afghani, "The Materialists in India," in Keddie, *An Islamic Response to Imperialism*, 177.

34. Ibid., 177.

35. Ibid., 178.

36. According to Afghani, *neicheris* spoke to "wicked souls whose final object is the attainment of bestial desires"—see Afghani, "The Truth about the *Neicheri* Sect," 151.

37. Afghani, "The Materialists in India," 178.

38. Ibid., 179.

39. Aziz Ahmad, "Sayyid Aḥmad Khān, Jamāl Al-Dīn Al-Afghānī and Muslim India," *Studia Islamica*, no. 13 (1960): 62.

40. Ibid., 65. Ahmad explains that Afghani's accusation that Sayyid Ahmad Khan sought rewards from the British is not substantiated by the writings of Indian Muslims, and in fact many of his supporters have made the argument that he refused to

accept confiscated property of other Muslims and that in fact he worked hard to refute anti-Muslim sentiments of civil servant historians such as Muir and Sir William Hunter (see ibid., 66).

41. Wilfred Cantwell Smith, *Islam in Modern History* (Princeton, N.J.: Princeton University Press, 1957), 49.

42. Jamal al-Din al-Afghani, "Lecture on Teaching and Learning," in Keddie, *An Islamic Response to Imperialism*, 102.

43. Ibid., 103.

44. Ibid., 105.

45. Ibid., 106–107.

46. Ibid., 107.

47. Ibid., 108.

48. Sayyid Ahmad Khan, "Lecture on Islam," in *Modernist Islam 1840–1940: A Sourcebook*, ed. Charles Kurzman (Oxford: Oxford University Press, 2002), 293.

49. Ibid., 293.

50. Ibid., 293.

51. Ibid., 294.

52. Ibid., 294–295.

53. Ibid., 296.

54. Jamal al-Din al-Afghani, "Commentary on the Commentator," in Keddie, *An Islamic Response to Imperialism*, 123.

55. Ibid., 126–127.

56. Ibid., 125.

57. Nikki R. Keddie, *Sayyid Jamal ad-Din "al-Afghani": A Political Biography* (Berkeley: University of California Press, 1972), 170.

58. Afghani, "Commentary on the Commentator," 125.

59. Keddie, *An Islamic Response to Imperialism*, 82.

60. The editor of this paper, Henri Rochefort, in fact writes about Afghani in his own autobiography and praises Afghani for his ability to speak to the masses and how he "developed in them the spirit of insurrection." Elie Kedourie, *Afghani and ʿAbduh: An Essay on Religious Unbelief and Political Activism in Modern Islam* (New York: The Humanities Press, 1966), 47.

61. Afghani, "Le Mahdi," *L'Intransigeant* (December 17, 1883), quoted in Keddie, *Sayyid Jamal ad-Din "al-Afghani"*, 207. The preceding discussion relies on Keddie, 205–207.

62. According to the editor of the journal, Henri Rochefort, Afghani not only asserted that the Sudanese Mahdi—who had never left Sudan—was a student of his at Al-Azhar, but also promised another journalist named Olivier Pain that he could help him enter Mahdist territory. Pain was not only unwelcome but was imprisoned as a spy, despite his proclamations of support for Mahdism. He eventually died from

maltreatment and disease in 1884 in El Obeid. See Kedourie, *Afghani and ʿAbduh*, 47. The point here is that Rochefort describes al-Afghani as "a reformer and revolutionist . . . a descendant of Mahomet, and himself regarded as somewhat of a prophet." Quoted in Keddie, *Sayyid Jamal ad-Din "al-Afghani"*, 211.

63. Kedourie, *Afghani and ʿAbduh*, 46–55; Keddie, *Sayyid Jamal ad-Din "al-Afghani"*, 205–214.

64. Keddie describes how Prince Halim, the last son of the early nineteenth century Egyptian leader Muhammad Ali, had been suddenly excluded from khedivate succession. Halim therefore turned to the masonic lodge as a place to plan to get back his succession rights—Keddie, *Sayyid Jamal ad-Din "al-Afghani"*, 92–93.

65. Ibid., 92–93. Keddie makes the point (as in her overall argument about Afghani's writings on religion) that Afghani's interest in Freemasonry was primarily political—Keddie, *Biography*, 93.

66. My discussion in this paragraph follows Keddie, *Sayyid Jamal ad-Din "al-Afghani"*, 92–96. Keddie notes that the development of the new "political journalism" was only made possible by the freedom of press granted by Ismail, who encouraged Syrians to help make Egypt an epicenter of Arabic journalism.

67. According to Karim Wissa, in the period of 1798–1921, the four most important leaders of the Grand Orient National d-Egypt (GONE) were Prince ʿAbd al-Halim (1867–1868), the youngest son of Muhammad Ali Pasha, whose position was taken by Ismail; an Italian Salvatore Avventore Zola (1873–?); Jamal al-Din al-Afghani (1878–1879); and Idris Ragheb (1889–1922), the successor to the Khedive Muhammad Tawfiq. Wissa claims that Afghani consciously chose a "European-structured" organization to engage in his political activities and gives a more specific trajectory for Afghani's connections to the various lodges: he was first a member of the Italian masonic lodge in Cairo, then the British-influenced lodge "Star of the East," and in 1875 he joined the United Grand Lodge of England and became its chairman in 1878—see Karim Wissa, "Freemasonry in Egypt 1798–1921: A Study in Cultural and Political Encounters," *Bulletin (British Society for Middle Eastern Studies)* 16, no. 2 (1989): 147–149.

68. Kedourie, *Afghani and ʿAbduh*, 21.

69. Carmela Baffioni, "Ikhwân al-Safâ'," *The Stanford Encyclopedia of Philosophy* (Fall 2016 Edition), ed. Edward N. Zalta, https://plato.stanford.edu/archives /fall2016/entries/ikhwan-al-safa/, accessed on 16 February 2022. Abbas Hamdani, "The Name 'Ikhwan Al-Safa,'" *Digest of Middle East Studies* 8, no. 2 (1999): 7. Baffioni writes that the "encyclopedia consists of 52 treatises divided into four sections— introductory, natural, psycho-rational, and metaphysical-theological sciences." Although there is no official consensus on the specific theological orientation of the *Ikhwan*, "the text's hierarchical structure of the universe, references to septenary cycles, distinction between elect and masses, and the use of Ismaʿili symbols" all

suggest an Ismaili orientation. According to Abbas Hamdani, the brethren were not just intellectuals but also political activists who were involved in a secret underground movement during the period of the Abbasid Caliphate. He contends that the Brethren of Purity was a group of thinkers working for the Fatimid *dawa*, similar to other Ismaili *dais* that were operating in Khurasan, Iran, southern Iraq, Syria, and North Africa at the time. The goal of the Brethren, according to the treatise, was to hold gatherings in secrecy, study the sciences and mysteries of knowledge, and to "know that for every State there is a time when it begins, a purpose to which it aspires, and an end—in which it finishes" (Hamdani, "The Name 'Ikhwan Al-Safa,'" 5).

70. Rashid Rida's obituary for Aghani in *Al-Manar*, vol. 8 (1905): 402–404, quoted in Kedourie, *Afghani and 'Abduh*, 22.

71. Kedourie, *Afghani and 'Abduh*, 9.

72. 'Abduh, "*Risalat al-waridat*," quoted in Kedourie, *Afghani and 'Abduh*, 10.

73. Muhammad 'Abduh, letter to Afghani, in Kedourie, *Afghani and 'Abduh*, 66. Rashid Rida was also scandalized by the terms 'Abduh uses to describe Afghani (Kedourie, *Afghani and 'Abduh*, 10).

74. Keddie, *Sayyid Jamal ad-Din "al-Afghani"*, 19.

75. Ibid., 20.

76. Baffioni, "Ikhwan al-Safa."

Chapter 2: Muhammad 'Abduh, Rashid Rida, and Bahai "Esotericists"

1. Oliver Scharbrodt, *Islam and the Baha'i Faith: A Comparative Study of Muhammad 'Abduh and 'Abdul-Baha 'Abbas* (London: Routledge, 2008), 49.

2. Scharbrodt, *Islam and the Baha'i Faith*, 50–51.

3. Itzchak Weismann, "The Sociology of 'Islamic Modernism': Muhammad 'Abduh, the National Public Sphere and the Colonial State," *Maghreb Review: Majallat Al-Maghrib* 32, no. 1 (2007): 104–121.

4. Ibid.

5. Ibid.

6. 'Abduh shared Afghani's vision that world politics was a struggle between an aggressive West and defenseless East. M. A. Zaki Badawi, *The Reformers of Egypt* (London: Biddles Ltd., 1976), 40–41.

7. Charles Clarence Adams writes specifically about 'Abduh's teaching of Ibn Khaldun: "Not only was the teaching of this work a new departure in Egypt, but the method of teaching it was also unheard of hitherto. The young professor took the ideas of the great historian on the causes of the rise and fall of nations, the principles of civilization and organization of human society, and made them a point of departure for adding ideas of his own on political and social affairs, drawn from modern

works, and applied the whole in a practical manner to the case of his own country." Charles Clarence Adams, *Islam and Modernism in Egypt* (London: Taylor & Francis, 2000), 45.

8. Jamal al-Din al-Afghani, "Answer to Renan," in *Modernist Islam 1840–1940: A Sourcebook*, ed. Charles Kurzman (New York: Oxford University Press, 2002), 108.

9. ʿAbduh's adoption of the Guizot framework could have been learned from Afghani or through Tahtawi, who commissioned its Arabic translation in 1857. Albert Hourani, *Arabic Thought in the Liberal Age 1798–1939* (Cambridge: Cambridge University Press, 1983), 132.

10. Ibid., 136.

11. For example, when the nationalist press attacked a Copt who was then Under-Secretary for Justice, ʿAbduh intervened to point out that criticism of one individual should not lead to an attack on the entire community, and that Muslims should cooperate with and accept help from non-Muslims. Ibid., 156.

12. Muhammad ʿAbduh, *The Theology of Unity*, trans. Ishaq Musaʾad and Kenneth Cragg (New York: Books for Libraries Press, 1980), 29.

13. Ibid., 30–31.

14. Ibid., 32.

15. Ibid., 33.

16. Ibid., 36.

17. Ibid., 39.

18. Ibid., 151.

19. Ibid., 151.

20. Ibid., 153.

21. Jamal al-Din al-Afghani, "The Truth about the *Neicheri* Sect and an Explanation of the *Neicheris*," in Nikki R. Keddie, *An Islamic Response to Imperialism: Political and Religious Writings of Sayyid Jamal ad-Din al-Afghani* (Berkeley: University of California Press, 1968), 173.

22. Juan Cole, "Muhammad ʿAbduh and Rashid Rida: A Dialogue on the Bahaʾi Faith," originally published in *World Order* 15, nos. 3–4 (1981): 15. Available at https://bahai-library.com/pdf/c/cole_abduh_rida_dialogue.pdf, accessed on 3 July 2018.

23. Cole writes: "In short, Bahaullah in his Ottoman exile developed a coherent program of institutional reform for societies that found themselves faced with the new world of the industrial revolution, the mass politics of the French Revolution, and the rise of industrial capital as the dominating factor in world affairs." Ibid., 7.

24. Ibid., 7.

25. Ibid., 9.

26. He believed that the Bahai were reformers of Shii Islam and fully supported Bahaʾuʾllah's reform projects, such as a new law that limited the number of wives to two rather than the traditional four supported by the Quran. Ibid., 10.

27. According to Cole, it demonstrates "a wide divergence in their outlooks and tendencies of thought." Ibid., 8.

28. Ibid., 12.

29. Ibid., 12.

30. Ibid., 13–14.

31. Regarding this term "miraculous rational faculty," Cole, by the way, explains that Rida made the following interjection in his notes: "It would have been more right to have said, "unusual psychological states and strange statements." Ibid., 13n23.

32. Ibid., 14.

33. Ibid., 13.

34. Ibid., 14.

35. Ibid., 14n24.

36. There is a long history of Sunni polemics against the *batinniyya* Ismailis that invokes the language of deception. Afghani deploys the same logic in his argument against the *neicheris* in the "Refutation." Rida references the Ismailis in his case against the Bahais, specifically with this issue of how they spread their religious message, what he calls "propaganda."

37. Cole, "A Dialogue on the Baha'i Faith," 15.

38. Rida writes: "(Then he expanded on this and referred to the destruction of households resulting from polygamy through the extension of the mutual hostility of the two wives, or more, to their children, making it impossible to train them up properly. He said in regard to sultáns and rulers:) 'If this large number of women is in any of their palaces, when will their thoughts become purified such that their deliberation upon the affairs of the Muslim community will improve?'" Ibid., 15.

39. Ibid., 16.

40. Ibid., 13.

41. 'Abduh, *Theology of Unity*, 130–131.

42. Hourani has argued that for all three, "it is impossible to exaggerate the importance of unity, and the scandal of disunity." He remarks further that unity for them was neither an affective unity nor was its ideal a single Muslim state, but "the agreement of hearts of those who accepted each other as believers and dwelt together in mutual tolerance, and the active cooperation of all in carrying out the commandments of religion." Hourani, *Arabic Thought*, 229.

43. Juan Cole, "Rashid Rida on the Bahai Faith: A Utilitarian Theory of the Spread of Religions," *Arab Studies Quarterly* 5, no. 3 (1983): 283–284.

44. Ibid., 284.

45. Ibid., 285–287. Juan Cole points out that there was, on Rida's part, a misreading of the Bahai faith because he did not draw the distinction between the early Bab ideas and those of the Bahai religion. The latter was rationalistic and modernist, and

it was these specific features of the religion that attracted modernists such as ʿAbduh as well as intellectuals such as Mustafa Kamil (1874–1908).

46. Cole contends that Rida's account of the Bahais is shortsighted and does not take into account both the early period of Babism in Iran, which included members of the Shaykhi ʿulama, as well as the later modernist development of ʿAbdul Baha, which drew the Azharite scholars as well as modernists such as ʿAbduh. Ibid., 288.

47. "Rashid Rida | Islamic Scholar," Encyclopedia Britannica (August 28, 2012), https://www.britannica.com/biography/Rashid-Rida.

48. For example, the Druze supported the British, the Maronites the French, and the Sunnis the Ottomans. Cole explains, "Given Rida's loyalty to the Ottoman caliphate, the Western imperialist connections of some of these millets were especially galling to him." Ibid., 289.

49. Hourani, Arabic Thought, 224–225.

50. Rashid Rida, al-Manar wa 'l-Azhar (Cairo: 1934–1935), 171–2, cited in Hourani, Arabic Thought, 225.

51. Hourani, Arabic Thought, 232. Rida attributed this second dangerous form of mysticism to Zoroastrianism, which he calls a religion that was meant to "corrupt the religion of the Arabs and pull down the pillars of their kingdom by internal dissension so that by this means they could restore the rule of the Zoroastrians and the domination of their religion to which the Arabs had put an end in Islam." Rashid Rida, Al-Manar 27 (1927–8), 1ff. Cited in Hourani, Arabic Thought, 232.

52. "Rashid Rida," Encyclopedia Britannica; Hourani, Arabic Thought, 230.

53. Rashid Rida, "Renewal, Renewing, and Renewers," trans. Emad Eldin Shahin, in Modernist Islam 1840–1940: A Sourcebook, ed. Charles Kurzman (Oxford: Oxford University Press, 2002), 78–80.

54. Ibid., 80.

55. Ibid., 84.

56. Ibid., 84.

57. When ʿAbdul Baha came to visit ʿAbduh in Beirut, ʿAbdul Baha was held as a prisoner by the Ottoman Empire and stationed in Akka, Palestine, on account of Bahai beliefs that first, Baha'u'llah received a new revelation from God that abrogated the laws of the Quran and, second, the teachings of the various prophets represent the progressive unfolding of religious truth according to the needs of the time. ʿAbdul Baha laid out these teachings after he was released from Ottoman imprisonment in 1908, after the Young Turk revolution. William McCants, "I Never Understood Any of This from ʿAbbas Effendi': Muhammad ʿAbduh's Knowledge of the Bahai Teachings and His Friendship with ʿAbdul-Baha ʿAbbas," in Studies in Modern Religions, Religious Movements and the Babi-Bahai Faiths, ed. Moshe Sharon (Boston: Brill, 2004), 277–278.

58. Rashid Rida, Ta'rikh al-Ustadh al-Imam al-Shaykh Muhammad ʿAbduh, vol. 1 (Cairo: al-Manàr Press, 1931), 407, quoted in McCants, "I Never Understood," 277–278.

59. Jamal al-Din al-Afghani, "The Truth about the *Neicheri* Sect and an Explanation of the *Neicheris*," in Keddie, *An Islamic Response to Imperialism,* quoted in Mc-Cants, "I Never Understood," 280.

60. Jamal al-Din al-Afghani, *Al-Radd 'ala al-dahriyyan,* trans. Muhammad 'Abduh [and Abì Turab] (Cairo: Dar al-Hilal, 1973), quoted in McCants, "I Never Understood," 280.

61. This is attested to in letters of correspondence between 'Abduh and 'Abdul Baha. In a letter 'Abduh writes to 'Abdul Baha in 1877, he addresses 'Abdul Baha as the "perfect master" (*al-mawla al-kamil*) and the "proof that the latter generation surpasses its forebears" (*hujjat al-awakhir 'ala al-awail*) (285). Moreover, he writes of his longing (*shawqi*) for 'Abdul Baha and conveys his wish to visit him on account of a "need to be illumined by your light." McCants, "I Never Understood," 287, 295.

Chapter 3: Muhammad Iqbal on the Question of Ahmadi Exclusion and Ismaili Inclusion

1. Muhammad Iqbal, *The Reconstruction of Religious Thought in Islam* (Stanford: Stanford University Press, 2012), 142.

2. Iqbal, *Reconstruction,* 116–117.

3. Iqbal uses Denison to establish the coordinates of his argument: the opposition between Christianity and Islam. In this instance, culture and civilization are interchangeable, but it is important to understand first the difference between culture and civilization broadly speaking and in relation to Iqbal. Amongst sociologists and theorists of culture there is a working assumption that civilization refers to technical, material, and social phenomena whereas culture is more refined: artistic, spiritual, and intellectual. For the most part, Iqbal does not use the language of civilization to define and describe Islam. He is far more interested in the intellectual and spiritual aspects of culture rather than the technical and material aspects of civilization.

4. Iqbal's preference for culture over civilization is corroborated by Javed Majeed's point that Iqbal is not interested in the practical application of science and technology or religiouus practices on the ground. Iqbal's focus on science, for example, stems from a theoretical interest in the nature of physics as well as larger themes of evolution. Like many other modernist Muslim thinkers, he posits that Islam had intervened prior to modern western science, i.e., with Asharite atomism, and also that, for example, theories of physics and evolution can be reconciled in the modern times with a spiritual way of living. This way of thinking about civilization/culture casts Iqbal's *Reconstruction* as much more speculative, "fluid and at times fragmented and improvisational" in style. Javed Majeed, "Introduction to Muhammad Iqbal's *The Reconstruction of Religious Thought in Islam,*" in ibid., xx–xxi.

5. Iqbal, *Reconstruction,* 117.

6. This reconstructed selfhood is key, according to Majeed, for Iqbal's reconstruction of Islam that is defined by a "modernizing anti-colonial self-affirmation." One way to think about a spiritual Islam as he conceives of it is as a possibility for self-cultivation. Majeed has argued that Iqbal's conception of "khudi" or self is at the center of his understanding of Islam. In Iqbal's view, Majeed argues, the self, as it approaches God, becomes more and more individuated and self-aware (as opposed to any kind of merging with the divine, as many Sufis explain through the concept of fana). This idea of selfhood is applied to God as well, who, like the human individual, is also an "ego." In this regard, humans and God are conceived of through the same terms. The difference is that the latter possesses greater degrees of selfhood. In this regard, there is room for the development of a new interpretation of the Sufi idea of "insan-e-kamil" or "perfect-man." Majeed, "Introduction," xxii.

7. Iqbal, *Reconstruction*, 117.

8. Ibid., 122.

9. Ibid, 117.

10. Ibid., 117–120.

11. Ibid., 120–121.

12. Reinhard Schulze, "Mass Culture and Islamic Cultural Production in 19th Century Middle East," in *Mass Culture, Popular Culture, and Social Life in the Middle East*, eds. G. Stauth and S. Zubaida (Boulder: Westview Press, 1987), 201.

13. Iqbal, by contrast, rarely engaged other Muslims, corroborating Shulze's points about how secularized elites were concerned more with European thought than with other Muslims.

14. Iqbal, *Reconstruction*, 122.

15. Islam is described in the following way: "a unity of the eternal verities of freedom, equality, and solidarity," which has "no fatherland." Ibid., 123–124.

16. Ibid., 124.

17. Ibid., 124.

18. Ibid., 124–129.

19. Muhammad Iqbal, "Islam as an Ethical and Political Ideal," *Columbia University*, http://www.columbia.edu/itc/mealac/pritchett/00islamlinks/txt_iqbal_1908 .html, accessed on 8 June 2022.

20. Ibid., 122.

21. Ibid., 124.

22. Muhammad Iqbal, *Islam and Ahmadism* (Lahore: Ashraf Printing Press, 1980), 66.

23. Ibid., 17.

24. In 1914, the Ahmadi movement was divided into two factions, the Qadianis and Lahoris. The Qadiani Ahmadis held that Mirza Ghulam Ahmad was a prophet, whereas the Lahori Ahmadis believed that he was only a renewer, *mujaddid*, not

prophet (*nabi*) or messiah (*mahdi*). For history of the Ahmadis, see Lavan, *The Ahmadiyyah Movement*. Although many Ahmadis claim that Iqbal too was an Ahmadi, Iqbal's writings do not indicate that this was the case. He was, however, especially early in his career, supportive of their organization and development, having praised the movement in his 1910 speech at Aligarh. Lavan, *The Ahmadiyyah Movement*, 172.

25. "The simple faith of Muhammad is based on two propositions—that God is One, and that Muhammad is the last of the line of those holy men who have appeared from time to time in all countries and in all ages to guide mankind to the right ways of living." Iqbal, *Islam and Ahmadism*, 17.

26. Ibid., 9–10.

27. Ibid., 15–17.

28. Ibid., 17–18.

29. Ibid., 22.

30. Ibid., 23–24.

31. Ibid., 21.

32. Georg Simmel, *Essays on Religion* (New Haven: Yale University Press, 1987), 114–115.

33. George Zito, "Toward a Sociology of Heresy," *Sociological Analysis* 44, no. 2 (1983): 125.

34. Lavan, *The Ahmadiyyah Movement*, 172.

35. Even in the literature on early Islam we find evidence of the idea that heresy and apostasy were functions of group dynamics instead of theological disputes. For instance, Frank Griffel writes in his article on al-Shafiʿi, Ghazali, and apostasy: "the status of a believer, which in those early days meant the membership of the community of Islam, was lost if a sin was committed or a key tenet on which the community agreed was denied. Membership of the community . . . is the oldest expression of Islamic soteriology."—Frank Griffel, "Toleration and Exclusion: al-Shafiʿi and al-Ghazali on the Treatment of Apostates," *Bulletin of the School of Oriental and African Studies* 64, no. 3 (2001): 339–354; 339. In other words, apostasy ought to be thought of in political and social terms, not exclusively within theological or doctrinal frameworks.

36. According to Peter Berger, there is a major difference between expressions and declarations of heresy in the modern versus pre-modern period. Berger makes the point that the existence of heresy in contemporary times is problematic insofar as modernity itself is predicated on the heretical ethos. He draws a fundamental contrast between heresy in early Christianity, where restricting choice (hairesis) was necessary for the existence of heresy, and heresy in the modern period where choice is the basis of social existence. "Modernity multiplies choices and concomitantly reduces the scope of what is experienced as destiny. In the matter of religion, as indeed in other areas of human life and thought, this means that the modern individual is faced not just with the opportunity but with the necessity to make

choices as to his beliefs. This fact constitutes the heretical imperative in the contemporary situation. Thus heresy, once the occupation of marginal and eccentric types, has become a much more general condition; indeed, heresy has become universalized."—Peter L. Berger, *The Heretical Imperative* (New York: Anchor, 1979), 30–31.

37. Pierre Bourdieu, *Outline of a Theory of Practice*, trans. Richard Nice (Cambridge: Cambridge University Press, 1992), 169.

38. Ibid., 168.

39. Another comparison with the public/private question can be seen with the Aga Khan. In *Islam and Ahmadism*, Iqbal expresses his support for the Aga Khan and in fact argues that the Aga Khan was capable of representing the Indian Muslim community, despite the fact that the Aga Khan, like Mirza Ghulam Ahmad, was a prophet-type figure. I have made the argument that one of the reasons why he supported the Aga Khan was that the Aga Khan was able to relegate his prophetic authority as Imam to a private domain while maintaining a public position that was inclusive of all Muslims and thus ecumenical. Furthermore, Iqbal believed that Ahmadis, by contrast to the Ismailis, were backward because their belief that Mirza Ghulam Ahmad was a prophet of the time was rooted in the premodern Magian tradition that Iqbal claimed was retrograde. For an elaboration of this argument about Iqbal's views of the Aga Khan compared to Mirza Ghulam Ahmad, see Teena Purohit, "Muhammad Iqbal on Muslim Orthodoxy and Transgression: A Response to Nehru," *ReOrient* 1, no. 1 (2015): 78–92.

40. Iqbal, *Islam and Ahmadism*, 54.

41. Ibid., 55.

42. Ibid., 56–57.

43. Jawaharlal Nehru, "The Solidarity of Islam," *Modern Review of Calcutta*, November 1935, 504.

44. Ibid., 505.

45. Ibid., 505.

46. Purohit, *The Aga Khan Case*.

47. Muhammad Iqbal, *The Development of Metaphysics in Persia: A Contribution to the History of Muslim Philosophy* (East Lansing: H. Bahai, 2001 [1908]), 57.

48. Devji, Faisal. "The Idea of Ismailism." Critical Muslim 10 (2013), https://criticalmuslim.com/issues/10-sects/idea-ismailism-faisal-devji.

49. Iqbal, *Development of Metaphysics*, 58–59.

50. Ibid., 59.

51. Ibid., 60.

52. Iqbal, *Islam and Ahmadism*, 25.

53. Iqbal, *Reconstruction*, 114–115.

54. Iqbal, *Islam and Ahmadism*, 59–60.

55. Javed Majeed, *Islam, Aesthetics, and Postcolonialism* (London: Routledge, 2009), 64.

56. Iqbal, *Development of Metaphysics*, 63–64.

57. I choose "monistic monotheism" because the language that Iqbal uses when he describes the Ismaili intervention is of "universal reason" and unity, which speaks much more to a kind of philosophical monism rather than the strict monotheistic understand of *tawhid*. I don't want to suggest these two are entirely incompatible, but that they reflect different emphases.

58. Iqbal, *Reconstruction*, 114–115.

59. Iqbal, *Islam and Ahmadism*, 25–31, 35.

60. Majeed, *Islam, Aesthetics, and Postcolonialism*. Javed Majeed provides extensive support to this argument through an exploration of Iqbal's idea of "khudi" (selfhood) in Iqbal's prose and poetry. Iqbal draws on the idea of *khudi* to imagine a postcolonial Muslim community, as well as develop the idea of the individual ethical self and the interiority of selfhood. For the latter, he draws very much from Sufism. *Khudi* is often about self-divinization, in which there is "an ontological equality between God and the individual human self" (31).

61. Iqbal, *Islam and Ahmadism*, 22.

62. Ibid., 22–23.

63. Ibid., 23.

64. Faisal Devji, *Muslim Zion: Pakistan as a Political Idea* (Cambridge: Harvard University Press, 2013). Faisal Devji has argued that Iqbal's problem with Mirza Ghulam Ahmad was not really about the defense of the finality of prophecy, nor was it about the God-man idea Mirza claimed for himself. What made the Ahmadis so dangerous was that "they would drag man back into the mists of occult wisdom while at the same time refusing to let him assume divinity by reserving this attribute for Mirza Ghulam Ahmad alone." Devji, *Muslim Zion*, 157.

65. Iqbal, *Islam and Ahmadism*, 29.

66. Ibid., 31.

67. Hadrat Mirza Ghulam Ahmad, *The British Government and Jihad*, trans. Tayyba Seema Ahmad and Lutfur Rahman (Surrey: Islam International Publications, 2006), 35.

68. Ibid., 35–36.

69. Iqbal, *Islam and Ahmadism*, 35.

Chapter 4: Abul Ala Mawdudi's Islamic State and Minority Ahmadis

1. Seyyed Vali Reza Nasr, *Mawdudi and the Making of Islamic Revivalism* (New York: Oxford University Press, 1996), 9–11.

2. Ibid., 12–15.

3. Ibid., 15–19. Nasr writes that he would no doubt have been accepted as an *'alim*, in terms of his training. However, the sticking point would have been his refusal to accept the *ijma* (consensus) of the *'ulama* before him. Nevertheless, he adopted many Deobandi positions, such as the importance of teaching law at the popular level, their criticisms of popular practices and Sufi festivals, and the emphasis on creating a normative religious way of life that Muslims could live by despite and outside of political order.

4. Ibid., 19–22.

5. Ibid., 23.

6. Ibid., 23–31.

7. Ibid., 31.

8. Ibid., 31–32.

9. Ibid., 40–41.

10. Sayyid Abul A'la Maududi, *The Islamic Law and Constitution*, trans. Khurshid Ahmad (Lahore: Islamic Publications, 1960), 125.

11. Maududi, *The Islamic Law and Constitution*, 128.

12. Ibid., 136.

13. This conception of *tawhid* shares some similarities with traditionalist views as well as earlier modernists' understandings of *tawhid* as social and political unity, but was a fundamentally singular configuration. Qasim Zaman has made the point that God's sovereignty was not originally an Islamist idea, nor was Mawdudi the first to describe Allah in such a manner. Many *'ulama* had invoked the language of God's sovereignty before Mawdudi, but Mawdudi was the first to seamlessly move between the concept of *hakimiyyat*, a neologism in Urdu, and the English word "sovereignty" in a way that made it appealing to those who were drawn to the concept of an Islamic state that upheld God's immutable law. Muhammad Qasim Zaman, "The Sovereignty of God in Modern Islamic Thought," *Journal of the Royal Asiatic Society* 25, no. 3 (July 2015): 389–418.

14. He writes: "the belief in the unity and sovereignty of Allah is the foundation of the social and moral system propounded by the prophets." Maududi, *The Islamic Law and Constitution*, 136.

15. Ibid., 136.

16. Ibid., 138.

17. Ibid., 129, 132–133.

18. Ibid., 138–140.

19. Ibid., 143.

20. Ibid., 146.

21. Ibid., 274–276.

22. Sadia Saeed, *Politics of Desecularization: Law and the Minority Question in Pakistan* (Cambridge: Cambridge University Press, 2017), 94–98.

23. Ibid., 99–102.

24. Sayyid Abul A'la Maududi, *The Qadiani Problem* (Lahore: Islamic Publications, 1979), 3–12.

25. Ibid., 59–60.

26. Muhammad Iqbal, "Qadianis and Orthodox Muslims," quoted in ibid., 64.

27. Iqbal, quoted in Maududi, *Qadiani Problem*, 64.

28. Iqbal, *Islam and Ahmadism*, 63.

29. Maududi, *Qadiani Problem*, 13–18.

30. Iqbal, *Islam and Ahmadism*, 56.

31. Maududi, *Qadiani Problem*, 22–25.

32. Sayyid Abul A'la Maududi, *A Short History of the Revivalist Movement in Islam* (New Delhi: Markazi Maktaba Islami Publishers, 2009), 36.

33. Ibid., 38–39.

34. Ibid., 40.

35. Ibid., 42.

36. Ibid.

37. Ibid., 43.

38. John Esposito, *Islam: The Straight Path*, 3rd edition (New York: Oxford University Press, 1998), 176–177.

39. Esposito describes the Muslim Brotherhood and Jamat-i-Islami as having started as an "ideological fraternity" that sought to combine religion with social activism. Both organizations were built upon the paradigm of the Prophet's early community, the *salaf*, and reinterpretations of *jihad* as social transformation. Esposito, 177.

40. Ibid., 181–182.

41. "I have written 'Milestones' for this vanguard, which I consider to be a waiting reality about to be materialized." Sayyid Qutb, *Milestones* (New Delhi: New Johar Offset Press , n.d.), 12.

42. Ibid., 12.

43. Qutb, like Mawdudi, adopted and reworked the concept of the vanguard from Lenin's theory of vanguardism, in which the most class-conscious sections of the working class would lead the masses toward a revolutionary politics against the bourgeois. Qutb explains that he wrote *Milestones* for the vanguard: "It is necessary that the vanguard should know the landmarks and milestones on the road toward this goal so that they may recognize the starting place, the nature, the responsibilities and the ultimate purpose of this long journey." Ibid., 12.

44. Ibid., 35.

45. Ibid., 23.

46. Ibid., 24.

47. Ibid., 31–32.

48. Ibid., 32.

49. Ibid., 11–12.

50. Ibid., 55.

51. Ibid., 9.

Chapter 5: Postcolonial Legacies of Modernist *Tawhid*: A Quest for Justice and the Nation-State

1. Fazlur Rahman, *Islam and Modernity: Transformation of an Intellectual Tradition* (Chicago: The University of Chicago Press, 1982), 2.

2. Ibid., 3.

3. Ibid., 3. Rahman writes, "This . . . extrinsic treatment of the Quran has not ceased in modern times; indeed, in some respects it has worsened. The pressures exerted by modern ideas and forces of social change, together with the colonial interregnum in Muslim lands, has brought about a situation in which the adoption of certain key modern Western ideas and institutions is resolutely defended by some Muslims and often justified through the Quran. . . . Against this background the evolving of some adequate hermeneutical method seems imperative." (Ibid., 4).

4. Ibid., 6.

5. Ibid., 134–135.

6. Ibid., 142.

7. Ibid., 132–133. Rahman is referring to the influence of Bergson and Whitehead on Iqbal.

8. Ibid., 142.

9. Ibid., 137.

10. Ibid., 143.

11. Amina Wadud, Islamic studies scholar of women and gender, has offered an inclusivist interpretative framework of *tawhid* that she has explicitly claimed to be shaped by the ethical approach of Fazlur Rahman. wadud is both a scholar of the Quran and an activist most recognized for her founding of the nongovernmental organization Sisters in Islam—a Malaysian organization that advocates for the rights of women within the terms of universal human rights as well as concepts of equality and freedom outlined in the Quran. She adopts Rahman's framework to convey a feminist theory of *tawhid* that is both political and theological. She writes, "Activating the tawhidic principle as a matter of personal practice and in the definitions, establishment, and sustenance of a just social order—the primary responsibility of being human—is the means for practicing a more egalitarian, humanistic, and pluralist Islam." Amina Wadud, *Inside the Gender Jihad: Women's Reform in Islam* (Oxford: Oneworld, 2006), 15. For wadud, "*tawhid*" operates as a fundamental principle of her working definition of Islam, which is to argue that Islam does not oppress women. The term functions at two interconnected levels: the physical and metaphysical

realms. At the metaphysical level, *tawhid* represents Allah's unicity, and in the physical world the unity and equality of all people. It is important to note that these two worlds are fundamentally intertwined, as she explains, "Allah is not only one and unique, Allah is uniform, and unites existing multiplicities or seeming dualities in both the corporeal and the metaphysical realm.... As an ethical term, tawhid relates to relationships and developments within the social and political realm, emphasizing the unity of all human creatures beneath one Creator. If experienced as a reality in everyday Islamic terms, humanity would be a single global community without distinction for reasons of race, class, gender, religious tradition, national origin, sexual orientation or other arbitrary, voluntary, and involuntary aspects of human distinction." (Wadud, *Inside the Gender Jihad*, 28). For wadud, therefore, there is a direct correlation between God's unicity and the social equity of humankind. In this regard, *tawhid* serves as an organizing principle of equality among all humans in the physical world that fully aligns with an original metaphysical equilibrium of God's unicity.

12. Ervand Abrahmian has argued that Shariati's thinking—devoted to synthesizing western sociological thought with traditional Shiism—can be understood in three parts: Shariati the sociologist interested in connections between ideas and social forces and practices; Shariati the devout believer in revolutionary Shiism; and Shariati the public speaker whose position was ever-threatened by secret police accusing him of "Islamic Marxism." Ervand Abrahamian, "Ali Shariati: Ideologue of the Iranian Revolution," *Middle East Research and Information Project* 12 (1982), http://www.merip.org/mer/mer102/ali-shariati-ideologue-iranian-revolution, accessed on 24 January 2016.

13. "Introduction: A Biographical Sketch" in Ali Shariati, *On the Sociology of Islam: Lectures by Ali Shari'ati*, trans. Hamid Algar (Berkeley: Mizan Press, 1979), 11–38.

14. Abdulaziz Sachedina expands on this position with an even more philosophical rendering of this idea of *nizam-i-tawhid*. Sachedina explains that Shariati uses the term *nizam-i-tawhid* (system based on unity) to describe the ethical ordering of the early society of the Prophet. *Tawhid*, according to Sachedina, is not just one principle (equivalent to prophecy and the day of judgment) but rather *the* foundational principle of all principles, as it represents the "foundation of the individual and social life of a Muslim.... All human activities and relationships, whether political, economic, literary, or artistic, ought to be firmly grounded on tawhid. It provides one, single direction, and it guarantees a unified spirit for its adherents." Abdulaziz Sachedina, "Ali Shariati: Ideologue of the Iranian Revolution" in *Voices of Resurgent Islam*, ed. John L. Esposito (New York: Oxford University Press, 1983), 200.

15. Shariati, *On the Sociology of Islam*, 82.

16. Ibid., 84–85.

17. Ibid., 86.

18. Ibid., 87.

19. Sachedina, "Ali Shariati," 200.

20. Ibid., 200.

21. Sachedina points out that Shariati read Iqbal's works extensively and was very much influenced by the idea that man was God's *khalifa*, vicegerent on earth. Shariati affirms the creation narrative in the Quran, which narrates how God created man out of clay and then breathed his spirit in the clay, thus creating man. Only man has the capacity to accept divine sovereignty because he has the ability to attain perfection. Only man can carry the burden of God's trust (*Amanah*), but he does so by exercising free will and acting responsibly. Ibid., 199.

22. Ali Shariati, "Mohammad Iqbal: A Manifestation of Self-Reconstruction and Reformation," (n.d.), http://www.shariati.com/english/iqbal.html, accessed on 24 January 2016.

23. Ibid.

24. Ibid.

25. Farid Esack, *Qur'an, Liberation, and Pluralism: An Islamic Perspective of Inter-religious Solidarity against Oppression* (Oxford: Oneworld, 2006), 83.

26. Ibid., 90–91, 101–103.

27. Quoted in ibid., 84–85.

28. Ibid., 90–91.

29. From there he asserts, "The conviction that *tawhid* is at the heart of a comprehensive socio-political worldview, although not entirely novel, has grown enormously in the last few decades, particular in some of the ideological currents in Iran that led to the 1979 revolution." Ibid., 91.

30. Ibid., 91.

31. Ibid., 91.

32. Quoted in ibid., 92.

33. Ibid., 92.

34. Although Mawdudi claimed that the Islamic state was a separate concept from the nation-state, it is obvious that his ideas of majority and minority relied wholly on the nation-state model, as I demonstrated in the previous chapter.

35. Quoted in Esack, *Qur'an, Liberation, and Pluralism*, 93.

36. Ibid., 93.

37. It is important to keep in mind that although Qutb was a participant in the Muslim Brotherhood, his thought broke from the early focus outlined by Hasan al-Banna. It was Nasser's authoritarian state that was emblematic of the *jahiliyya*, "a society ruled by an iniquitous prince who had made himself an object of worship in God's place and who governed an empire according to his own caprice instead of ruling on the basis of principles inspired by the Book and the Sayings of the

Prophet"—Gilles Keppel, *Muslim Extremism in Egypt: The Prophet and the Pharoah* (Berkeley: University of California Press, 1985), 46–47.

38. Roxanne L. Euben and Muhammad Qasim Zaman, eds., *Princeton Readings in Islamist Thought: Texts and Contexts from al-Banna to Bin Laden* (Princeton: Princeton University Press, 2009), 432–433. The phrase "more episodic than systemic" seems to be from Mamoun Fandy, *Saudia Arabia and the Politics of Dissent* (New York: St. Martin's Press, 1999), 193, as cited by Euben and Zaman (432).

39. Osama Bin Laden, "Declaration of War Against the Americans Occupying the Land of the Two Holy Places," in *Princeton Readings in Islamic Thought*, eds. Euben and Zaman, 436–437.

40. Ibid., 442.

41. Ibid., 448.

42. Ibid., 454.

43. Ibid., 458.

BIBLIOGRAPHY

'Abduh, Muhammad. *The Theology of Unity*, trans. Ishaq Musa'ad and Kenneth Cragg. New York: Books for Libraries Press, 1980.

Abrahamian, Ervand. "Ali Shariati: Ideologue of the Iranian Revolution." *Middle East Research and Information Project* 12 (1982), http://www.merip.org/mer/mer102/ali-shariati-ideologue-iranian-revolution, accessed on 24 January 2016.

Adams, Charles Clarence. *Islam and Modernism in Egypt*. London: Taylor & Francis, 2000.

Ahmad, Aziz. *Islamic Modernism in India and Pakistan, 1857–1964*. Oxford: Oxford University Press, 1967.

Ahmad, Aziz. "Sayyid Aḥmad Khān, Jamāl Al-Dīn Al-Afghānī and Muslim India," *Studia Islamica*, no. 13 (1960): 55–78.

Ahmad, Hadrat Mirza Ghulam. *The British Government and Jihad*, trans. Tayyba Seema Ahmad and Lutfur Rahman. Surrey: Islam International Publications, 2006.

Ahmad, Hadrat Mirza Ghulam. *The British Government and Jihad*. Islam International Publications, 2006.

Ahmad, Irfan. *Religion as Critique: Islamic Critical Thinking from Mecca to the Marketplace*. Chapel Hill: UNC Press, 2017.

al-Afghani, Jamal al-Din. "Answer of Jamal ad-Din to Renan." In Nikkie R. Keddie, *An Islamic Response to Imperialism: Political and Religious Writings of Sayyid Jamal ad-Din "al-Afghani"*. Berkeley: University of California Press, 1968.

al-Afghani, Jamal al-Din. "Answer to Renan." In *Modernist Islam 1840–1940: A Sourcebook*, ed. Charles Kurzman. New York: Oxford University Press, 2002.

al-Afghani, Jamal al-Din. "Commentary on the Commentator." In Nikki R. Keddie, *An Islamic Response to Imperialism: Political and Religious Writings of Sayyid Jamal ad-Din "al-Afghani"*. Berkeley: University of California Press, 1968.

al-Afghani, Jamal al-Din. "Le Mahdi," *L'Intransigeant* (December 17, 1883).

al-Afghani, Jamal al-Din. "Lecture on Teaching and Learning." In Nikki R. Keddie, *An Islamic Response to Imperialism: Political and Religious Writings of Sayyid Jamal ad-Din "al-Afghani"*. Berkeley: University of California Press, 1968.

al-Afghani, Jamal al-Din. "The Materialists in India." In Nikki R. Keddie, *An Islamic Response to Imperialism: Political and Religious Writings of Sayyid Jamal ad-Din "al-Afghani"*. Berkeley: University of California Press, 1968.

al-Afghani, Jamal al-Din. "The Truth about the *Neicheri* Sect and an Explanation of the *Neicheris*." In Nikki R. Keddie, *An Islamic Response to Imperialism: Political and Religious Writings of Sayyid Jamal ad-Din al-Afghani*. Berkeley: University of California Press, 1968.

al-Afghani, Jamal al-Din. *Al-Radd ʿala al-dahriyyan*, trans. Muhammad ʿAbduh [and Abi Turab]. Cairo: Dar al-Hilal, 1973.

Alavi, Seema. *Muslim Cosmopolitanism in the Age of Empire*. Cambridge: Harvard University Press, 2015.

Aydin, Cemil. *The Idea of the Muslim World*. Cambridge: Harvard University Press, 2017.

Badawi, M. A. Zaki. *The Reformers of Egypt*. London: Biddles Ltd., 1976.

Baffioni, Carmela. "Ikhwân al-Safâʾ." *The Stanford Encyclopedia of Philosophy* (Fall 2016 Edition), ed. Edward N. Zalta, https://plato.stanford.edu/archives/fall2016/entries/ikhwan-al-safa/, accessed on 16 February 2022.

Bauer, Thomas. *A Culture of Ambiguity: An Alternative History of Islam*. New York: Columbia University Press, 2021.

Berger, Peter L. *The Heretical Imperative*. New York: Anchor, 1979.

Bourdieu, Pierre. *Outline of a Theory of Practice*, trans. Richard Nice. Cambridge: Cambridge University Press, 1992.

Cole, Juan. "Muhammad ʿAbduh and Rashid Rida: A Dialogue on the Bahaʾi Faith," *World Order* 15, nos. 3–4 (1981), https://bahai-library.com/pdf/c/cole_abduh_rida_dialogue.pdf, accessed on 3 July 2018.

Cole, Juan. "Rashid Rida on the Bahai Faith: A Utilitarian Theory of the Spread of Religions." *Arab Studies Quarterly* 5, no. 3 (1983): 276–291.

Devji, Faisal. *Muslim Zion: Pakistan as a Political Idea*. Cambridge: Harvard University Press, 2013.

Devji, Faisal. "The Idea of Ismailism." *Critical Muslim* 10 (2013).

Esack, Farid. *Qurʾan, Liberation, and Pluralism: An Islamic Perspective of Interreligious Solidarity against Oppression*. Oxford: Oneworld, 2006.

Esposito, John. *Islam: The Straight Path*, 3rd edition. New York: Oxford University Press, 1998.

Euben, Roxanne L., and Muhammad Qasim Zaman, eds., *Princeton Readings in Islamist Thought: Texts and Contexts from al-Banna to Bin Laden*. Princeton: Princeton University Press, 2009.

Fandy, Mamoun. *Saudia Arabia and the Politics of Dissent*. New York: St. Martin's Press, 1999.

Friedmann, Yohanan. *Prophecy Continuous: Aspects of Ahmadi Religious Thought and Its Medieval Background*. Berkeley: University of California Press, 1989.

Griffel, Frank. "Toleration and Exclusion: al-Shafiʿi and al-Ghazali on the Treatment of Apostates." *Bulletin of the School of Oriental and African Studies* 64, no. 3 (2001): 339–354.

Hamdani, Abbas. "The Name 'Ikhwan Al-Safa.'" *Digest of Middle East Studies* 8, no. 2 (1999): 1–11.

Hannegraff, W.J. *New Age Religion and Western Culture: Esotericism in the Mirror of Secular Thought.* New York: SUNY Press, 1997.

Haq, S. Nomanul. "Salman Rushdie, Blame Yourself." *The New York Times* (23 February 1989), https://archive.nytimes.com/www.nytimes.com/books/99/04/18/specials/rushdie-haq.html, accessed on 15 February 2022.

Hasan, Mehdi. "Why Islam doesn't need a reformation." *The Guardian* (17 May 2015), https://www.theguardian.com/commentisfree/2015/may/17/islam-reformation-extremism-muslim-martin-luther-europe, accessed on 28 January 2022.

Hourani, Albert. *Arabic Thought in the Liberal Age, 1798–1939.* Cambridge: Cambridge University Press, 1983.

Hussain, Khurram. *Islam as Critique: Sayyid Ahmad Khan and the Challenge of Modernity.* London: Bloomsbury Academic, 2019.

Iqbal, Muhammad. *Islam and Ahmadism.* Lahore: Ashraf Printing Press, 1980.

Iqbal, Muhammad. *The Development of Metaphysics in Persia: A Contribution to the History of Muslim Philosophy.* East Lansing: H. Bahai, 2001 [1908].

Iqbal, Muhammad. *The Reconstruction of Religious Thought in Islam.* Stanford: Stanford University Press, 2012.

Keddie, Nikki R. "The Pan-Islamic Appeal: Afghani and Abdülhamid II." *Middle Eastern Studies* 3, no. 1 (1966): 46–67.

Keddie, Nikki R. *An Islamic Response to Imperialism: Political and Religious Writings of Sayyid Jamal ad-Din "al-Afghani".* Berkeley: University of California Press, 1968.

Keddie, Nikki R. *Sayyid Jamal ad-Din "al-Afghani": A Political Biography.* Berkeley: University of California Press, 1972.

Kedourie, Elie. *Afghani and ʿAbduh: An Essay on Religious Unbelief and Political Activism in Modern Islam.* New York: The Humanities Press, 1966.

Keppel, Gilles. *Muslim Extremism in Egypt: The Prophet and the Pharoah.* Berkeley: University of California Press, 1985.

Kerr, Malcolm. *Islamic Reform: The Political and Legal Theories of Muhammad ʿAbduh and Rashid Rida.* Berkeley: University of California Press, 1966.

Khan, Sayyid Ahmad. "Lecture on Islam." In *Modernist Islam 1840–1940: A Sourcebook,* ed. Charles Kurzman (Oxford: Oxford University Press, 2002), 293.

Laden, Osama Bin. "Declaration of War against the Americans Occupying the Land of the Two Holy Places." In *Princeton Readings in Islamist Thought: Texts and Contexts from al-Banna to Bin Laden,* eds. Roxanne L. Euben and Muhammad Qasim Zaman (Princeton: Princeton University Press, 2009).

Lavan, Spencer. *The Ahmadiyyah Movement: A History and Perspective*. New Delhi: Manohar Book Service, 1974.

Majeed, Javed. "Introduction." In Iqbal, Muhammad, *The Reconstruction of Religious Thought in Islam*. Stanford: Stanford University Press, 2012.

Majeed, Javed. *Islam, Aesthetics, and Postcolonialism*. London: Routledge, 2009.

Maududi, Sayyid Abul A'la. *A Short History of the Revivalist Movement in Islam*. New Delhi: Markazi Maktaba Islami Publishers, 2009.

Maududi, Sayyid Abul A'la. *The Islamic Law and Constitution*, trans. Khurshid Ahmad. Lahore: Islamic Publications, 1960.

Maududi, Sayyid Abul A'la. *The Qadiani Problem*. Lahore: Islamic Publications, 1979.

McCants, William. "I Never Understood Any of This from 'Abbas Effendi': Muhammad 'Abduh's Knowledge of the Bahai Teachings and His Friendship with 'Abdul-Baha 'Abbas." In *Studies in Modern Religions, Religious Movements and the Babi-Bahai Faiths,* ed. Moshe Sharon. Boston: Brill, 2004.

Nasr, Seyyed Vali Reza. *Mawdudi and the Making of Islamic Revivalism*. New York: Oxford University Press, 1996.

Nehru, Jawaharlal. "The Solidarity of Islam." *Modern Review of Calcutta*, November 1935.

Purohit, Teena. "Muhammad Iqbal on Muslim Orthodoxy and Transgression: A Response to Nehru." *ReOrient* 1, no. 1 (2015): 78–92.

Purohit, Teena. *The Aga Khan Case: Religion and Identity in Colonial India*. Cambridge: Harvard University Press, 2012.

Qutb, Sayyid. *Milestones*. New Delhi: New Johar Offset Press, n.d.

Rahman, Fazlur. *Islam and Modernity: Transformation of an Intellectual Tradition*. Chicago: The University of Chicago Press, 1982.

"Rashid Rida | Islamic Scholar." *Encyclopedia Britannica* (August 28, 2012), https://www.britannica.com/biography/Rashid-Rida.

Rida, Rashid. "Renewal, Renewing, and Renewers," trans. Emad Eldin Shahin. In *Modernist Islam 1840–1940: A Sourcebook*, ed. Charles Kurzman. Oxford: Oxford University Press, 2002.

Rida, Rashid. *al-Manar wa 'l-Azhar* (Cairo: 1934–1935).

Rida, Rashid. *Ta 'rikh al-Ustadh al-Imam al-Shaykh Muhammad 'Abduh*, vol. 1 (Cairo: al-Manàr Press, 1931).

Sachedina, Abdulaziz. "Ali Shariati: Ideologue of the Iranian Revolution." In *Voices of Resurgent Islam*, ed. John L. Esposito (New York: Oxford University Press, 1983).

Saeed, Sadia. *Politics of Desecularization: Law and the Minority Question in Pakistan* Cambridge: Cambridge University Press, 2017.

Scharbrodt, Oliver. *Islam and the Baha 'i Faith: A Comparative Study of Muhammad 'Abduh and 'Abdul-Baha 'Abbas*. London: Routledge, 2008.

Schulze, Reinhard. "Mass Culture and Islamic Cultural Production in 19th Century Middle East." In *Mass Culture, Popular Culture, and Social Life in the Middle East*, eds. G. Stauth and S. Zubaida. Boulder: Westview Press, 1987.

Shariati, Ali. "Introduction: A Biographical Sketch." In Ali Shariati, *On the Sociology of Islam: Lectures by Ali Shari'ati*, trans. Hamid Algar (Berkeley: Mizan Press, 1979).

Shariati, Ali. "Mohammad Iqbal: A Manifestation of Self-Reconstruction and Reformation." (n.d.), http://www.shariati.com/english/iqbal.html, accessed on 24 January 2016.

Simmel, Georg. *Essays on Religion*. New Haven: Yale University Press, 1987.

Smith, Wilfred Cantwell. *Islam in Modern History*. Princeton, N.J.: Princeton University Press, 1957.

Smith, Wilfred Cantwell. *The Meaning and End of Religion*. Minneapolis: Fortress Press, 1991.

Wadud, Amina. *Inside the Gender Jihad: Women's Reform in Islam*. Oxford: Oneworld, 2006.

Weismann, Itzchak. "The Sociology of 'Islamic Modernism': Muhammad 'Abduh, the National Public Sphere and the Colonial State," *Maghreb Review: Majallat Al-Maghrib* 32, no. 1 (2007): 104–121.

Wissa, Karim. "Freemasonry in Egypt 1798–1921: A Study in Cultural and Political Encounters," *Bulletin (British Society for Middle Eastern Studies)* 16, no. 2 (1989): 143–161.

Zaman, Muhammad Qasim. *Modern Islamic Thought in a Radical Age*. Cambridge: Cambridge University Press, 2012.

Zaman, Muhammad Qasim. "The Sovereignty of God in Modern Islamic Thought." *Journal of the Royal Asiatic Society* 25, no. 3 (July 2015): 389–418.

Zito, George. "Toward a Sociology of Heresy," *Sociological Analysis* 44, no. 2 (1983): 123–130.

INDEX

'Abd al-Halim, Prince, 55, 197n64, 197n67

Abdel Fattah al-Sisi, 1

'Abduh, Muhammad, 4; and 'Abdul Baha, 62, 88–90, 201n57, 202n61; Afghani as influence on, 8, 13, 23, 57–58, 60, 64–67, 71–72, 89; appropriation of esoteric ideas by, 23–24, 58–59; Bahais as supported and respected by, 23–24, 62–63, 73–81, 89; batiniyya excluded by, 61–62, 70–71, 76, 174; biography and background of, 62–66, 68; and civilizational progress, 23, 66–67, 69–71; and continuous prophecy, 76–77; debate with Rida regarding Bahais, 23–24, 73–81, 89; and education, 66–67, 76; and Egyptian political reforms, 65; on equality of religions, 80–81; and esoteric groups as regressive and destructive of Islam, 70–71; and ijtihad, 12, 72, 78; Ismailism excluded by, 61–62; and leadership aspirations, 72–73; as mujaddid, 13–14; and persistence as evidence of validity, 76–77; and progressive revelation, 80–81; and rationality of Quran, 69–70; Rida as biographer of, 62–63, 64; as Rida's teacher, 23, 62; on sectarian groups as threat to Muslim unity, 70; Shariati on, 179; Shiism excluded by, 23, 61,

73 (see also batiniyya under this heading); and Sufism, 62, 63, 64, 66; and Sunni normative bias, 16; and tawhid as social or political unity, 21, 23–24, 61–62, 68–69, 71–73, 81, 168, 176–177 (see also Theology of Unity ('Abduh)); and temporal bifurcation, 68–70; 'ulama and, 64, 66–67

'Abdul Baha, 6, 18, 19, 74; 'Abduh as sympathetic to, 62, 88–90, 201n57, 202n61

'Abdu'l Baha Abbas, 74

Abdulhamid II, Sultan of Ottoman Empire, 34–35, 194n14

Abdullah ibn Maiman, 123

Abrahmian, Ervand, 210n12

Abu Bakr Al Baghdadi, 1

Adams, C. C., 64

al-Afghani, Jamal al-Din, 4, 12, 22; 'Abduh influenced by, 8, 13, 23, 31, 57–58, 60, 63–64, 67, 71–72, 89; appropriation of esoteric ideas and beliefs, 16–17, 23–24, 29, 52, 56–59, 60, 73; and Babism and, 29–31, 58; biography and background of, 29–31, 58–59; as canonical reformer, 62; and civilizational progress, 35–36, 39–42, 66–67; and colonial contexts, 21, 22, 27–31, 46–47, 53–54, 60, 156, 194n13; and continuous prophecy, 29; debates with European scholars, 27; and education, 30–31, 43, 47–48,

al-Afghani, Jamal al-Din (*continued*)
50–52, 60; and Freemasonry, 29,
55–56, 59, 197n66; Guizot as influence
on, 36, 40, 68; *ijtihad* and, 12; as
influence on Rida, 8, 62; leadership
aspirations of, 16, 22–23, 29, 31, 46,
51–55, 57–60, 64, 156, 184, 196n62;
and link between unified religions
and progress, 30, 34–36, 39; and
Mahdi role, 29, 52–55, 57–60;
materialism rejected by, 22–23,
27–28; and Muslim orthodoxy, 28,
29, 34–35, 59–60; and nationalism,
29, 31, 56; on *neicheri* and *neicheris*
(see *neicheri*, batiniyya as); and Pan-
Islam, 34–35, 66–67; and political
activism, 22, 29, 30–31, 46, 52–53,
55–56, 59, 60; and progress, 23, 39, 42,
47, 50–51; and prophetic authority,
51–52; rationalism and evolutionary
concept of religion, 30, 195n20;
and rationality, 43; and religion
as distinct from society (Islam *vs.*
people/Muslims), 39–42; response
to Renan, 43, 47, 67; role in Egypt,
68; Sayyid Ahmad Khan as target of
critique, 22–23, 27–30, 43–52, 54–55,
59–60; science as advocated by,
27–28, 30–31, 33, 40–42, 47, 51, 57, 60,
67; Shariati on, 179; Shii (Shaikhi)
influences on, 58–59; and Sultan
Abdulhamid, 34–35; and Sunni
normative bias, 16, 28, 62–63; on
tawhid, 23–24, 28, 34–36, 39, 71–72,
168; and *ulama*, contentious relationship with, 46, 48, 55; and unified
Islam, 38–39, 43, 60
Aga Khan: dual religious and secular
leadership roles of, 18, 120–122, 205;
and inclusion, 205n39; Iqbal on, 25,
117–122, 131, 133, 205n39; and Muslim
unity, 118, 119, 121–122; Nehru on,
120–121; and prophetic authority,
120, 133, 205n39; and Sunni normative
bias, 121–122, 131

Ahmad, Hadrat Mirza Ghulam. *See*
Mirza Ghulam Ahmad (Ahmad,
Hadrat Mirza Ghulam)
Ahmad, Irfan, 5–6
Ahmadis: and continuous prophecy, 24,
133; contributions to Islam elided
or neglected, 14–15; as elided in
traditionalist scholarship, 14–15;
and esotericism, 18; as heretics, 20,
22, 93, 110–111; Iqbal as anti-Ahmadi,
20, 22, 24–25, 104, 106–107, 108, 110,
118–119, 123, 125, 148–150; leadership of
(*see* Mirza Ghulam Ahmad (Ahmad,
Hadrat Mirza Ghulam)); Mawdudi
and exclusion of, 137, 146, 147–153,
166; modernist reformers and
exclusion of, 4–5, 6; Munir Report
and inclusion of, 148; and Muslim
identity, 18; as Qadianis, 104, 106–107,
108, 110, 118–119, 123, 125, 148–150,
153, 160, 166, 203n24; as regressive,
24–25, 93, 120, 130, 133–134; as threat
to unity, 133–134; *ulama* and exclusion of, 147–149; violence against, 137
Alavi, Seema, 192n9
Al-Hallaj, 116
"Answer to Renan" (Afghani), 27, 40–43,
47, 67
apartheid, 26, 169, 179–184, 189
Ayaan Hirsi Ali, 1
Aydin, Cemil, 9, 192n5
Azzam, Sheikh Abdullah Yusuf, 185–186

Babism: 'Abdul's endorsement of, 74,
76, 88–90; Afghani and, 30, 38–39,
58; Bahaism contrasted with, 74;
foundation and tenets of, 74; Rida's
rejection of Bahais linked to, 76, 82,
201n46
Bahais: 'Abduh sympathetic or supportive of, 23–24, 62, 73–81; blamed
for assassination of Nasir ud-Din
Shah, 75; conflicting attitudes among
canonical reformers, 62; and
continuous prophecy, 78–79;

contributions to Islam elided or neglected, 14, 18; and esotericism, 18; foundation and history of, 74–75; Gulpaygani's role in, 74–75; and Magian revival, 125; modernist reformers and exclusion of, 4–5, 6, 62; as modernist reform movement, 74, 200n45; and Muslim identity, 18; as propagandists in Rida's analysis, 76–79, 81–83, 88, 90

al-Banna, Hasan, 85, 158–159

batiniyya: ʿAbduh and exclusion of, 61–62, 70–71, 76, 174; Afghani and batiniyya as neicheri, 38–40, 89, 174; and esoteric groups as threat to Islam unity, 173–174; Rahman and exclusion of, 173–174; Rida on Bahais and, 76

Bauer, Thomas, 192n6

Berger, Peter, 113, 204n36

Bourdieu, Pierre, 24, 93, 106, 114–117

British Government and Jihad (Mirza Ghulam Ahmad), 129–130

Call of Islam (group), 180

canonical reformers, 6–7, 15–17, 19–21, 62, 90

Charlie Hebdo, 1

Cole, Juan, 75, 79, 83, 90

colonialism and colonial contexts: and al-Afghani's career, 21, 22, 27–31, 46–47, 53–54, 60, 156, 194n13; and decline of Muslim empires, 3, 4, 8; and emergence of nation-states, 25, 136–137, 149, 156, 158–159; Iqbal and Indian Muslim solidarity, 91–92, 103–104, 106–108, 112–113, 117, 119–121, 127–128, 133, 150; and minority/majority dynamics, 103, 136–137; and modernist redefinition of tawhid, 8–9, 12, 25, 132, 165–166; modernist reformers and, 3, 12–14, 157–158; Muslim elites and ijtihad in, 98; Sayyid Ahmad Khan as pro-British, 28, 46, 59–60, 193n2; Shariati and

anti-colonial revolutionary thought, 174–175

"Commentary on the Commentator" (Afghani), 28, 50, 52, 60

cumulative tradition and diversity within Islam, 10, 20, 71–72, 177

"Declaration of War against the Americans . . ." (bin Laden), 187–189

The Decline of the West (Spengler), 126

Denison, J. H., 94–95, 202n3

The Development of Metaphysics in Persia (Iqbal), 121–125

Devji, Faisal, 123, 206n64

doxa, 114–116

dualism, 99, 117, 126, 131

education: ʿAbduh and modern pedagogy, 66–67; al-Afghani and, 30–31, 43, 47–48, 50–52, 60; modernist perspectives on, 3–4, 11–12; modernists' critique of traditional institutions of, 11, 82–83; Muslim intellectuals and western, 65–66; and progress, 50–51, 59–60; as Rahman's primary focus, 170–173; Rida on, 82–83, 87; traditionalists (ʿulama) and, 3, 12–13

Egypt, 23, 25, 27, 185, 187; European influences in, 64–65; Freemasonry in, 8, 29, 55–57, 59, 60, 197n67; Gulpaygani and Bahais in, 74–75; Islamism and Egyptian nationalism, 90; Qutb's role in, 136, 157–158

equality, 92–93, 96–102, 104, 152, 169, 183–184

Esack, Farid, 26, 169, 179–184

esotericism, 17–21, 78–80; and atheism, 70–71; and charismatic leaders, 14; and continuous prophecy, 18–20, 29; distinction between canonical and esoteric modernists, 21; and heresy, 22; and living religious leadership, 18; modernists and appropriation of esoteric ideas and beliefs, 16–17, 20–24,

esotericism (*continued*)
22, 29, 52, 56–59, 60, 73; as regressive
or barrier to progress, 24–25, 33–34,
39–40, 70–71, 84, 117, 124–127,
130–134, 205n39; scholarly neglect
of, 90; and *tajdid*, 14; as threat to
Muslim unity, 38, 61–62; as threat
to *tawhid*, 10, 28, 36–39, 73, 101, 133.
See also specific minority groups.
Esposito, John, 159
exclusion/inclusion: ʿAbduh and
exclusion of esoteric groups, 61–62,
70–71, 76, 174; ʿAbduh on equality
of religions, 80–81; Afghani's *neicheri*
concept and, 37–38; apartheid, 26, 169,
179–184, 189; *batiniyya* as excluded,
61–62, 70–71, 76, 173–174; and
canonical reformers, 19–20, 62; and
definition in opposition, 115–116;
excommunication, 106; heresy
and inquisition, 107–108; and
heterodoxy/orthodoxy dynamics,
114–115; Iqbal and Ahmadi exclusion,
20, 22, 24–25, 106–107, 150–151, 166,
204n24, 205n39; Iqbal and contradictory logic of, 103, 110–111, 112; Iqbal
and Ismaili inclusion, 24–25, 93,
117–126, 131–133; Iqbal and Sufi inclusion, 22, 97, 109–110, 113, 115, 116, 128;
Islam as diverse and inclusive, 10, 71,
103, 152–153, 177–178; Islamism and,
159, 166, 186–187; Mawdudi and
Ahmadi (Qadiani) exclusion, 137, 146,
147–153, 166; modernist reform and,
4–6, 20–21, 29 (*see also specific thinkers
under this heading*); Munir Report
and, 148; progressive Islamism and,
183–184; Qutb on Muslim identity
and *tawhid*, 161; Rahman and, 174;
Shii Marxism and, 184; Sunni normative bias and, 2–3, 20; *ulama* and
judgements on Muslim identity,
147–149; and Wadud's feminist
framework of *tawhid*, 209n11

freedom, 92–93, 96–104, 108, 134,
141–142, 152
Freemasonry, 8, 29, 55–57, 59, 60, 197n67

al-Ghazali, Abu Hamid, 2, 83
"Golden Age" of Islam, 9–10, 13, 48,
69–70, 161–162, 172; and Muslim
unity in ideal past, 39–40, 69–70;
salafi and understanding of, 84–85
Guizot, François, 36, 40, 68
Gulpaygani, Mizra Abul-Fadl, 73–76

Hajji Muhammad Karim Khan Qajar
Kirmani, 58
Hamas, 186
Hasan, Mehdi, 1
Hasan al-Banna, 85, 158–159
heresy: Al-Hallaj condemned for, 116;
and contemporary call for reform
of Islam, 1; and esotericism, 22;
exclusion and inquisition, 107–108;
as intrinsic to Islam per Nehru,
107–108; Iqbal and Ahmadi trans-
gressions as, 92–93, 105–115, 117,
132–133, 150; prophetic continuity as
heretical transgression, 6–7; Sayyid
Ahmad Khan as "neicheri" heretic,
22–23; sociological theories of, 93,
111–113; Sunni normative bias and
framing of, 6–7, 110–113; and temporal
context, 113; as threat to unity, 86,
116–117
Heretic: Why Islam Needs a Reformation
(Hirsi Ali), 1
Hinduism, 17–18, 36, 102, 139–140, 149
History of Civilization in Europe
(Guizot), 67–68
Hourani, Albert, 28
Hussain, Khurram, 5–6

Ibn ʿAbd al-Wahhab, Muhammad, 98,
140. *See also* Wahhabism
Ibn ʿArabi, Muhyuddin, 109–110, 112–113,
115–116, 178

Ibn Khaldun, 67, 126–127, 198n7

Ibn Saud, 'Abd al-'Aziz, 140

Ibn Taymiyya, 73, 97–98

ijtihad (reinterpretation): 'Abduh and, 12, 72, 78; Afghani and, 12; Iqbal and, 12, 97–99, 101–102; Islamists and, 159, 165, 176–177, 181; Mirza and, 14; Rahman and, 169, 170, 172; and renewal of Islam, 12; Rida and, 12; Sayyid Ahmad Khan and, 12, 46; Shariati and, 176–177; traditionalist reformers and, 12, 46; *'ulama* as incapable of, 46

Ikhwan, 29, 56, 59, 197n69

'ilm al-kalam, 45–46, 48–49

inclusion. *See* exclusion/inclusion

India, 12, 138, 139, 149–150

Iqbal, Muhammad, 4, 9–10, 12, 13–15; on Aga Khan, 25, 117–122, 131, 133, 205n39; and Ahmadi exclusion, 20, 22, 24–25, 106–107, 150–151, 166, 204n24, 205n39 (*see also* and heresy accusations against Ahmadis *under this heading*); biography and background of, 91–92, 112; Christianity contrasted with Islam by, 94–96, 202n3; and civilizational theories, 92, 94–96, 134, 202nn3–4; and continuous prophecy, 22; contradictory logics of exclusion, 103, 110–111, 112; and cultural diversity of Muslims, 103–104; and dynamic nature of Islam, 92, 94–99, 102, 104, 134; and ethical components of *tawhid* (freedom equality solidarity), 92–93, 96–102, 104, 152; and finality of prophecy (*khatm-i-nabuwwat*), 93, 104–106, 108, 110, 113, 115, 128–130, 133, 150, 206n64; and freedom as value, 97–104, 101, 108, 134; and "heathenism" as threat, 100–101, 104; and heresy accusations against Ahmadis, 92–93, 105–115, 117, 132–133, 150; on Ibn 'Arabi, 109–110, 112–113,

115–116; and *ijtihad*, 12, 96–99, 101–102; on Imamate as institution, 118–120, 122–123, 131; and Indian Muslim contexts (minority), 103; as influence on Mawdudi, 150; and Islam as indivisible, 99–100; Ismailism included by, 24–25, 93, 117–126, 131–133; *khudi* (selfhood), 203n6, 206n60; and Magianism as regressive, 117, 124–127, 130–132, 134, 205n39; and majoritarian logic, 151–152; and Mawdudi, 25, 137, 138; and Mirza as rival authority, 93, 109–111, 113, 130–131, 133; as *muhaddid*, 13–14; and Muslim legal institutions, 97–98, 101–102; and Muslim political unity, 9–10; and Muslim solidarity, 106–107, 112, 117–120, 150–151; and nationalism, 21, 99, 107, 125–126, 136, 168; Nehru's argument with, 106–110, 118–121; and orthodoxy, 104, 110–113, 115–116, 118–122, 131–133; political roles of, 91–92; on prophecy, 22, 24; and prophetic authority, 205n39; and "prophetic consciousness" as unsound, 109–110, 112, 115–116; and public/private distinction, 109–112, 113, 115–116, 131, 133, 205n39; on Qadianis, 150–151; Rahman on, 173; and rationality, 97, 122–126, 131; and rejection of liberal tolerance, 150–151; and science, 99–100, 202n3; and sectarian division as threat, 102–104, 132; Shariati on, 178–179; and Sufi inclusion, 22, 97, 109–110, 113, 115, 116, 128; and Sunni normative bias/orthodoxy, 16, 121–122, 131, 132, 152; *tawhid* in, 9–11, 21–22, 92–104, 132–134, 168, 176–177; and transition to politically united Islam, 117–118; and Turkey as example, 99–102, 119; on *'ulama* as political and religious authority, 127–128, 151; and women's rights, 145

ISIS, 1

islah (repair), 2, 13–14

Islam and Ahmadism (Iqbal), 24, 92–93, 102–104, 104–111, 117, 131, 205n39

Islam and Modernity (Rahman), 169

"Islam and Science" (Afghani), 40–41

Islam as Critique: Sayyid Ahmad Khan and the Challenge of Modernity (Hussain), 5–6

"Islam as Moral and Political Ideal" (Iqbal), 102–103

The Islamic Law and Constitution (Mawdudi), 140–141, 153, 166

Islamic state: as goal of Islamism, 21, 25, 158, 164–165; *Mahdi/Mujaddid* role in, 153, 155–156, 167; and majoritarian logic, 136, 146, 166, 211n34; Mawdudi and proposed, 25, 135–137, 140, 142, 144–146, 152–153, 165–167; and minority exclusion, 136; Qutb and vanguard's role in, 160, 164, 188–190; and sovereignty of God, 135, 142, 144, 153, 160–163, 165–166; as "theo-democracy," 144

Islamism, 1; Al-Qaeda and, 26; and holistic view of Islam, 159, 182; and Islamic state as goal, 21, 25, 164–165; and *jahiliyya* (ignorance) as threat to Muslim unity, 159, 160, 163–165, 186; and *jihad*, 159; majoritarian logic and exclusion in, 159, 166; Mawdudi and, 25, 135–137, 139, 156, 165; modernism contrasted with, 159–160, 165; and Muslim Brotherhood, 157–159; and Muslim self-sufficiency, 135, 159, 165; progressive Islamists, 181–184; Qutb and, 136, 157–158, 165; Rahman's critique of, 172–173; *tawhid* and, 21, 23, 25–26, 136, 189, 207m13; and vanguard as leadership, 25, 160–161, 163–165, 167, 169, 188–190 (*see also* Al Qaeda ("the base")); western influence rejected by, 85, 135, 145, 165

Ismailism: 'Abduh and exclusion of, 61–62; Aga Khan's leadership (*see* Aga Khan); contributions to Islam elided or neglected, 14, 18; and esotericism, 18; Iqbal's inclusion of, 24–25, 93, 117–126, 131–133; modernist reformers and exclusion of, 4–5, 6; as *neicheri* in Afghani, 28, 38, 43–44; Rida and exclusion of, 23, 57, 75–76, 78–79, 83, 90

jahiliyya, 159, 160, 163–165, 186

Jalal, Ayesha, 105

Jamat-i-Islami, 137, 140, 147, 158–159, 208n39

Jamiat Ulama-i-Hind (JUH), 139, 140

jihad, 127; and Islamist worldview, 159; and liberation theology, 180; Mirza and rejection of, 129–130; Al Qaeda, the *mujahideen* and, 169, 185–190; Qutb's formulation of, 161, 164–165, 169, 186–187; and vanguard (van-guardism), 165, 169

Jones, William, 17

justice: Islam as essentially rational and just, 144–145; *jihad* as response to injustice, 187, 189–190; liberation theology and, 169, 180; Qutb on, 157, 162; Shariati and Marxist, 175–176; *tawhid* as response to injustice, 25–26, 169, 175–176, 180, 182

kalam, 45, 74–75, 139

Keddie, Nikki R., 28–30, 34–35, 52–54, 58, 194nn13–15

Kedourie, Elie, 54, 56

Khan, Sayyid Ahmad: Afghani's attacks on, 20, 45; biography and back-ground of, 46; and education, 8, 50–51, 60; as heretical "neicheris," 22–23, 43–44; political orientation and colonial contexts, 12, 46, 193n2, 195n40; response to *neicheri* accusations, 49–50; as rival leader,

22–23, 29, 43–44, 60; and science as
compatible with Islam, 45, 60
Khedive Ismail, 55, 66, 68
Khilafat movement, 139–140
*Khutabat-i-Ahmadiyya (Essays on Life
of Mohammed)* (Sayyid Ahmad
Khan), 45
Kurzman, Charles, 7–8

Laden, Osama bin, 185–189
leadership: esoteric as rival to modernist authority, 11, 16, 18–19, 22–23, 29,
43–44, 60, 82–83, 93, 119–120, 166;
Imamate and institutional, 118–120,
122–123, 131; Mahdi role and (*see*
Mahdis); millenarianism and,
189–190; modernist reformers
concerns regarding, 1–2, 5–7, 10–11,
19, 74, 86, 90, 166 (*see also specific
thinkers*); *mujaddid* role (see
mujaddids (agents of reform)); and
"Muslim Martin Luther," 1–2, 13, 43;
prophecy and legitimacy of, 14, 18, 24,
29; and Qutb's vanguard, 160–167,
169, 185, 186, 188–190, 208n43; *taqlid*
(traditional authorities), 64, 82, 98,
159; and *tawhid*, 10–11, 23, 156–157;
Twelver Shiism and theory of, 58–59
"Lecture on Teaching and Learning"
(Afghani), 47–48
"liberating praxis," 181
liberation theology, 169

Madani, Mawlana Husain Ahmad, 140
madrasa, 3
Magianism, 117, 119, 124–127, 130–134,
205n39
Mahdis, 29; Afghani and Mahdi role,
29, 53–55, 60, 156, 184, 196n62;
Mawdudi and Mahdi role, 22, 137,
153–156, 160, 167, 184; Mirza Ghulam
Ahmad as *mahdi* and *masih-i-mawud*,
15, 22, 105, 129–130; as revolutionary
reformers, 137; Rida and Sudanese

Mahdism as sectarian threat to
Islam, 82
Majeed, Javed, 125–126, 202n4, 203n6,
206n60
Majlis-i-Ahrar al-Islam (Ahrar), 147–148
majoritarian logic, 6–7, 13, 15; and
Islamic state, 146, 166, 211n34. *See also*
exclusion/inclusion
Martin Luther (as model reformer), 1,
2, 13, 36, 39, 40, 43, 52
Marxism, 26, 169, 184, 189
materialists. See *neicheri, batiniyya* as,
"The Materialists in India" (Afghani),
28, 42–44
Mawdudi, Sayyid Abul Ala, 4, 25; and
Ahmadi (Qadiani) exclusion, 137, 146,
147–153, 166; biography and background of, 137–140; and civilizational
progress, 135, 145, 166; and freedom,
141–142; God's sovereignty as
conceived by, 25, 135, 140–144,
156–157, 165–166, 207n13; and heresy
charges against rival leaders, 156; on
human dominion as error, 143–144,
153; Iqbal as influence on, 25, 137,
138, 149–152, 166; Islamic state as
envisioned by, 25, 135–137, 140, 142,
144–146, 152–153, 165–167; and
Islamism, 25, 135–137, 139, 156, 165;
Jamiat Ulama-i-Hind (JUH), 140,
147, 158–159; as journalist, 138, 139;
leadership aspirations of, 25, 153;
and Mahdi/*mujaddid* role, 22, 137,
153–156, 160, 167, 184; and majoritarian logic, 136–137, 146, 151–153, 166,
211n34; and nationalism, 136, 139–140;
political organization and activism
of, 137, 139; and Quran as authority,
141–144; Qutb as influenced by,
136, 156–157, 159–161, 163, 167; and
secularism as threat to Islam, 135,
140, 144; and Sunni normative bias, 16,
151–152; on *tawhid*, 21, 23, 25, 141 (*see
also* God's sovereignty as conceived

Mawdudi, Sayyid Abul Ala (*continued*) by *under this heading*); and temporal bifurcation, 166; on "theo-democracy," 144–145; and *ulama* as authorities, 148–149; and vanguard concept, 189–190, 208n43; western influences rejected by, 135, 138–139, 144–145; and women's rights, 140, 145

Mazdak (Zoroastrian leader), 37–38

McCants, William, 90

messianism: Afghani and, 30, 52–55; Aga Khan and, 131; Iqbal and messianic expectation as Magian, 125–127; Mirza Ghulam Ahmad and, 14–15, 22, 24, 105, 127–130, 204n24; Shii, 52–54, 58, 73, 156

Milestones (Qutb), 136–137, 156, 157, 160–164, 208n43

Mirza Ghulam Ahmad (Ahmad, Hadrat Mirza Ghulam): as anti-colonial, 14–15; Ibn 'Arabi compared to, 109–110, 112–113, 115–116; and *ijtihad*, 14; Iqbal's leadership authority threatened by, 93, 109–111, 120, 130–131, 133, 205n39; as messianic *buruz*, 15, 128–130, 192n11; modernist critiques of, 6; as *mujaddid, mahdi*, and messiah, 14–15, 22, 105, 127, 128–130, 203n24; as regressive, 120, 130; and *risalat* (prophetic calling), 14–16; scholarly neglect of, 14–15; and *tawhid*, 15–16

Mirza Husayn Ali Nuri (Baha'u'llah), 74

The Mission of the Poet in Life and Poetry of the Present Generation (Qutb), 157

"Mohammad Iqbal . . ." (Shariati), 178–179

monistic monotheism, 126, 206n57

monotheism, *tawhid* and, 9–11, 142, 175–177

Muhammad Ahmad, Sudanese Mahdi, 29, 53–54, 82, 156

Muhammad Ali, Egyptian leader, 65–66

Muhammad Ibn 'Abd al-Wahhab, 98

Muir, William, 45

mujaddids (agents of reform), 2; Mawdudi on, 137, 139, 153–156, 167; Mirza Ghulam Ahmad and claims of prophetic authority, 129; modernist reformers recognized as, 13–14; Rida on, 63, 88, 185; role in Islamic state, 153, 155–156, 167

mujahideen, 169, 185–190

Muslim Brotherhood, 85, 90, 157–159, 185–186, 211n37

Muslim (JUH periodical), 139

Muslim League, 91–92, 140

Muslim Youth Movement (MYM), 181–183

Mutazilites, 37–38

Nasir ud-Din Shah, 75

nationalism, 8–9; al-Afghani and, 29, 31, 56; and anti-British movements in India, 139; and exclusion, 136–137; Iqbal and, 21, 99, 107, 125–126, 136, 168; Mawdudi and, 136, 139, 140; Nehru and, 119, 121; and pan-Islamic politics, 194nn13–15; Rida and, 21, 85–87, 90, 136, 157, 168; Turkish, 99, 101

"The Nature of the Quranic Method" (Qutb), 161–162

Nehru, Jawaharlal, Iqbal's argument with, 106–110, 118–121

neicheri, batiniyya as, 38–40, 89, 174; and civilizational decline, 32–33, 38–40, 73; as communists, 37, 45; definitions and uses of term, 22–23, 28, 32–33; Ismailism as, 28, 38, 43–44; and materialism, 27–28; Sayyid Ahmad Khan as, 43–44 (*see also* Khan, Sayyid Ahmad); as threat to Islam, 38–39; as threat to unity, 36–39, 73; Zoroastrians as, 37–38

nizam-i-tawhid (system based on unity), 175, 178, 210n14

"One Islam," 1–2

On the Sociology of Islam (Shariati), 175–176

Orientalists, 2, 9, 17–18, 27

orthodoxy, 116; al-Afghani and, 28, 29, 34–35, 59–60; exclusion and heterodoxy/orthodoxy dynamics, 114–115; Iqbal and, 104, 110–113, 115–116, 118–122, 131–133; Sunni, 121–122, 171 (*see also* Sunni normative bias)

Ottoman Empire, 3, 12

Pakistan: Ahmadi exclusion and persecution in, 147–150; as nation state, 136–137, 147, 166; and Qadiani separatist nation state, 152–153; Rahman exiled from, 169

Palestinian Liberation Organization (PLO), 182–183, 186

pan-Islamism, 34–35, 194nn13–15

Party of Religious Reform, Turkey, 99

persistence theory, 81–82

piety, 12–14

PLO, 182–183, 186

political unity, 81, 136, 166, 168–169, 192n5

"The Principle of Movement in the Structure of Islam" (Iqbal), 94

progress, civilizational, 3–4, 6, 20; 'Abduh and theories of, 61, 66–67, 79–81; al-Afghani and theories of, 30, 34–37, 35–36, 39, 40, 42, 47–48, 66–67; Bahais as progressive, 79–81; and education, 50–51, 59–60; esoteric groups as regressive or destructive of, 24–25, 33–34, 39–40, 70–71, 84, 117, 124–127, 130–134, 205n39; Iqbal and theories of, 92, 94–96, 134, 202nn3–4; Ismailism as progressive, 93; Mawdudi and Islamist theory of, 135–136, 145–146, 166; and *tawhid*, 6, 10, 22–25, 34–35, 92, 166, 189, 192n5; *'ulama* and tradition as obstacle to, 48

progressive revelation, 80–81, 89–90

Prolegomena (Ibn Khaldun), 67

"Propaganda Is the Life of Religions" (Rida), 81–82

prophecy: 'Abduh's view of, 76–77, 80–81, 90; al-Afghani's view of, 29; Aga Khan as prophet, 120; Ahmadis and continuous, 24, 133; Bahais and continuous, 78–79; *buruz* or reappearance, 15, 128–130, 192n11; continuous, 6–7, 18–20, 22, 24, 29, 58–59, 64, 76–79, 90, 120, 132, 133; esotericism and charismatic leadership, 18–20, 22, 29; finality of prophecy (*khatm-i-nabuwwat*) as orthodox doctrine, 5, 6, 93, 104–106, 108–110, 113, 115–116, 128–130, 133, 150, 206n64; Iqbal and finality of prophecy, 24, 93, 104–106, 108–110, 113, 115, 128–130, 133, 150, 206n64; Iqbal's critique of "prophetic consciousness," 109–110, 112, 115–116; Ismailism and, 24, 120; and leadership authority, 14, 18, 24, 29; Mirza Ghulam Ahmad and prophetic calling, 14–15, 120, 132; Muhammad as messenger of God (*nabi*), 11, 19, 24, 69–70, 104–105 (*see also* finality of prophecy (*khatm-i-nabuwwat*) as orthodox doctrine *under this heading*); and Muslim reform, 14–15, 132; progressive revelation, 80–81, 89–90; Qutb and Meccan period of revelation, 162–163; *risalat* (prophetic calling), 15–16; Shaikhi concepts and, 58–59; Sufism and continuous, 22, 64; Sunni normativity and (*see* finality of prophecy (*khatm-i-nabuwwat*) as orthodox doctrine *under this heading*)

"Qadiani Problem" (Mawdudi), 136, 148–150, 153, 166

Qadianis (Ahmadis): Iqbal on, 104, 106–107, 108, 110, 118–119, 123, 125, 150; and Magian revival, 125; Mawdudi on, 136, 148–150, 153, 166

"Qadianis and Orthodox Muslims" (Iqbal), 104, 118–121, 143

Al Qaeda ("the base"), 169, 184–185, 186, 189–190; ethics of, 189–190; and *jihad* as goal, 186–190; Mawdudi as influence on, 169; and Muslim unity, 189–190; post-colonial context and, 21; Qutb as influence on, 169, 185–187; and *tawhid,* 21; and vanguard concept, 26, 184–190

Quran: ʿAbduh on the essential rationality of, 58, 69–71; al-Afghani and reference to, 34–35, 39, 44–45; as authority, 10, 69–70; as both unchanging and dynamic, 95–96; as coherent text, 69, 171–174, 189; and education of the masses, 12–13; *ijtihad* and individual interpretation of, 170, 172, 176–177; mediating figures and authority of, 10–11, 176–177, 180–181; Prophet Muhammad and Quranic revelation, 69–70; Protestant approach to scripture, 12–13; Rahman's two-step interpretive process, 171–172, 209n3; traditional methods of exegesis, 170–171; unified Quranic worldview, 170–171

Qurʾan, Liberation, and Pluralism . . . (Esack), 179–180

Qutb, Sayyid: biography and background of, 156–157, 159, 185; execution of, 185–186; as influence on Al Qaeda, 169, 185–187; and Islamism, 21, 25, 135–136, 165; and *jihad,* 161–165, 169, 186–187; Mawdudi as influence on, 136, 156–157, 159–161, 163, 167; and Meccan period as critical to Islam, 162–163; *Milestones* and political views of, 136–137, 156, 157, 160–164, 208n43; and Muslim Brotherhood, 156, 211n37; as political prisoner, 159; political rather than theological focus of, 25, 161; and prophecy, 161–162; *tawhid* as formulated by, 21, 136, 160–161, 168; and temporal bifurcation, 161, 163–165; and vanguard concept, 160–167, 185, 186, 188–190, 208n43; western culture rejected by, 135, 157

Rahman, Fazlur, 21, 169; Afghani as influence on, 174; biography and background of, 169, 170, 189; as distinct from earlier modernist reformers, 172–173, 177–178; education as primary focus of, 170–173; and esoteric groups as threat to unity, 174; and *ijtihad,* 169, 170–174; as influence on Wadud, 209n11; Iqbal as influence on, 21, 173–174; on Islamism, 21, 172, 173, 189; and Mawdudi, 169; and nationalism, 21; post-colonial context and, 21; and Quran as totalizing ethical guide, 25–26, 170–174, 177–178, 189; and Sunni normative bias, 26, 174; *tawhid* as formulated by, 26, 169–172; and two-step interpretive process, 171–172, 209n3

Rasa ʾil Ikhwan al-Safa, 56, 59

Rasool, Ebrahim, 183

rationalism: ʿAbduh and essential rationality of Quran and Islam, 58, 69–71; Afghani and Islam as inherently rational, 38–40, 195; Iqbal and, 97, 122–126, 131; Islam as essentially rational, 38–40, 144–145; Ismailism and, 122–126; Quranic interpretation and, 176–177; Rationalist movement, 97; religion and suppression of, 42; Rida's critique of "miraculous rational faculty," 77–78, 80, 82, 88, 200n31; and *tawhid,* 10, 70–71, 176, 179; Twelver Shiism and, 58; and western enlightenment, 7, 40, 43, 60

Reconstruction of Religious Thought in Islam (Iqbal), 93–98, 104, 125, 172–173

"The Refutation of the Materialists" (Afghani), 22–23, 27–28, 32–34, 42–44, 59–60, 71–72, 73, 89

Religion as Critique: Islamic Critical Thinking from Mecca to the Market-place (Ahmad), 5–6

"Religions' Three Beliefs" (Afghani), 34

"Religious Propaganda" (Rida), 81–82

Renan, Ernest, 17–18, 27, 40–43, 47, 67

"Renewing, Renewal, and Renewer" (Rida), 63, 85–87

"Response to Renan" (Afghani), 27, 40–43, 47, 67

Rida, Muhammad Rashid, 90; as 'Abduh's biographer, 62–64, 83, 88–90, 157; 'Abduh's influence on, 23, 62; Afghani as influence on, 8, 13, 62–63; as anti-western, 86–87; Bahais excluded by, 23, 62, 74–79; biography and background, 75; biography and background of, 83; as canonical reformer, 62–63; and civilizational progress, 84–85; and colonial context, 21, 62; debate with 'Abduh regarding Bahais, 23–24, 62–63, 73–81, 89; al-Ghazali's influence on, 83; and heresy against esoteric groups, 63; and heretics or false renewers as threat to unity, 63, 83–84, 86–89; *ijtihad* and, 12; as influence on Islamism, 158; as influence on Muslim Brotherhood, 90; Ismailism excluded by, 23, 57, 75–76, 78–79, 83, 90; leadership aspirations of, 62–63; and "miraculous rational faculty" of charismatic leaders, 77–78, 88; and nationalism or the nation state, 21, 85–87, 90, 136, 157, 168; and orthodoxy, 83; on propagandists and esoteric religions, 62, 76–79, 81–83, 88, 90; and rationality, 8, 77–78; and rejection of *batiniyya* groups, 89; on secularism as heretical, 86–88; and Sudanese

Mahdism as sectarian threat to Islam, 82; and Sufi exclusion, 23, 74, 83–84, 90; and Sunni normative bias, 16, 62–63, 90; and *tawhid* as political unity, 9–11, 21, 81, 168

Risalah al-Tawhid (*Theology of Unity* 'Abduh), 23, 61–62, 68–69, 71–73, 81, 89, 162

Risalat al-Waridat (*Treatise of Mystical Inspirations*, 'Abduh), 57

Rochefort, Henry, 53

Roula Khalaf, 1

Sachedina, Abdulaziz, 178, 210n14

Saeed, Sadia, 147

Said Halim Pasha, Ottoman Vizier, 99–100

Sanusiyya, 64, 82

Schulze, Reinhart, 98

science, 4; Afghani as advocate of, 27–28, 30–31, 33, 40–42, 47–48, 51, 57, 60, 67; Iqbal and, 99–100, 202n3; Renan and Islam as opposed to, 41; Sayyid Ahmad Khan and, 46

"sect" and sectarian as terms inapplicable to Islam, 16–17

secularism: Aga Khan's dual roles and, 120–122, 205; and Bahais, 75, 87; and elites, 88, 98; and esotericism, 17; and heresy, 98, 111; Mawdudi and threat of, 135, 140, 144; Mirza Ghulam Ahmad and, 113; modernist reformers and, 3–4, 165; and Muslim elites, 98, 203n13; Rida on secularism as heretical, 86–88; Sayyid Ahmad Khan accused of, 50–51; secular/religious dichotomy, 182, 193n14; *tawhid* and secular sphere, 182; as threat in Mawdudi, 135; and western cultural influence, 3–4, 192n6

selfhood (*khudi*), 203n6, 206n60

Sevea, Iqbal Singh, 105

Shaikh Ahmad Ahsai, 58

sharia, 66, 84, 101, 145, 146, 165

Shariati, Ali: biography and background of, 169, 174–175; as distinct from earlier modernist reformers, 177–178; *ijtihad* and rationalist interpretation of Quran in, 176–177; and Iranian revolution, 175; and Marxist inclusivity, 174–176; and *nizam-i-tawhid* (system based on unity), 175, 178; post-colonial context and, 21; and Shii Marxism, 26, 169, 174–176, 184, 189; *tawhid* as formulated by, 21, 26, 174–176, 178–179; and unity as natural order, 176–177

Shaykh Darwish al-Khadir, 64

Shiism: 'Abduh on threat to Muslim unity, 23; Afghani and, 29–30, 52, 58–59; as esoteric group, 19, 61–62, 76; minority status and framing of unity, 174; modernist reformers and exclusion of, 4–5, 6; scholarly neglect of, 15; and Shaikh school, 50, 58–59; Shii Marxism, 26, 169, 174–176, 184, 189; Twelver Shiism and theory of leadership, 58–59. See also *batiniyya*

A Short History of Revivalist Movements in Islam (Mawdudi), 153–156, 166

Simmel, George, 93, 106, 111–112, 116

Smith, W. C., 10, 46

Social Justice in Islam (Qutb), 157

Soviet-Afghan war, 185

Spengler, Oswald, 126

Sufism, 12; 'Abduh as sympathetic toward, 62, 63, 64, 66; and continuous prophecy, 22, 64; as esoteric group, 19; Iqbal and inclusive sympathy for, 22, 97, 109–110, 113, 115, 116, 128; Islamism as anti-Sufi, 159; Rahman on, 171; and reform, 64; Rida and exclusion of, 23, 74, 83–84, 90; scholarly neglect of, 15

Sunni normative bias, 6–7; Afghani and, 16; Aga Khan and Sunni orthodoxy, 121–122; Asharite Sunni orthodoxy, 171; and definition of Islam, 115–116;

and exclusion, 2–3, 6–7, 16, 20, 174; Iqbal and, 16, 152; and majoritarian logic, 6–7, 13; Mawdudi and, 16, 152; and modernist reformers, 2–7, 15–16, 19, 20, 90, 166, 174; and Pakistani nation-state, 137; Rahman and, 171, 174; Rida and, 16, 62; and traditionalist reformers, 16; and unified Islam, 20–21

al-Tahtawi, Rifa, 65–66

tajid (renewal), 2, 13–14

Tanzimat reforms, 30–31

taqlid, 64, 82, 98, 159

Tarikh al-Ustadh . . . (Rida), 63

Tawfik Pasha, Khedive, 31

tawhid: 'Abduh's formulation of, 21, 23–24, 61–62, 68–69, 71–72, 71–73, 81, 168, 176–177; as "absolute postulate" in Mawdudi, 141; Afghani's formulation of, 23–24, 28, 34–36, 39, 71–72, 168; apartheid as violation of, 26, 169, 179–184, 189; as belief in unity, 141; and civilizational progress, 6, 10, 22–25, 23, 25, 34–35, 92, 166, 189, 192n5; Esack's formulation of, 179–184; ethical components of (freedom/equality/solidarity), 92–93, 96–102, 104, 152; and ethical practice, 23, 25–26, 169–171, 178–179; and exclusion, 2–3, 21, 61–62, 72–73 (*see also under specific groups*); as God's sovereignty, 23, 25, 136, 140–144, 142, 160–161, 163, 165–166, 188, 207n13, 207n131; God's unity, Quranic theological term, 6, 35, 72, 115, 121–122, 130, 182; and "Golden Age" of Islam, 9, 39–40; heresy as threat to, 111–112, 116; and *ijtihad*, 96–97, 99, 101, 102, 104, 134; Iqbal's formulation of, 9–11, 21–22, 92–104, 132–134, 168, 176–177; Islamism and, 21, 23, 25–26, 136, 189; bin Laden's *mujahideen* and restoration of, 186–188; and leadership concerns, 10–11; and liberation theology, 169, 179–183; Magianism as threat to, 130–131; and Marxist inclusivity, 23, 174–176; Mawdudi's formulation of, 21, 25, 136, 140–144, 160–161, 165–166, 168, 207n13; modernist formulations of, 6, 9–13, 21 (*see also specific thinkers under this heading*); and monotheism, 9–11, 126, 142, 175–177, 206n57; and Muslim solidarity, 96, 112, 130, 133; and *nizam-i-tawhid* (unitary society), 175, 178; as political unity, 6, 10, 13, 21, 23–28, 192n5 (*see also specific thinkers under this heading*); and postcolonial contexts, 25–26, 168–169; and progressive Islamism, 184, 189; and prophetic authority, 130; Al Qaeda and, 23, 169, 184–188, 186–187; Qutb's formulation of, 21, 136, 160–161, 168; Rahman and unified Quranic worldview, 170–172; as response to injustice, 25–26, 169, 175–176, 180, 182 (*see also* apartheid as violation of *under this heading*); Rida's formulation of, 9–11, 21, 81, 168; and *risalat* (prophetic calling), 15–16; Shariati's formulation of, 21, 26, 174–176, 178–179; and social equality, 35–36, 169, 183–184; as social unity, 9–10, 21, 24, 28, 34–36, 72, 96, 102, 165–166, 188 (*see also specific thinkers under this heading*); and Sunni orthodoxy normative bias, 2, 20–21, 115, 121–122; and temporal bifurcation, 10, 15–16, 40–41, 61, 68–69, 71, 96, 136, 142, 164–166, 183, 184; as threatened by esoteric minority groups, 10, 28, 36–39, 73, 101, 133; traditionalists and, 12–13, 19; Wadud and inclusive feminist theory of, 209n11; as world-view, 175–177

temporal bifurcation, 10, 15–16, 40–41, 61, 68–69, 71, 136, 142, 164–166, 183, 184

Theology of Unity ('Abduh), 23, 61–62, 68–69, 71–73, 81, 89, 162

theophany *(zuhurullah)*, 75, 82

Tipu Sultan, 85–86, 127

traditionalist reform, 3; contrasted with modernists, 12–13; as mentors of modernists, 13; and Muslim institutional culture, 3, 12; *tawhid* individual piety as focus of, 13

Treatise of Mystical Inspirations (Risalat al-Waridat, 'Abduh), 57

"The Truth and the Neicheri Sect . . ." (Afghani), 22–23

'ulama, 12; 'Abduh and, 64, 66–67; Afghani's contentious relationship with, 31, 46, 48, 55; and Ahmadi exclusion, 147–149, 151; as authorities on Muslim identity and exclusion, 147–149; as incapable of responding to western science, 46; Iqbal's critique of, 98–99, 127–128, 151; Islamism and authority of, 181; Mawdudi's Deobani studies with, 139, 147, 207n3, 207n13; and mediation or interpretation, 10–11, 180–181; modernist critiques of, 11–12, 46, 48–49, 82–83, 85, 127; and Muslim institutions, 12; Rahman's critiques of, 169, 170; Rida on failed religious authority of, 82–83, 85; Sayyid Ahmad Khan's critique of, 46, 48–50; and traditionalist reform, 3, 12–14, 191n3

'Umar Bin 'Abd al-'Aziz, 2, 154

unity. See *tawhid*

Urabi Pasha and Urabi revolt, 29, 68, 88

Urdu, 12, 13, 138, 139

'Uthman ibn Affan, 70

vanguard (vanguardism): Al Qaeda and concept of, 26, 169, 184–190; and global *jihad*, 165, 169; and Mawdudi, 167, 169; *mujahideen* as, 188–189; and Qutb, 160–167, 169, 185, 186, 188–190, 208n43

Vasil, Muhammad, 32–33

Wadud, Amina, 209n11
Wahhabism, 98, 102–103, 140
the West: Afghani and link between
    Christianity and progress in, 35–36,
    39–42; Afghani's debates with Euro-
    pean scholars, 27; cultural Islam
    defined in opposition to Europe, 46,
    94; as declining civilization, 126–127;
    Egypt and European influence,
    64–65; enlightenment values as
    influence on modernist reformers,
    3–5, 7–9, 19–20, 43, 67–68, 92;
    Islamism and rejection of western
    modernity, 157–159; Islamism as
    response to threat of, 158–159, 165,
    187–189; materialist tradition in
    western culture, 28, 33–34, 37; mod-
    ernist reformers' engagement with,
    2, 4, 27, 172–173; Protestant Reforma-
    tion as example of reform, 2, 35–36,
    39–42; Rahman on Western influence
    and need for hermeneutical method,

209n3; Rida as anti-western, 85–87;
    and Soviet-Afghan proxy war, 185;
    as a threat to Islam, 85; women's
    rights and, 145. *See also* colonialism
    and colonial contexts
Wissa, Karim, 197n67
women: disunity linked to rights of,
    85; polygamy and concubinage, 79;
    Wadud's feminist framework of
    tawhid, 209n11; women's liberation
    as threat, 85, 145
"The World-View of Tauhid" (Shariati),
    175–176

Zafarullah Khan, 147, 151
Zaman, Muhammad Qasim, 207n13
Zimmel, Georg, 93, 106, 116
Zito, George, 24, 93, 106, 111–112,
    116
Ziya Gökalp, Mehmet, 101
Zoroastrians, 23, 28, 32, 37, 43, 81–82,
    126, 131, 201n51

A NOTE ON THE TYPE

This book has been composed in Arno, an Old-style serif typeface in the
classic Venetian tradition, designed by Robert Slimbach at Adobe.